IMMORTAL, INVISIBLE

Immortal, Invisible: lesbians and the moving image is the first collection to bring together leading film-makers, academics and activists to discuss films by, for and about lesbians and queer women.

The contributors debate the practice of lesbian and queer film-makers, from the queer cinema of Monika Treut to the work of lesbian film-makers Andrea Weiss and Greta Schiller. They explore the pleasures and problems of lesbian spectatorship, both in mainstream Hollywood films, including *Aliens* and *Red Sonja*, and in independent cinema from *She Must Be Seeing Things* to *Salmonberries* and *Desert Hearts*.

The authors tackle tricky questions: Can a film such as *Strictly Ballroom* be both pleasurably camp and heterosexist? Is it okay to drool over dyke icons like Sigourney Weaver and kd lang? What makes a film lesbian, or queer, or even post-queer? What about showing sex on screen? And why do lesbian screen romances hardly ever have happy endings?

Immortal, Invisible is splendidly illustrated with a selection of images from film and television texts.

Tamsin Wilton is Senior Lecturer in Health and Social Policy at the University of the West of England, where she also teaches Women's Studies and Lesbian Studies.

IMMORTAL, INVISIBLE

Lesbians and the moving image

Edited by Tamsin Wilton

London and New York

First published 1995
by Routledge
11 New Fetter Lane,
London EC4P 4EE

Simultaneously published in the USA and Canada
by Routledge
29 West 35th Street, New York, NY 10001

Typeset in Times by J&L Composition Ltd, Filey, North Yorkshire
Printed and bound in Great Britain by Biddles Ltd, Guildford and King's Lynn

British Library Cataloguing in Publication Data
A catalogue record for this book is available from the British Library

Library of Congress Cataloging in Publication Data
Immortal, invisible: lesbians and the moving image / [edited by]
Tamsin Wilton.
p.   cm.
Includes bibliographical references and index.
1. Lesbianism in motion pictures.   I. Wilton, Tamsin.
PN1995.9.L48I45   1994
791.43'6520643–dc20
94-11401

ISBN 0–415–10724–5 0–415–10725–3 (pbk)

In queer memory of
Tessa Boffin and Derek Jarman

A code is not the destiny of the history that mobilizes it,
but only the trace of the histories that precede it.
Alison Butler (1994, p. 368)

CONTENTS

List of illustrations   ix
Notes on contributors   xi
Acknowledgements   xv

Introduction:
On invisibility and mortality   1
Tamsin Wilton

 1 What is a Nice Lesbian Like You
   Doing in a Film Like This?   20
   Cindy Patton

 2 The Meaning of Treut?   34
   Julia Knight

 3 *Oranges are not the Only Fruit:*
   Reaching Audiences Other Lesbian Texts
   Cannot Reach   52
   Hilary Hinds

 4 *Salmonberries*: Consuming kd lang   70
   Louise Allen

 5 Sex in the Summer of '88   85
   Susan Ardill and Sue O'Sullivan

 6 'If You Don't Play, You Can't Win'
   Desert Hearts and the Lesbian
   Romance Film   92
   Jackie Stacey

 7 Portrait of a Production   115
   Penny Florence

 8 The Space Between:
   Daughters and Lovers in *Anne Trister*   131
   Lizzie Thynne

CONTENTS

 9 On Not Being Lady Macbeth:
   Some (Troubled) Thoughts on
   Lesbian Spectatorship   143
   Tamsin Wilton

10 Girl's Camp? The Politics of Parody   163
   Paula Graham

11 Looking at *Pumping Iron II: The Women*   182
   Jocelyn Robson and Beverley Zalcock

12 Desire and Design – Ripley Undressed   193
   Ros Jennings

13 Visible Mortals:
   Andrea Weiss and Greta Schiller   207
   Interviewed by Nazreen Memon

Filmography   225
Index   228

LIST OF ILLUSTRATIONS

1 Susie Sexpert enthuses over her dildo collection to Dorothee
in *Virgin Machine*   35
2 Monika Treut and her masculine 'other'   47
3 Sexual desire: the image from *Virgin Machine* used for the
poster   49
4 Roswitha's whiteness is visually compounded by her white
coat and the white snow   78
5 The difference between Roswitha and Kotzebue is articulated
within the discourse of race   80
6 Cay admires Silver's engagement ring   99
7 The public rituals of heterosexuality   101
8 Image used in the poster for *Desert Hearts*   104
9 A final moment of uncertainty for Cay and the professor   110
10 Vita and Violet at Knowle   115
11 Vita and Harold at Sissinghurst   126
12 Anne forces a kiss on Alix when she visits her studio   134
13 Alix reestablishes a connection symbolically by taking Sarah's
hand   135
14 Anne is again left alone in an empty space   138
15 *The Living End*'s Luke and Jon in a typical interchange   150
16 Scott's heterosexual masculinity is uncompromised by his camp
get-up in *Strictly Ballroom*   154
17 Jean Peters' swashbuckling tomboy hits off the not-so-
innocently androgynous charm of the principal boy   169
18 Anne Bancroft's sexy defiance of Margaret Leighton's
repressed, bossy lesbian gets smoke in our eyes   176
19 Disavowing the lack? Well, I think this one just about covers it!   179
20 Tiny from *Tiny and Ruby: Hell Divin' Women*   209
21 *Maxine Sullivan: Love To Be In Love*   211
22 *Woman of the Wolf*, directed by Greta Schiller   213
23 Greta and Andrea shooting studies in the Berlin Olympic
Stadium for *Ticket to Anywhere*   222

24 Greta and Andrea at work on *Ticket to Anywhere*   223

Plates courtesy of: Contemporary Films and the British Film Institute Stills Department (12–14); BBC (10–11); British Film Institute Stills Department (4–9, 15–20); Out on a Limb film and video distributors (1–3); Andrea Weiss (23–4); Jezebel Productions (21–22).

CONTRIBUTORS

Louise Allen is a postgraduate research student in the Department of Sociology at Lancaster University. Her research is concerned with lesbian readings of kd lang, and the emergence of country and western lesbian culture. She is currently engaged in theorizing lesbian identities in relation to how country and western reworks forms of white masculinity that have developed through the genre of the western film, and is queerying queer theory in the process. Her favourite star is Doris Day and her favourite director is Sergio Leone. She has no cats, as they always sit in front of the TV.

Susan Ardill is an Australian-born director/producer who lived in London from 1982 to 1992. For four years she worked on *Spare Rib* magazine and then freelanced as a writer and editor. In 1988 she developed the lesbian and gay series *Out On Tuesday* for Channel 4 and was coproducer of the first two series. She directed a number of films for television, including *Stand On Your Man* (on the dyke cult of country and western music) which won Best Documentary Award at the 1992 Torino Film Festival. In 1991 she was director on the weekly Channel 4 series *Free For All*. She returned to live in Australia in 1992 and has since been working as a documentary producer.

Penny Florence is an independent scholar and film-maker. She describes her film career as chequered and is now working mainly on her own in Hi 8 video. She is author of *Mallarmé, Manet and Redon, Visual and Aural Signs and the Generation of Meaning* (Cambridge University Press, 1986), editor (with Dee Reynolds) of *Media, Subject, Gender* (Manchester University Press, 1994), and author of various articles on painting, women's film, photography and writing. Her current interests include exploring the boundaries between fiction and theory through the idea of the daughter's patricide as a missing mythological theme.

Paula Graham is researching a D.Phil. thesis at Sussex University on lesbian readings of popular film, and teaches media, cultural and lesbian studies in higher and adult education. She is currently writing a book on images of female dissidence in popular cinema, and has contributed 'Looking lesbian: amazons and aliens in science fiction cinema' to the forthcoming book edited by Diane Hamer and Belinda Budge, *The Good, the Bad and the Gorgeous* (Pandora, Autumn 1994). She is also involved in programming film screenings for lesbian audiences.

Hilary Hinds teaches Literature and Women's Studies at Fircroft College of Adult Education in Birmingham. She is co-editor, with Elspeth Graham, Elaine Hobby and Helen Wilcox, of *Her Own Life: Autobiographical Writings by Seventeenth Century Englishwomen* (London: Routledge, 1989) and, with Ann Phoenix and Jackie Stacey, of *Working Out: New Directions for Women's Studies* (London: Falmer Press, 1992). She is currently completing a study of seventeenth-century radical sectarian women's writing.

Ros Jennings is a teaching assistant in the Department of Film Studies at Warwick University. Before this she completed an MA in Women's Studies at the University of York while working full time as a care assistant in a residential home for the elderly. She is presently completing her Ph.D. on female audiences and their response to television series featuring strong women as leading characters.

Julia Knight worked in the independent film and video sector for four years and now lectures in Media Studies at the University of Luton. She was a commissioning editor for independent *Media Magazine* before its demise, and has contributed to various journals including *Sight & Sound* and *Screen*. She is currently on the management committee of the women's film distributor Cineova. She is also UK corresponding editor for the Australian contemporary music and popular culture journal *Perfect Beat*.

Nazreen Memon is a born and bred Londoner of Pakistani and Italian parents. A degree in History of Design and the Visual Arts, majoring in Film Studies, fuelled her passion for the arts in general and cinema in particular. She spent eight years working on the South Bank in London, first as an arts publicist promoting music, dance, theatre, poetry and exhibitions, and then as the National Film Theatre Press Officer. Following her work with the British Film Institute she became press officer for a London local authority. Alongside this work she has freelanced as a journalist, PR consultant, researcher and flower arranger. She is on the Board of Directors of Gay Sweatshop theatre company.

Sue O'Sullivan is a writer and health activist and has been working primarily around HIV/AIDS while residing temporarily in Australia. She plans to return to London in 1995. Her most recent work includes an essay on lesbians in mainstream culture, published in Diane Hamer and Belinda Budge's book, *The Good, the Bad and the Gorgeous* (Pandora, Autumn 1994), and she is presently working on a collection of her own writing for Virago.

Cindy Patton is an activist, cultural critic and holds the position of Assistant Professor of Rhetoric and Communications at Temple University in Philadelphia. She is the author of numerous books and articles on the HIV pandemic and on sexual representation, and on changing representations of sexuality in the 1980s.

Jocelyn Robson was born and brought up in New Zealand. She came to London to study film at the Slade School of Art in the early 1970s. Since then she has worked in further and higher education as a teacher and as a trainer of teachers, setting aside small (but precious) amounts of time to pursue projects in film studies and feminism.

Greta Schiller is an award-winning independent film-maker. She recently wrote, directed and produced a half-hour drama, *Woman of the Wolf* (1994) based on a short story by lesbian poet Renee Vivien. Funded by ITVS (PSB), it premiered at the 1994 Berlin Film Festival. Prior to this she produced and directed *Maxine Sullivan: Love To Be In Love* (1991), a portrait of the once famous but now largely forgotten jazz singer, which was coproduced with Channel 4 and La Sept Television. With Andrea Weiss she has produced and directed *International Sweethearts of Rythm* (1986), which won awards worldwide (including the Blue Ribbon first prize at the American Film Festival) and *Tiny and Ruby: Hell Divin' Women* (1988) which premiered at the 1989 Berlin Film Festival (where it won the Gay Teddy Bear Award). Her ground-breaking, feature-length documentary *Before Stonewall: The Making of a Gay and Lesbian Community* (1984) was a hit in Berlin, London, Toronto and other major film festivals. It was released theatrically in North America and Europe and won numerous awards including an Emmy Award for Best Historical Program and an Emmy nomination for Best Director. Greta moved to London in 1988 as the first ever recipient of a Fulbright Fellowship in Film.

Jackie Stacey teaches Women's Studies and Film Studies in the Department of Sociology at Lancaster University. She is author of *Star Gazing: Hollywood Cinema and Female Spectatorship* (Routledge, 1994) and co-editor of *Working Out: New Directions for Women's Studies* (Falmer Press, 1992) and *Off Centre: Feminism and Cultural Studies* (Harper Collins/Routledge, 1991). She has recently become an editor of *Screen*.

Lizzie Thynne is a freelance film-maker and writer. She has worked on several drama and documentary productions including *Out* for Channel Four. She teaches part-time at the University of Northumbria and edited *Studying Film* for the British Film Institute.

Andrea Weiss is a writer, historian and film-maker. She won an Emmy Award for Outstanding Individual Achievement: Best Research for her work on the award-winning feature documentary *Before Stonewall: The Making of a Gay and Lesbian Community* (1984) and co-authored the companion book of the same title. Her subsequent book, *Vampires and Violets: Lesbians in the Cinema* was published in 1992 by Jonathan Cape and in 1993 by Penguin Books in the USA. With Greta Schiller, Andrea founded the New York/London-based production company Jezebel Productions and coproduced *International Sweethearts of Rythm* (1986) and *Tiny and Ruby: Hell Divin' Women* (1988). In 1992 she lived in Berlin on a German Artist Programme (DAAD) fellowship in film, and began developing a lesbian feature film *Ticket to Anywhere* which is nearing production. In the meantime she is working on a companion book to the film *Paris was a Woman*, to be published in 1995 by Pandora (UK) and Harper, San Francisco (US). She holds a Ph.D. in History and has taught Women's Studies and History at the City University of New York.

Tamsin Wilton is Senior Lecturer in Health and Social Policy at the University of the West of England in Bristol, where she also teaches Women's Studies and Lesbian Culture and Society. She currently calls herself a radical queer feminist (but who knows how long that will last?) and has taught and written widely on Lesbian Studies and sexualized representation. She has also been active in HIV/AIDS training and safer sex education since 1987. Publications include *Antibody Politic: AIDS and Society* (Cheltenham: New Clarion Press, 1992), *A Lesbian Studies Agenda* (London: Routledge, forthcoming) and (edited with Lesley Doyal and Jennie Naidoo) *AIDS: Setting a Feminist Agenda* (London: Taylor & Francis, 1994). She is currently at work on *Engendering AIDS: The Sexual Politics of an Epidemic* for Taylor & Francis, and a book about lesbian sex for Cassell. Her five cats tend to sit *on* the TV.

Beverley Zalcock was a child in the fifties, a student in the sixties, a feminist in the seventies, a postmodernist in the eighties and now, in the nineties, is 'queer', which isn't to suggest that she's ceased to be any of the above. She was born and continues to live in London where she works part time teaching film studies. She is also involved in making films. She thinks the personal is still political and believes in a critical practice that allows a hundred flowers to bloom.

ACKNOWLEDGEMENTS

This book is the result of many people's hard work, enthusiasm and support. It is also, of course, firmly situated on the bedrock of previous work. I am indebted to the pioneering work of Vito Russo, Richard Dyer, Teresa de Lauretis, Jackie Stacey and (especially) Andrea Weiss, whose earlier forays into the field have made this one possible, and whose enthusiasm for *Immortal, Invisible* was extremely encouraging. Andrea's own book, *Vampires and Violets* (1992), was not only informative and entertaining but an immense source of inspiration, and Richard Dyer's continued productivity, in particular his book *Now You See It* (1991), was also something from which I learnt much. Journals of the moving image, *Screen*, *Film Quarterly*, *Jump Cut*, *Cineaste* and *Sight & Sound* among others, have a willingness to incorporate lesbian and gay material that is noticeably lacking in other areas (I speak as someone currently working in the profoundly heterosexist field of Health and Social Policy), and as such have helped shape lesbian film studies. This book owes them, too, a debt.

I am also indebted to Richard Dyer, Laura MacGregor, Pratibha Parmar and Jackie Stacey for help in tracking down potential contributors, and to Jo Bristow and Angie Wilson for making it possible for me to recruit still more contributors at their 1992 conference.[1] Detective work is unearthing useful material on lesbians and the moving image was carried out by Lesley Doyal, for whose support and friendship I am deeply grateful. Although a truly Thomas Hardyesque saga of letters gone astray prevented Mary Wings from contributing, her enthusiasm for the project was a timely antidote to the despair that I suspect seizes all editors of such collections from time to time.

Participants in my workshop/seminar at York University, 'The Politics of Lesbian Looking', and students on my Lesbian Studies Dayschools at the University of Bristol Department of Continuing Education, have been instrumental in challenging my thinking about lesbians and the moving image, as have those lesbian friends who have responded surprisingly positively to me arguing the toss with them when they thought they were just accompanying me on a pleasant and restful trip to the movies!

Most of all, thanks are due to the contributors, all of whom have been remarkably patient during the extended and somewhat rocky ride of getting the book together, and whose enthusiasm and willingness to take risks have been exemplary. The fact that so many women (seven in all) were in the end unable to submit their planned contributions says much about the conditions of women's labour. Many of those who stayed the course have had to write in the gaps left over from the double burden of paid work and domestic labour, or have taken precious time out from film projects, truly a labour of love. A special mention here for Jackie Stacey, without whose additional support the book would never have seen the light of day, and for Nasreen Memon, who performed a veritable labour of Hercules at short notice.

Patience and enthusiasm have also been the hallmark of Rebecca Barden's editorial support from the Routledge end, during what seemed like an endless series of delays and set-backs. Thank you Rebecca! And of course I know that I speak for many of the contributors when I acknowledge the help of the British Film Institute's unfailingly friendly and efficient stills department.

Finally, on a personal level, I must acknowledge the love and practical support of my son, Tom Coveney, whose tea-making skills were taxed to the limit at times.

Any faults, omissions and failings are my own.

Hilary Hinds, '*Oranges Are Not The Only Fruit*: reaching audiences other texts cannot reach' originally appeared in Sally Munt (ed.), *New Lesbian Criticism: Literary and Cultural Readings*, Brighton: Harvester Wheatsheaf. We are grateful to Harvester Wheatsheaf and Columbia University Press for permission to reprint here. Susan Ardill and Sue O'Sullivan, 'Sex in the summer of '88', originally appeared in Feminist Review 31, Spring 1989.

NOTE

1 'Activating Theory: Lesbian, Gay, Bisexual Politics' at the University of York, October 1992.

INTRODUCTION

On invisibility and mortality

Tamsin Wilton

Lesbian cinema is on an invisible screen
(Hammer 1994 p. 70)

The magic of the moving image is perhaps no longer so magical to a more sophisticated, cinema-literate generation that not only takes its extra-ordinary special effects for granted but also has access to domestic video technology. No longer do the immortals – Garbo, Deitrich, Bette Davis – perform fleeting visitations into our lives, glowing on the silver screen in the dark of the local cinema. Rather, we may purchase them cheaply, carry them home on video and make them dance in our own living rooms as often as we like. The highly charged ritual of communal worship has been displaced by mundane communion with a set of personal gods, a kind of Protestantization of the moving image.

Then, too, we have acquired skills, knowledges and competencies concerning film that enable us to engage more actively with the film-maker in what I have called the *cinematic contract* (see pp. 143–62). We do not so much suspend disbelief as believe in the unreality of what we see: I sometimes think of that early audience that fled the cinema in terror as a steam train rushed towards them 'out of' the screen. What would they do if transported, naivety intact, to a cinema showing *Star Wars* or *Alien*?

Yet, as the great screen goddesses of Hollywood's golden age join one another (and River Phoenix) in the grave, the power of the moving image to confer a different kind of immortality becomes clear. In millenial western culture we live in a truly strange relationship with certain of our dead. The bodily death of Garbo seems insignificant when we can push a switch and watch her, still young and entrancing, moving, speaking, breathing, weeping, even dying in front of our eyes. Such immortality is partial, not granted to everyone. It is not, for example, granted to lesbians. That the pantheon of Hollywood goddesses included some lesbians among their number we know (although the naming of dykes is a curious matter, and their 'lesbian' is not ours, nor ours that of dykes to come), but because immortality was conferred upon them precisely as heterosexual icon, the 'lesbian'

1

remained invisible. Although, of course, the 'lesbian' tended to leak out across the screen at odd moments, moments now precious as archaeological treasures to dyke fans: Garbo kissing her maidservant in *Queen Christina*, Deitrich kissing a female member of her nightclub audience in *Morocco*. Of such fleeting moments is the flickering shape of lesbian cinematic in/visibility made.

Lesbian invisibility is not only a screen presence. Despite the recent flowering and proliferation of lesbian/gay/queer studies – Ken Plummer (1992) calls this the 'golden age of gay and lesbian studies' – this volume is the first collection, to my knowledge, of essays on lesbians and the moving image (by which I mean not only film, but also TV and video). It is also, let us not forget, the first such collection despite the decades-old explosion and (beleaguered) establishment of feminism and women's studies, and despite the similar explosion and (more secure) establishment of film studies. Writers and theorists interested in women, sexuality or film have clearly been looking somewhere else. People usually do; it is somewhat of a political and theoretical truism that lesbian oppression is preeminently marked by invisibility, and invisibility is a somewhat potent problematic in the context of the moving image!

ON BEING PIG IN THE MIDDLE

Lesbians have, at least since the so-called 'second wave' of women's liberation in the 1960s, been suspended, theoretically and politically, somewhere between the women's movement and gay liberation, between feminism and queer, between a position that privileges gender as paradigmatic site of oppression (and the sexualization of gender as significant) and of resistance and a position that privileges sexuality as that site (and the gendering of sexualities as significant). For lesbians of colour there has, of course, always been a third pull, towards a black theory and politics which similarly privileges race (and sees the sexualization of race as significant). This trinity has given rise to an increasing complexity of political, social and cultural interlocutions, and this is as true within the academy as elsewhere. Those organizing around gender, feminism and women's studies have been obliged to recognize and engage with questions of 'race' and sexual deviance, while black studies, organized around 'race', has been obliged to recognize and engage with issues of gender and sexuality, and most recently queer activism and theory has been taken to task for not incorporating issues of 'race' and gender. Meanwhile, the newly confident disability rights movement has begun to add a fourth voice to the interweavings of these vectors of oppression. This collection is inevitably marked by these collisions, conflicts and competing demands; as much in the shape of its exclusions, silences and absences as by what it includes.

Importantly, 'lesbian' is a contested sign and a privileged site of enquiry within discourses of both gender and sexuality. This is largely due to the elision of gender and sexual orientation in mainstream thinking, an elision which has been challenged by and within both feminism and queer theory, and which continues to demand both careful scrutiny and a critical praxis that takes account of the ideological and political codependency of gender and the erotic. As Judith Butler insists:

> Precisely because homophobia often operates through the attribution of a damaged, failed, or otherwise abjected gender to homosexuals, that is, calling gay men 'feminine' or calling lesbians 'masculine', and because the homophobic terror over performing homosexual acts, where it exists, is often also a terror over losing proper gender ('no longer being a real or proper man' or 'no longer being a real or proper woman'), it seems crucial to retain a theoretical apparatus that will account for how sexuality is regulated through the policing and shaming of gender.
>
> (Butler 1993, p. 27)

I would add that, since the binary paradigm of gender (either being masculine or feminine) and that of sexuality (either being queer or straight) are codependent and intercalate, we need also to pay attention to how *gender* is regulated through the policing and shaming of *sexuality*. Lesbians, defined and oppressed by and within the interstices of gender and the erotic, are positioned quite differently from either non-lesbian women or gay men, and have been poorly served by feminism and queer. This collection is, among other things, concerned to make space in film studies and cultural studies for the specificity of lesbian thinking, lesbian oppression and lesbian resistance, refusing any longer to 'add lesbians on' to work which privileges non-lesbian women or gay men. It is also concerned to make space for thinking about film in arenas such as women's studies, lesbian studies and queer studies, where film may still be marginalized,[1] perhaps because film theory has gained a (deserved) reputation for obscurity. The contributors to this volume speak from an unusually wide range of positions and are all concerned with demystification and clarity. Perhaps above all else, the collection is an attempt to open up the relationship between lesbians and the moving image, and to bring to that task a diverse assortment of theoretical tools. Perspectives from sociology, cultural studies, literary criticism, feminism, queer theory, psychoanalysis and a dash of 'straight' film theory here combine to present a rich and challenging approach to a subject elsewhere marginalized.

ASKING THE PRIMAL QUESTION?

It is by now obligatory to preface any exploration of lesbian issues with what I think of as the catechism of undecidability: the formula of question and response which problematizes the definition of 'lesbian'. When considering the moving image the meaning of 'lesbian' becomes particularly acute. What *is* this book about? How may we adequately define a lesbian film, a lesbian film-maker, a lesbian spectator? Of course, unless we resort to essentialism we are forced to conclude that these things are contingent, strategic, in constant flux, marked by undecidability.[2] Luckily this set of questions has by now been asked often enough that undecidability has itself left firm traces in the literature (for example, Weiss 1992; Olivieri 1992), and it no longer seems simply a cop-out to insist that 'lesbian' is both 'real' and 'unreal', both a densely significant moment in sociocultural time and a fleshly woman with desires that expose her to discipline and punishment (and to pleasure) in the 'real' here and now.

This collection does not adhere to a standard policy for defining 'lesbian', whether as producers or consumers of the moving image, or as descriptive of content or form. Indeed, put all the contributors in a room together and we would almost certainly argue passionately about our understanding of these meanings. It would be worrying if this were not the case, for these meanings are, and must continue to be, characterized by contestation. For Barbara Hammer, the form must be radical and innovative for a film to be a lesbian film, for traditional films (and she refers to *Lianna* (1982), *Personal Best* (1982) and *Desert Hearts* (1985) specifically) offer 'no lesbian to deconstruct, as the discourse of the gendered subject is within a heterosexist authority system' (Hammer 1994, p. 71). This, for Hammer, obliges us to renounce conventional cinematic forms:

> It is my belief that a conventional cinema, such as classical narrative, is unable to address the experiences or issues of lesbian and gay perceptions, concerns and concepts. . . . Even if the characters are lesbian, the script projects lesbian characters within a heterosexual world of role-playing, lovemaking, and domestic and professional life.
>
> (ibid., p. 70)

While lesbian form for lesbian cinema may be an ideal – and Hammer's work was and remains crucially important in challenging the heterosexist authority system that she rejects – many lesbians would argue that it is equally important to break into conventional narrative cinema precisely in order to destroy its monolithic heterosexism. Still others would argue that the pleasure which lesbian audiences gain from films such as *Desert Hearts* (see Stacey, this volume) are important both socially and politically.

While debate may rage over what constitutes lesbian form, surely it is easier to determine lesbian content, lesbian spectatorship or the presence of a lesbian auteur? Well, no. Writing about lesbian film-makers Ellen Spiro, Donna Deitch, Patricia Rozema, Andrea Weiss, Greta Schiller and Cheryl Dunye, Alisa Lebow admits that 'sexuality is an important criterion by which to aggregate these film/video makers, but its multifaceted and

4

mutable character makes it a less than certain criterion', and she asks, 'even if the lesbian artist is "out", must her subject matter or treatment be lesbian-specific?' (Lebow 1993, p. 19). The question of lesbian auterism and content are debated in many chapters in this book, notably by Julia Knight, whose piece interrogates and finds inadequate the description of Monika Treut as a 'lesbian' film-maker, and Hilary Hinds, who discusses the refusal of heterosexual critics to recognize the lesbian content in the television adaptation of Jeanette Winterson's *Oranges Are Not The Only Fruit*. Clearly, neither a lesbian writer nor a lesbian director automatically produce a 'lesbian product'; equally clearly, the making of lesbian meaning is a contested process determined as much by lesbian/non-lesbian reading as by lesbian/non-lesbian text. We may not unproblematically locate lesbian meaning at any one point of the hermeneutic cycle/circle.

Lesbian spectatorship is, then, of central importance in 'making' lesbian film, video or TV, and the question of lesbian spectatorship opens up yet another can of theoretical worms. Clearly we may not assume that the lesbianness of a 'lesbian spectator' is a taken-for-granted constant on any level. As Andrea Weiss cautions, 'there is a danger in using the term "lesbian spectator", or even worse, "lesbian identity", which assumes a coherent, unified position of identification among all lesbians, despite wide cultural, racial, class and generational differences' (Weiss 1992, p. 3). Yet, as my own piece in this book sugests, there are important social, cultural and political specificities that attach to being lesbian, and that impact upon the subjectivity of 'real' lesbians who watch films/videos. Yvonne Rainer agrees: 'to "call myself" a lesbian is not only a statement of sexual preference, it is a way of pointing to where I – and others like me, for the same, also different, reasons – live: outside the safe house, on the edge, in the social margin' (Rainer 1994, p. 13). An anti-essential, social-constructionist perspective on sexual 'identity' does not make 'lesbian' a redundant label, rather it obliges us to recognize and deploy 'lesbian' as an avowedly strategic sign.

> Fundamentalism and essentialism aside, I therefore call myself a lesbian, present myself as a lesbian, and represent myself as a lesbian. This is not to say that it is the last word in my self-definition. 'Lesbian' defines not only sexual identity but also the social 'calling', or resistance, made necessary by present social inequalities.
>
> (Rainer 1994, p. 15)

Conceptualizing 'lesbian' strategically has important consequences for studying the moving image. Not only does it imply a long overdue incorporation of a sociological perspective into film studies, it also poses a unique theoretical challenge to the hegemony of traditional heterobinarism which has for so long been the dominant paradigm for thinking about film (and representation more generally).

5

In the context of theorizing a gaze unbounded by rigid gender polarities, the figure of the 'lesbian' is, it seems to me, a privileged site of inquiry. As both subject and object of desire, she embodies the potential desiring modality of all viewing subjects, her body displacing the binary economy enforced by heterosexual ideology.

(Traub 1991, p. 311)

The 'lesbian spectator' must, then, be foregrounded in order to reinscribe the materialities of oppression on to a discourse which is too often characterized by textual determinism (Stacey 1994), and in order to eradicate the troublesome and troubling inadequacies of heterobinarism.

WE'RE HERE, WE'RE QUEER, WE'RE ALL GIRLS TOGETHER?

Questions such as these have recently been further complicated by the arrival on the scene of the New Queer Cinema (Rich 1992), prompting a questioning of the meaning of 'queer', and the place of 'lesbian' within queer. For Ellis Hanson, queer is a perspective rather than a cinematic practice, a perspective which enables him, for example, to return to Stanley Kubrick's *2001: A Space Odyssey* (1968) for a queer rereading:

By 'queer' I mean the odd, the uncanny, the undecidable. But, more importantly, I refer to 'queer' sexuality, that no-man's land beyond the heterosexual norm, that categorical domain virtually synonymous with homosexuality, and yet wonderfully suggestive of a whole range of sexual possibilities (deemed perverse or deviant in classical psychoanalysis) that challenge the familiar distinctions between normal and pathological, straight and gay, masculine men and feminine women.

(Hanson 1993, pp. 137–8)

One of the problems for lesbians looking to queer for a new direction is that queer, that 'no-man's land beyond the heterosexual norm', is in fact more like a no-woman's land. While Derek Jarman is optimistic, 'queer seems to me to be a democratic word: it is not so obviously gender-based, and has united lesbians and gays' (Jarman 1992, p. 34), B. Ruby Rich remains cautious, pointing to gender inequalities in access to systems of production and distribution:

Surprise, all the new movies being snatched up by distributors, shown in mainstream festivals, booked into theatres, are by the boys. Surprise, the amazing new lesbian videos that are redefining the whole dyke relationship to popular culture remain hard to find. . . . The Queer New Wave has come full circle: the boys and their movies have arrived. But will lesbians ever get the attention for their work that gay men get for theirs? Will queers of colour ever get equal time?

(Rich 1992, pp. 33–4)

Rich is not alone in her perception that queer excludes lesbians. Alisa Lebow notes that 'even within the queer cinema movement, in spite of the abundance of lesbian films and videos, lesbian work still tends to be ignored by critics' (Lebow 1993, p. 19), and Cherry Smyth highlights the material inequalities submerged within queer which, she suggests, are one reason why lesbians are currently more active in photography than in cinema: 'It is hardly surprising, in terms of economics alone, that more queer women are working in photography than in film or video. In the New Queer Wave, lesbians are drowning' (Smyth 1992, p. 39). Amy Taubin suggests that queer is even more exclusive of women than heterosexual film, and implicates the construction of queer desire in this exclusivity:

queer cinema is figured in terms of sexual desire and the desire it constructs is exclusively male. . . . Indeed, women are even more marginalised in 'queer' than in heterosexual film; at least in the latter they function as objects of desire.

(Taubin 1992, p. 37)

Taubin's comment identifies something other than simple sexism at work in queer's marginalization of lesbians. In addition to the (gendered) material realities of lesbian oppression, including both lack of funding and critical neglect, there is a set of (gendered) ideological/imaginary differences at work. The sexual desire celebrated in queer cinema is not only 'exclusively male', it is profoundly phallocentric. Then, too, queer is characterized by a re-visioning of camp, traditionally a gay men's paradigm (though see Graham, this volume), and by the parodic engagement with preexisting cultural artefacts so typical of postmodernism, artefacts which are themselves products of androcentrism. B. Ruby Rich suggests that, while gay men may *unearth* gay material, lesbians must conjure it, invent it, in a process she dubs the Great Dyke Rewrite:

A new kind of lesbian video surfaced . . . and with it, a contemporary lesbian sensibility. Like the gay male films now in the limelight, this video has everything to do with a new historiography. But where the boys are archaeologists, the girls have to be alchemists.

(Rich 1992, p. 33)

In many ways, this is a familiar conflict. For women, whether lesbian or not, it has never been enough to proclaim that 'transgressive' sex was, in and of itself, politically radical. The erotic is most certainly instrumental in women's oppression, and asserting women's (and specifically lesbian) sexual agency is equally certainly radical in feminist terms. but sexual politics does not end there. For many, myself included, gay men having sex with one another impacts at best tangentially (at worst not at all) on men's power over and control of women. It is hard to disagree with Constantine Giannaris when he insists that 'what gay was and what queer is [is] intrinsically transgressive sexuality which will always be in conflict with the status quo' (Giannaris 1992, p. 35), but – lest we forget – transgressive does not equal politically radical. For Amy Taubin, for example, the struggle against homophobia and racism is not adequately politicized in *Tongues Untied* (1989): 'Where does the politics of *Tongues Untied* – that "black men loving black men is *the* revolutionary act" leave lesbians of colour? I'd say high and dry' (Taubin 1992, p. 37). The lesbian response to queer cinema has almost unanimously been that it has not served lesbians well, if for no other reason than that the different experiences and practices of lesbian and gay film/video-makers are not acknowledged within queer. 'As the histories of lesbians and gay men differ, so, too, do their film and video movements' (Lebow 1993, p. 19).

On a more fundamental level, the relationship between 'lesbian' and femaleness is radically different to the relationship between 'gay' and maleness. The hegemony of the male narrative is all but absolute in western cultures. Every text other than the subversive few tells a tale by men, about men and for men. Heterosexuality is constructed around, and deployed (within economic, political, cultural, textual and sexual discourse and practice) to enforce, the subordination of women to men. Lesbians challenge this status quo in a way that gay men, I suggest, don't. In classical Athens (simplistically perceived as being 'accepting' of homosexuality) free, adult, male citizens fucked whoever they wanted to fuck as long as the object of their intentions was *of a lower social status*. Such people included women, boys, slaves and foreigners (Halperin 1989), and gender was relatively immaterial. The social and political power of the free, adult, male citizen not only constituted all his social inferiors as sex toys, but was expressed and maintained precisely through his doing so. Sexual agency, erotic desire and sexual object choice were the prerogative and property of the dominant class of men, something which is arguably no different today. For men to regard other men as sexually desirable and sexually available to them represents a threat of a very different, and less radical, order than for women to do so.

A curious set of intersections between a certain strand of androcentrism (which, phallocentrically, regards lesbian desire as castrated, ultrafeminine and hence harmless) and a certain strand of feminism (which, phalloeccentrically, regards lesbian desire as the bonding of women against and without penile penetration, ultrafeminine and hence revolutionary), results in a general tendency to construct a particular 'lesbian' as a kind of excessive femaleness. Male homosexuality, on the other hand, is generally seen in problematic relation to maleness, as Richard Dyer notes in relation to 1970s lesbian feminist documentary film-making:

> [there is] a perception of continuity between femininity, or woman-hood, and lesbianism. A similar argument for men would be hard to make, because gay male identity has more often been constructed as oddly placed in relation to masculinity, seen as either departing from it towards effeminacy, or else as play-actingly exaggerating it in clonedom.
>
> (Dyer 1990, p. 194)

For a multiplicity of reasons, then, lesbians and gay men may not easily be incorporated into a generic (gender-resistant) queer. On the other hand, neither may we be incorporated into a generic 'woman', nor into feminism.

FEMINISM – HOW TO BE A WOMAN-CENTRED WOMAN

OK, so what about feminism and women's studies? Apart from the stubborn heterosexism of women's studies (see Wilton 1993), the major problem with feminist theory, and feminist film theory in particular, is that it is by and large taken up with notions of sexual difference, in a more or less obedient dialogue with psychoanalysis. This, as Cindy Patton suggests in this volume, is perhaps largely due to simple historical accident: 'Film became a . . . popular entertainment form simultaneously with the establishment of pop-Freudianism as the 'modern' way of understanding human behaviour.' In other words, it is not just film theory but film itself that has absorbed the tenets of psychoanalysis. Liz Kotz believes that this renders most feminist film theory obsolete:

> In recent years, issues of lesbian representation and of the lesbian spectator have become nagging questions posed to feminist theories of film, which have become codified around semiotic and psychoanalytic discourses. . . . In many instances, this has represented a closed system, one open neither to new lines of analysis nor to works which don't fit the predominant theoretical models.
>
> (Kotz 1994, p. 86)

Predicted as it is upon heterobinarism, indeed valorizing heterobinarism as non-pathological (normal, healthy, mature), psychoanalytic film theory is not only fundamentally antagonistic to lesbian existence, but utterly unable (by definition) to incorporate 'lesbian' into thinking about discursive/textual production, construction or consumption without implicit reproduction of hegemonic doctrines of homophobia/heterosexism. It has proved difficult enough to write female subjectivity into the paradigm, let alone disobedient/deviant lesbian subjectivity. As Alison Butler comments, 'working within the confines of difference theory's binary structuration,

9

feminist theory has become – for a time – gridlocked by its own conceptual topography' (1994, p. 368). The sad result of this is that what may (with some irony) be called 'mainstream' feminist film theory has had little to offer lesbians. Within the phallocentric heterobinary paradigm of psycho-analysis, lesbianism is constituted as lack/fetish. As Barbara Hammer points out, what lesbians lack is not a phallus but a presence in the semiotic field, and the act of 'stepp[ing] into the void, the invisible, the blank screen, and nam[ing] ourselves "lesbian"' constitutes a radical inscription of that presence.

> There could be no semiotics if there were no sign. The lack we felt as we began this early naming process was not the lack of the phallus but the singular and significant lack of any representations. The image did not exist, the picture was not made, the word scarcely heard in discourse nor seen in text.
>
> (Hammer 1994, p. 71)

She adds that feminism has been complicit in this erasure of lesbian cinema: 'Until recently, the dominant discourse of feminist criticism has not addressed this issue but has continued to ignore it, and by doing so perpetuates the invisibility and repression of lesbian cinema.'

It is important to remember that feminist critical praxis mounted a potent challenge to patriarchal thinking about film, gender and sexuality, and that insistent lesbian intervention into feminism has resulted in the development of a much less monolithic, more troubled and nuanced feminist film theory which I suspect will in the end serve lesbians and lesbian cinema better than queer. (In this I may be proved wrong.) However, at the present moment, neither feminism nor queer may be relied upon to do justice to lesbians.

AS ON A DARKLING PLAIN?

The heady excitement of engaging with the meanings, location and pleasures of 'lesbians and the moving image' must not distract us from the risky business of survival, playing as we queers do the monstrous abject in the ubiquitous homophobic narrative that is millenial western culture. Only three decades ago the British Board of Film Censors played a major part in determining the final content of Basil Dearden and Michael Relph's film *Victim* (1961), commenting not only on the finished film itself, but on both the synopsis and the script at an earlier stage. The film, which stars Dirk Bogarde as a guilt-ridden gay barrister closeted in a conventional marriage and focusses on gay men's vulnerability to blackmail, is now widely regarded as a significant intervention in the struggle for the decriminalization of homosexuality in Britain. At the time the film was recognized to be an extremely risky venture, and Dearden and Relph worked in close cooperation with the BBFC to ensure that it was given a certificate. The comments of the Board make clear just how radical *Victim* was at the time: 'Great tact and discretion will be needed if this project is going to come off, and the "queerness" must not be laid on with a trowel . . . the less we have of "covens" of queers lurking about in bars and clubs the better' (cited in Robertson 1992, p. 120). Their concern was not solely, as might be assumed, that the British cinema-going public might be exposed to too many 'queers', but also that the film might catalyse homophobia and result in *more* harm done to gay men. Although there was a specific worry, that 'we have never had . . . such a great number of different types of "Queer" assembled in one film', they were especially concerned that the blackmailers should not be seen to be unduly successful:

Anyone who doesn't pay up, sooner or later gets cut up or beaten up . . . it is an element which adds an undesirable 'spiciness' to the story and will bring in just the type of customer who cannot claim to be a serious student of social problems, except the social problem of how to enrich oneself by blackmail and violence at other people's expense.

(cited in Robertson 1992, p. 121)

Hitherto the subject of queerness had been very much silenced in Britain, but the Wolfenden Report was current at the time the BBFC was considering *Victim*. Debate about homosexuality was thus much more open, and indeed liberal, than was the case in the United States, where the Hays Code remained inflexible in its prohibition of gay subject matter on screen. This battle has in no sense been won. There are still many powerful voices urging a return to those days of absolute prohibition. Those voices, like so many opportunistic social/cultural infections, have made cynical capital out of the HIV epidemic and the AIDS crisis (the one a biological reality, the other a social disaster on a monumental scale, driven by the terrifyingly familiar engines of prejudice, intolerance and cant). Martha Gever, John Greyson and Pratibha Parmar remind us that, although 1989 was a year that seemed 'ripe with possibilities' for lesbian and gay film and video, at the same time it was a moment of attrition: 'The resurgent right wing was opportunistically using AIDS to declare a take-no-prisoners war on queer expression. Funding was slashed, screenings were censored, films were banned. What's to savor when we suffer so?' (Gever *et al.* 1994, p. xiii).

Whatever the theoretical and political complexities of struggling to make space for 'lesbian' within queer and feminism, misogyny and homophobia continue to structure the lived experience of lesbians. So too do the material constraints of living and working within patriarchal capitalism, as Alison King's video *Switching Tracks* (1993) clearly demonstrates. Screened at the 1994 BFI Lesbian and Gay Film Festival in London, *Switching Tracks* documents the experiences of three New York City lesbians of colour, two of whom have AIDS and a third who is HIV+, and makes explicit the crushing economic burden which AIDS entails when healing is located within the for-profit infrastructure of western scientific medicine. One of the women explains that 'there is a helluva lot of money to be made out of AIDS', pointing out that the minimum dose of foscarnet (the medication of choice for gancyclovir-resistant cytomegalovirus, an AIDS-related opportunistic infection) costs $22,200 per year, and that her medication annually adds up to $65,000 per year. One of the many lessons that the queer community has learnt from AIDS is that the economic structures of capitalism do not make any exceptions for the sick and dying.

Those same economic structures, aligned as they are along sexist and racist lines, have a powerful influence on the kinds of moving images available by/for/about lesbians. The technology of representation comes expensive, and men have far greater access to money than women. The datasphere is as subject to (straight, white, ruling-class) male domination as any other facet of life on this planet. This means that there is a general scarcity of lesbian texts available and that lesbians are more likely to have to employ low-cost technologies such as video than high-cost ones such as film. It also means, in the increasingly market-orientated world of television, that programmes aimed at lesbian audiences (presumed to be tiny) or with lesbian content (presumed to be offensive to the non-lesbian majority – see Hinds, this volume), are resourced poorly if at all.

TAKING IT ALL ON

With an agenda as complex as the one outlined above, it is unsurprising that the essays in this book do not fit very neatly into distinct themes. Very little is taken for granted; there is no unitary perspective, no agreement about what constitutes a lesbian film/video or a lesbian spectator, no single position with regard to psychoanalytic film theory, poststructuralism, feminism or queer. There is certainly no editorial policy at work here, other than the determination to deal as openly and flexibly as possible with lesbians and the moving image. There is no unified address, few assumptions about you, our reader.

As Cindy Patton's piece makes clear, cinematic representation of lesbians and gay men has shifted over time, a shift that is influenced both by the changing sociopolitical position of lesbians and gays and by the changing sociopolitical context of film more generally. Patton suggests that mainstream cinema may make use of lesbian characters to perform specific diagetic and scopic functions, and offers a critique of the part played by the lesbian cop in *Internal Affairs* (1988). Pointing out that the film 'adopts the structural position of lesbian as a space and knowledge beyond the "straight mind" . . . [and] actually situates a lesbian character as the film's reference point for the normal psyche' (a radical innovation in mainstream cinema), Patton goes on to suggest that the figure of the lesbian has stepped in to resolve a moment of crisis in the genre:

> the lesbo cop of *Internal Affairs* (1988) enters the historical scene to announce the demise of a particular heteromasculine logic which may yet be recuperated, but can no longer proceed as if misogyny and homophobia are the presumptive frame of reference for the audience.
>
> (p. 20)

Within this analysis, a lesbian character in a mainstream movie – and by implication any movie – is greater than the sum of her parts, referencing and expressing a moment in the political history of both gender and the erotic. Patton insists that we 'must understand that "signs" refer to something larger than the description of the character who wears them' (p. 23).

Hilary Hinds and Julia Knight, approaching from quite different positions, debate the notion of the lesbianness of text and auteur, focussing respectively on Beeban Kidron's television adaptation (1990) of *Oranges Are Not The Only Fruit* and the films of Monika Treut. Knight, privileging questions of address, provocatively suggests that Monika Treut – whose work has been called 'post-queer' – is *not* a lesbian film-maker. Indeed, to call her such risks ghettoizing her work. Reminding the reader that Treut herself rejects being 'claimed' by the gay community, Knight suggests that her self-promotion as a controversial director is the means to reach a wider audience and concludes that 'her films are not addressing a *purely* lesbian and gay audience. And thus to categorize Treut as a "lesbian filmmaker" is to deny the broader appeal and, more importantly, the wider relevance of her work' (p. 46). Since Monika Treut 'is' a lesbian and a film-maker, Knight's calculated refusal to call her a lesbian film-maker poses a dramatic challenge to many taken-for-granted assumptions about lesbian film-making, the kinds of assumptions that, for example, lead to Dorothy Arzner being identified as a lesbian film-maker (Dyer 1990, Archivi Lesbici Italiani 1992).

Hinds, on the other hand, shows how difficult it is to insist on the lesbianness of content in the face of the liberal-humanist refusal to see anything other than the broadly *human*. The doctrine *nihil humanum mihi alienum puto* is as efficient as erasing 'lesbian' from the record as any right-wing censorship, and the status of *Oranges* as 'high art', Hinds argues, allowed reviewers and critics to ignore or brush over its lesbian content and stress its universalist nature. The question of lesbian readings comes in here. Lesbians watching *Oranges* 'read the text through a specific set of codes apparently undiscerned by other audiences' (p. 65), and Hinds believes that an understanding of the wider social moment is also key to making sense of the reception of what was, after all, an extraordinarily forthright lesbian text. She reminds us that the television adaptation was shown at a time when censorship and freedom of expression were very live issues. Salman Rushdie was (and at the time of writing still is) hiding after the Ayatollah's *fatwah*, and Hinds suggests that, in consequence, 'lesbian-ism became an otherness preferable to the unacceptable otherness of fundamentalism' (p. 62). In addition, the high profile 'arts lobby' which had organized to protest against Section 28 (see p. 57) had established 'high-cultural "art" . . . as having a meaning separable from questions of politics, sexual or otherwise'. Lesbian meanings cannot, then, be separated from their socio-political context.

One important factor structuring that wider context is the question of racialization and ethnicity. Critics of lesbian film and lesbian cultural commentators are beginning to question how/whether 'racial' difference functions to introduce an erotic tension thought by some to be otherwise absent in relations between women (for example, Longfellow 1993). Louise Allen's piece on *Salmonberries* (1991) takes us beyond the film to reference the significance within the lesbian community of out lesbian country singer kd lang, the film's star and a cult figure to many lesbians. She also, importantly, draws attention to the ways in which 'performative racial identities in *Salmonberries* are interconnected with performative roles of butch and femme' (p. 82), and the way in which the film seems to set up resonance between lesbian identity and ethnic identity, a reso-nance that condenses in the figure of Kotzebue (played by lang) as she seeks out her Native American roots. Allen's piece is important in pointing the way forward to a 'critique of white lesbian culture/theory in terms of its investments in class, racial and gender privileges' (p. 83).

The lesbian 'community' is in itself a complex and conflict-ridden social context for the production and consumption of the moving image. Susan Ardill and Sue O'Sullivan's piece, which was written shortly after the events they describe, reminds us that this community can be very active in its attacks on (or defence of) work that deals with politically sensitive issues. Sheila McLaughlin's film *She Must Be Seeing Things* (1987) provoked heated reaction from lesbian audiences in Britain who went to great lengths to try and prevent it being shown, claiming that it glorified violence against women and butch–femme role play (seen as mimicking and perpetuating heterosexual relations of power). In my own city, Bristol, a small group of lesbians leafletted women's venues instructing women not to go to see the film, and demonstrated outside the independent cinema where it was being screened. Many women (me included, I must confess)[3] were too intimidated to risk seeing the film, while those who defended it were subject to vigorous censure. Ardill and O'Sullivan's article is included here in its original form, because I believe that it is essential to developing an understanding of the relation-ship between lesbians and the moving image that we take note of such extraordinary historical (hysterical?) moments. Ardill and O'Sullivan also set the film within a wider lesbian intertextuality, referencing Joan

Nestle's book *A Restricted Country* (1987) and local (London) lesbian community events.

Taking as her subject a film that was received quite differently by lesbian audiences, Jackie Stacey asks why *Desert Hearts* (1985) has not been followed by a spate of lesbian romance films, and why, despite its popularity within both a lesbian milieu and the mainstream (the film has been a box office success), it failed to move its lesbian viewers. The answer, Stacey concludes, lies in the different obstacles that structure lesbian and heterosexual romance narratives. While the obstacles to heterosexual romance appear in general to be less easily overcome than the obstacles which *Desert Hearts* flings in the path of its heroines – obstacles which are overcome with almost farcical ease – the 'real life' obstacles to lesbian romance are of a different order. It would take an unwieldy epic indeed to narrativize the defeat of the heteropatriarchy! 'Lesbian romance', suggests Stacey, 'has been defeated by problems too great to resolve in narrative terms' (p. 98).

Also significant in Stacey's account of *Desert Hearts* is the extraordinary story of how Donna Deitch pieced together the funding. The resulting budget set severe limitations on production, limitations which, according to Penny Florence, are too often ignored by feminist critics. There is, she writes, 'a need within feminist TV and film criticism . . . [for] incorporating issues around production, including finance, into the critique of finished films, videos, or broadcast productions' (p. 116). Discussing the BBC production *Portrait of a Marriage* (1990), which dealt with the affair between Vita Sackville-West and Violet Trefusis, Florence demonstrates quite unequivocally how the deregulation of broadcasting services currently underway in Britain has serious implications for lesbians, and indeed for all women. She also suggests that production issues may prove to be the way to resolve the tensions between the sociological and the psychological in film criticism: 'production issues have implications for the use of psychoanalytic frameworks in film criticism, and possibly have a contribution to make to crossing the boundary between psychoanalytic and sociological arguments' (p. 117).

It is a boundary which may be traced through several pieces in this collection. While Lizzie Thynne's piece on *Anne Trister* (1986) accepts that psychoanalysis is a 'valuable tool' which needs to be reformed, other pieces such as my own on *The Living End* (1992) and *Strictly Ballroom* (1992) and Paula Graham's on lesbian camp, reject psychoanalysis outright. Thynne makes use of Luce Irigaray's notion of the female homosexual economy to approach psychoanalysis afresh, suggesting that *Anne Trister* questions the Freudian phallocentric paradigm whereby a maturing girl must transfer her affection from her mother to her father, a paradigm which implicitly pathologizes lesbian desire. In *Anne Trister*, the association between a woman's desire for the mother and her desire for a woman

15

lover is understood to be considerably more complex than Freud allowed for.

Arguing for a more complete escape from the Freudian/Lacanian paradigm, my piece suggests that text-deterministic notions of identification are inadequate to account for lesbian viewing pleasure. I propose the notion of the *cinematic contract*, by which the spectator tacitly agrees to make use of a variety of engagement strategies in order to 'make sense of' the film in question. My suggestion is that such engagement strategies derive less from the unconscious and more from the social location of the spectator, and that hence sociology rather than psychology is the exemplary paradigm for thinking about lesbians and the moving image.

Paula Graham foregrounds questions of gender in her discussion of lesbian camp. Asserting that 'the effort to mould a grown-up, healthy, female lesbian out of the stuff of psychoanalysis often seems a losing battle' (p. 165), she points to the role of gender in the constitution of camp. 'Camp', she writes, 'expresses the relation of gay men *to* male authority, *mediated by* a relationship to representations of "the feminine"' (p. 168), and hence is not amenable to cooption by lesbians. Exploring such 'camp' classics as *Red Sonja* (1985) and *Anne of the Indies* (1951), Graham suggests that the pleasure they give to lesbian audiences is not unproblematic. For example, lesbians watching *Red Sonja* enjoy and identify with the heroine, Sonja, who is not only tamed into heterosexuality by Arnie Schwartzenegger, but is dedicated to overthrowing the lesbian queen, Gedren. Similar unease is expressed in my own critique of *Strictly Ballroom*, which I see as a profoundly anti-gay narrative. Graham concludes that gender should not be displaced in studying lesbian reading practices: 'To apply terms such as "camp" or "queer" to lesbian reading practices is likely to obscure both the diversity and specificity of the practices themselves, as well as the power relations which structure them' (p. 180).

Picking up on the theme of camp, Jocelyn Robson and Beverly Zalcock ask whether the radical elements of drag, as personified by the late lamented Divine are echoed by body-builder Bev Francis, subject of *Pumping Iron II: The Women* (1984). Situating the film in the milieu of postfeminism (while insisting that feminism is 'not dead, only deconstructing'), Robson and Zalcock ask whether postmodernism is radical or reactionary, and focus on the 'masculinized' female body of Bev Francis to ask some important questions about the relationship between body, gender and desire. 'The body is simultaneously the locus of gender definition and the site of sexuality' (p. 185), which means, by implication, that female body-building represents and is a product of a crisis in gender and sexuality that coalesces around the – damaged? abrogated? rejected? disguised? – femininity of Bev Francis. This potent mix of anxieties around gender and sexuality offers a dense and problematic text for lesbian readings.

A less problematic pleasure for lesbians has long been their enjoyment of Sigourney Weaver's playing of the character Ripley in the *Alien* films, a pleasure which Ros Jennings explores in detail. The three films have little in common except Weaver. There have been three directors, Scott, Cameron and Fischer, and three different genres: the first a slasher film, the second a war film, the third almost avant-garde. Weaver, the consistent factor linking the three, is seen by Jennings as demonstrating the changing issues of sexuality and gender that the films reflect: 'the special significance of Weaver and her role as Ripley has been in providing a distinctive site of change and engagement with film and sexual difference' (p. 194). Although never coded as lesbian, Ripley has been something of an icon within certain lesbian communities, and Jennings's analysis (happily and unusually) adds to rather than detracts from the subversive lesbian pleasure invested in the character.

The book concludes with Nazreen Memon's interview with lesbian film-makers Greta Schiller and Andrea Weiss, whose discussion both throws open a rich diversity of issues and at the same time adds an extra element to the more straightforwardly academic commentary of other pieces. As lesbian practitioners in the field, Schiller and Weiss engage perhaps more directly than most with the complexity of issues raised in this book. It is not a complexity that admits of easy answers (nor even of easy questions). The relationship between that contested site of cultural intervention, 'lesbian', and that most seductive of representational practices, the moving image, is and will long continue to be marked pre-eminently by undecidability. While looking at the screen, we are obliged to search for absence as well as presence, for shadow as well as light, for the invisible as well as the visible. As Andrea Weiss says (in her other guise as writer), in a passage that neatly sums up the social, political and theoretical difficulties that coalesce around any attempt to study lesbians and film:

> Violet, as a sign of love between women, serves as an indicator of what lies beyond the visible spectrum and as a means by which to become visible to each other. It suggests a way for getting at the problem of actually finding lesbian visual images: to consider invisibility as well as visibility as a form of representation, and to look for signs that have different meanings for lesbians than they do for western culture at large.
>
> (Weiss 1992, p. 2)

This collection, it is hoped, will contribute to the alchemical enterprise of making lesbian meaning out of invisibilities as well as visibilities. I have been very excited by the scope and perspicacity of the pieces collected here, and mightily cheered by reflecting on Cindy Patton's comment that 'if there is spectatorial pleasure to be gained in deconstructing the politically repressive dimensions of long-standing genres, then a little bit of lesbian goes a long way'!

NOTES

1 For example, I teach on an MA in women's studies which has little or no discussion of film. This is not unusual.
2 I cannot and will not resort to essentialism, both because my own experience, and that of most lesbians I know, makes the notion of inherent or essential lesbianism laughable and because essentialism is a political dead-end for feminism and for lesbians. Anyone who is naive enough to believe that if we are 'born that way' the heterosexuals will have to stop oppressing us and start being tolerant hasn't thought about racism or disability too clearly. We consider it entirely ethical and appropriate to abort disabled foetuses, and I have yet to meet the racist who renounces racism once they realize that black people are 'naturally' like that . . .
3 That was a long time ago, I am braver now! *She Must Be Seeing Things* remains one of my favourite films of all time and it troubles me greatly that a vocal minority should attempt to suppress discussion of the issues it raises with such grace and intelligence.

REFERENCES

Archivi Lesbici Italiani (1992) *Guida al Cinema Lesbico*, Rome: Centro Femminista Separatista.

Butler, A. (1994) '*She Must Be Seeing Things*; An interview with Sheila McLaughlin', in M. Gevver *et al.* (eds), *Queer Looks: Perspectives on Lesbian and Gay Film and Video*, London: Routledge.

Butler, J. (1993) 'Critically queer', *GLQ* 1, 1: 17–32.

Dyer, R. (1990) *Now You See It: Studies on Lesbian and Gay Film*, London: Routledge.

Gever, M., Greyson, J. and Parmar, P. (1994) 'Introduction: on a queer day you can see forever', in M. Gever *et al.* (eds), *Queer Looks: Perspectives on Lesbian and Gay Film and Video*, London: Routledge.

Giannaris, C. (1992) Statement on 'The New Queer Cinema', *Sight & Sound*, September 1992, p. 35.

Halperin, D. M. (1989) 'Sex before sexuality: pederasty, politics and power in classical Athens', in M. B. Dubermann, M. Vicinus and S. Chauncey (eds) *Hidden from History: Reclaiming the Gay and Lesbian Past*, Harmondsworth: Penguin.

Hammer, B. (1994) 'The politics of abstraction', in M. Gever *et al.* (eds), *Queer Looks: Perspectives on Lesbian and Gay Film and Video*, London: Routledge.

Hanson, E. (1993) 'Technology, paranoia and the queer voice', *Screen* 34, 2: 137–61.

Jarman, D. (1992) Statement on 'The New Queen Cinema', *Sight & Sound*, September 1992, p. 34.

Kotz, L. (1994) 'An unrequited desire for the sublime: looking at lesbian representation across the works of Abigail Child, Cecilia Dougherty, and Sue Freidrich', in M. Gever *et al.* (eds), *Queer Looks: Perspectives on Lesbian and Gay Film and Video*, London: Routledge.

Lebow, A. (1993) 'Lesbians make movies', *Cineaste* XX, 2: 18–23.

Longfellow, B. (1993) 'Lesbian phantasy and the Other woman in Ottinger's *Johanna d'Arc of Mongolia*', *Screen* 34, 2: 124–36.

Olivieri, G. (1992) Opening Statement in Archivi Lesbici Italiani, *Guida al Cinema Lesbico*, Rome: Centro Femminista Separatista.

Plummer, K. (1992) 'Speaking its name: inventing a lesbian and gay studies', in K. Plummer (ed.), *Modern Homosexualities: Fragments of Lesbian and Gay Experience*, London: Routledge.

Rainer, Y. (1994) 'Working round the L-word', in M. Gever *et al.* (eds), *Queer Looks: Perspectives on Lesbian and Gay Film and Video*, London: Routledge.

Rich, Ruby B. (1992) 'New Queer Cinema', *Sight & Sound*, September 1992, pp. 31–4.

Robertson, J. C. (1992) *The Hidden Cinema: British Film Censorship in Action 1913–1975*, London: Routledge.

Smyth, C. (1992) 'Trash femme cocktail', *Sight & Sound*, September 1992, p. 39.

Stacey, J. (1994) *Star Gazing: Hollywood Cinema and Female Spectatorship*, London: Routledge.

Taubin, A. (1992) 'Beyond the sons of Scorsese' *Sight & Sound*, September 1992, p. 37.

Traub, V. (1991) 'The ambiguities of "lesbian" viewing pleasure: the (dis)articulations of *Black Widow*', in J. Epstein and K. Straub (eds), *Body Guards: The Cultural Politics of Gender Ambiguity*, London: Routledge.

Weiss, A. (1992) *Vampires and Violets: Lesbians in the Cinema*, London: Jonathan Cape.

Wilton, T. (1993) 'Queer subjects: lesbians, heterosexual women and the academy', in M. Kennedy, C. Lubelska and V. Walsh (eds), *Making Connections: Women's Studies, Women's Movements, Women's Lives*, London: Taylor & Francis.

1

WHAT IS A NICE LESBIAN LIKE YOU DOING IN A FILM LIKE THIS?

Cindy Patton

The mid- to late 1980s produced conflicting accounts of the impact of the previous two decades of feminism: mainstream commentators pronounced the women's movement dead, while some feminist academics, dismayed by the prominence of discussions of masculinity in women's studies, feared that women's issues would once again be eclipsed, this time by a 'feminism without women'. While each account contains a partial truth, something even more complicated was occurring, at least in mass-consumption popular culture. Apparently radically affected by feminism's critique of gender roles and of gendered representational regimes, popular culture partially exhausted the tired misogynist tropes of the sexual terror *of* woman (in, for example, *Fatal Attraction* and its many clones) and moved instead to examine the pathology which lurked within men. Tentative efforts to move away from sexist and heterosexist images made clear the extent to which traditional genres had been premised on the very psychologies which underwrote those stereotypes. Ironically, purging a familiar genre such as the cop film of its misogyny and homophobia opened the door to incorporating not so much 'positive' counter images of lesbians, but a space in which lesbian knowledge could organize a film. Granted, her screen time is limited, and she in no way fits the call for 'lesbian visibility', but the lesbo cop of *Internal Affairs* (1988) enters the historical scene to announce the demise of a particular heteromasculine logic which may yet be recuperated, but can no longer proceed as if misogyny and homophobia are the presumptive frame of reference for the audience.

SEXUAL RISK

Internal Affairs was only one of a spate of films which showed a renewed interest in male psychopathology, a phenomenon clearly related to media discourse surrounding AIDS. Initially, the media omnipresence of the nice gay boy-next-door and/or professional now tragically afflicted with AIDS may have made gay men and the disease erroneously associated with them

20

less scarey to heterosexuals. But this politically equivocal form of visibility also reinforced the belief that the average person could easily identify who was gay (male). Similarly, female sex workers were visible as the already known figures of direct danger to heterosexual men and of indirect danger to white middle-class femininity and innocence (hazily figured in terms of risk to the wives and children of johns). But these two initial figures in the gendered matrix of sexual danger proved to be unsuccessful at explaining the *direct* danger HIV posed *to* women of the white middle class. An additional sign of sexual danger was required, and a new concept of the bisexual male was introduced.

Like prior notions of bisexuality – the polymorphous experimenters of the 1960s or the swinging singles of the 1970s – the new bisexual was preeminently seen as the 'active' partner and hence, always male. But unlike these earlier constructs – the quintessentially heterosexual men who 'chose' both male and female partners or the 'fence sitters' on their way to actually 'coming out' as gay – these AIDS-era bisexuals became the new figures of sexual undecidability, replacing gay men as the principle inhabitants of the 'closet'. Where bisexual males once had a home in heterosexuality and only dallied in another world, the bisexual male who emerged in the context of AIDS discourse (and largely in the aftermath of Rock Hudson's much publicized AIDS diagnosis in 1985) were represented as living in a netherworld *in between* two clearly marked identities. This AIDS-era construction of male bisexuality suggested that US culture had begrudgingly accepted and stabilized two positive sexual identities – gay and straight – based on gender of object-choice plus a 'lifestyle', and supported by two completely separate sexual economies. The bisexual who fell in between was shadowy, indeterminate, unrepresentable because he might *look* gay or straight.

A new genre of films stepped into this breech in the conventions for representing sexual danger. Although they did not thematize the culturally terrifying figure of the undecidable bisexual male, films like *Blue Velvet* (1987) and its more generically legible mainstream cousin, *Internal Affairs* (1988), were most significantly about whether to, how to and who could tell that an apparently straight man might harbour an invisible pathology. Male pathology which had once been representable as homosexuality or as a consequence of men's relation to women no longer had clear and stable signs. The discourse about 'ordinary men' who secretly engaged in HIV risk-relevant behaviours (as 'bisexuals' or as recreational drug-injectors), the increased demands for and debates about gay civil status and rights, and the recognition that misogyny, rather than women themselves, were to blame for much male acting out, narrowed the psychological attributes which could stand as markers of male pathology. How, then, could a film be about heterosexual male pathology in its own right? If part of AIDS discourse concerned liberated straight women's difficulty in identifying

21

sexually dangerous males, then who could occupy the cinematic space of recognition? Who could 'know' which straight men are dangerous? Paradoxically enough, the answer is The Lesbian.

Having freed the homosexual of her/his role in representing sexual deviancy, and probably unknowingly adopting Monique Wittig's proposition that 'lesbians are not women', *Internal Affairs* seizes this precise moment of representational crisis. Not only does the film adopt the structural position of lesbian as a space and knowledge beyond the 'straight mind' of the heteromasculine regime, but it actually situates *a* lesbian *character* as the film's reference-point for the normal psyche. Unlike the spate of films in the early 1980s which took up gay and lesbian life and oppression as their theme, or used homophobia to further their plot, *Internal Affairs* employs its lesbian character because, (psycho)logically, she is the only person not implicated in prior representations (queer men, steamy straight women) of masculinity gone off the rails. I want to briefly describe some relevant aspects of the interplay between genre formation and film censorship which shaped this particular possibility for lesbian representation.

REWRITING FILM HISTORY

It has been widely argued that the so-called 1930 Hays Code and its vigilant, if often inconsistent, administration effectively censored the portrayal of lesbians and gay men until film-content standards gave way to increasing social tolerance toward African Americans and Jews in the late 1940s, and then toward homosexuals and non-conforming women in the 1950s. While tracing this history of the exclusion of images of lesbians and gay men from film has been an important liberationist project, it is important to recognize that lesbians and gay men have in no way been coherent categories. The Hays Code sometimes worked together with, and sometimes against, a series of shifting psychological theories of sexuality.

The initial turn-of-the-century inscriptions and subsequent connotative meanings of 'lesbian', 'gay man', and 'homosexual' have distinct, if intertwined, representational histories. While changing meanings of male homosexuality occurred more or less in direct relation to social attitudes about and activism by gay men, lesbians were caught between two political tides more socially legible than the one they attempted to forge as their own. Although particular lesbians have attempted to wrest control over the meaning of their image, at least for themselves, the social concept of lesbian has been influenced in complex ways by changing attitudes both about heterosexual women's social role and about the relative deviance of male homosexuality. From the 1950s through the 1970s, lesbians formed useful if often difficult alliances both with straight women and with gay men. The anti-feminist backlash and the emergence of AIDS made lesbians' relation to both straight women and gay men even more contentious. Apparently, mainstream culture had similar difficulties: while still viewed as queer, lesbian sexuality was 'clean', tainted neither by the sordid sex which produced AIDS nor by the messy sex which produced babies. In the United States, the media and private citizens tacitly recast lesbian baby boomers as the angels of mercy in the gay community and as the solution to the two-career, working-mom(s) family. Lesbians became the new superwomen who tended to the sick while being both thirty-something and (more or less) married with (immaculately conceived) children.

The historical trajectory of film lesbians shows the schizophrenic logics which underwrite the idea of female homosexuality. Although the idea of lesbian is always linked with sex, precisely *how* that linkage is made has changed radically from Nazimova's scandalous role in *Salome* (1975), in which her prototype liberated lesbian character is constituted through orientational nonconformity (though figured as decadence rather than psychological trait), to the liminal lesbian who served for decades to police the boundaries of heterofemininity, to the lesbians of *Desert Hearts* (1985), whose explicit desires could provide the warrant for a love plot in a film with a substantial heterosexual crossover audience.

The problem with approaches which dehistoricize 'stereotype' in the service of recovering a hidden history is that they treat images as if they exist outside the stories which organize them. Saussure's semiotics suggested that the sign and its referent are inherently arbitrary, and that the mental concepts to which images refer can slide and realign. Pierce's semiotics suggests that there are gradations of arbitrariness in the sign. Feminist film critic Teresa de Lauretis develops Pierce to suggest that the image woman, and the particular signs she carries, may be iconic (standing for a cultural belief about women), symbolic (suggesting the presence of sexuality or of femininity), but is almost never indexical, that is to say, almost never stands for a particular woman herself.

Separating film from historicized concepts and self-concepts of homosexual, gay and lesbian identities has resulted in overemphasis on the search for and critique of 'stereotypes', both the classic negative ones like the predator–dyke in *The Killing of Sister George* (1968) and pablum counterstereotypes like the yuppy gay men in *Making Love* (1982). To simply hunt down stereotypes and attempt to replace them fails to understand that narrative film works precisely through loading up characters with signs which refer to something larger than the description of the character who wears them. Signs stand for class traits, issues, and even stand as boundary lines between forms of human being: changing the constellation of these signs doesn't automatically produce more acceptable representations, as critical reception of *Making Love* and *Desert Hearts* showed.

Claims about invisibility are complex, suggesting both a lack of specific images, but also a lack of interpretive practices. What lesbians and gay men mean when they demand visibility is control over interpretation of the images they have chosen to represent themselves; we want the mainstream to make of 'our' images what we want them to. But lesbian and gay visibility has not worked this way: even our best shot at positive images seem to fold back into the homophobic interpretive scheme – the men in *Making Love* traded the stereotype that gay men are promiscuous, non-domestic and perverted for the stereotype that they are economically privileged narcissists. Once it was permissible to present images of lesbians and gay men, they turned out to look like everyone else. It was difficult to make lesbians and gay men legible without marking them as different using the very signs – like gender nonconformity – which were viewed as stereotypical and damaging to the social status of lesbians and gay men in the first place. There was a lack of cinematic language to tell us that characters were gay or lesbian without at the same time reifying unconscious or inarticulate stereotypes.

The problems of queer representation are importantly different from, though contingent upon, the problems of producing non-stereotypical images of, for example, African Americans. Even with the demise of the enforced, self-abnegating acting styles and standard race-marking props (from watermelons to shack set to clothes and movements), black characters could be ineluctably legible as black by enforcing casting decisions about skin tone. This visual regime was unchanged by films about passing (where the passing character was virtually always played by a white actor) and even in the long reign of stardom granted to Sydney Poitier, the single black actor who got to be a black *person*. But where black *actors* cannot help but signify the problem of race, gay *characters* (with the exception of Harvey Firstein in his own *Torch Song Trilogy*, always played by reputedly 'straight' actors) could not be identified unless they were intentionally signified, either through gender nonconformity or, if they were 'ordinary', as victims in homophobic episodes in the narrative.

FILM GENRE AND POPULAR PSYCHOLOGY

Film became a viable and popular entertainment form simultaneously with the establishment of pop-Freudianism as the 'modern' way of understanding human behaviour (Walsh 1984). By the 1920s, film characterizations relied on popularized Freudian concepts and by the 1930s and 1940s, Freudian notions of the sexual basis of neurosis and psychopathology were virtually synonymous with film techniques for representing sexuality, desire, the relationship between work and sex, developmental concepts about masculinity and femininity and, in a broader sense, the dangerous line between civilization and primitive life which could be symbolically ruptured through gender nonconformity and mislocation of black characters. Of course, the popular version of Freudian psychology bore increasingly little resemblance to the master's work, and as psychological film theories emerged in the 1940s and 1950s and reemerged as psychoanalytic theory in *Screen* in the late 1970s, the literal link between the film practices under study and the film theory developed to analyse them began to be forgotten.

As film and film theory developed, film censorship had its own views on the psychological effects of film, and especially of 'talkies'. The older, sin-based theories of sexual and gender deviance which Freud sought to displace were all too present in the Hays Code, rereading psychologically challenging films about polymorphous desire into lurid morality tales about the hazards of queerness. Nevertheless, bastardized versions of Freud are evident in entire genres of film, for example: *Gaslight* (1939/43), and the gothic genre which makes it legible, testify that the female psyche will become unstable ('hysterical') if it is not anchored to that of a normal male; maternal dramas about unresolved Oedipal and Electral complexes (*Mildred Pierce*, 1945); career-woman comedies demonstrating the defeminizing and deheterosexualizing effects of breached domestic spaces and of women's entry into the public sphere of work; and film noir, which depicted suspiciously feminized and misogynist men as psychotic killers (*Rope*, 1948). Ironically, having situated sexual pathology largely within or in relation to women, two masculine genres – cop films and westerns – featured male homoerotic bonds and centred around male domesticity (the life of the station and around the camp fire). Apparently, the virtual absence of women from these films signified the absence of sexuality, leaving a wide space for now embarrassingly unselfconscious masculine desires directed at other men.

These genres emerged subsequent to the self-censoring film code, though perhaps not in any conscious effort to subvert it. In part because the Hays Code specifically forbade the depiction of 'perversion', but equally importantly because the early twentieth-century concept of homosexuality, still evident today, profoundly confused gender and sexuality, there are few overt representations of gay or lesbian characters in any major film until the 1960s. Not coincidentally, films which begin to address the 'problem' of homophobia appear concurrent with the articulation of homosexuals to the notion of minority identity in the homophile and later gay liberation and gay civil rights movements. Because society had yet even to approach consensus on the status of homosexuality – was it a property of persons or a temporary and controllable desire? – the Hays Code, which forbade both 'miscegenation' (specifically black–white, and not Asian–, Latino–, or Native-American–white relations, or any crossing within the 'non-white' categories) and perversion (in effect, failure to achieve heterosexual identity, but also overproduction of heterosexual practice, including kissing) was unclear on what the Code meant to police. Censors made increasingly minute distinctions about gestures, looks, content of dialogue, and even acting styles in its attempt to weed out queerness (Russo 1981).

At the time of the Hays Code, film was widely viewed as a fantasy with the power to evoke bodily pleasure and transgression: the 'reality' in film was phenomenological not representational. In effect, the Code adopted a psychological rather than sociological definition of homosexuality and miscegenation, proscribing representation of feared pathologies rather than the erasure of certain types of people. In a sense, there were not yet homosexual persons to be banned. Even films about passing permitted the appearance of the 'mulatto' person, but went to great lengths to avoid explaining the perverse congress which allowed their conception. Paradoxically, it was possible to fill the screen with homosexual and cross-race desire but never represent a stably homosexual person or miscegenating couple. Homosexuality as a psychic structure could appear and disappear in a single individual, and entire plots could centre around working out gender/sexuality confusions without these being construed as depicting homosexuality (Russo 1981; Dyer 1982).

In the post-Second World War years a range of 'message' films sympathetic to their 'gay' characters stabilized these fleeting representations of desire into fully fledged stereotypes. These films made humanistic appeals to the 'straight' world by showing homosexuals either as the victim of negative social attitudes (*Sunday, Bloody Sunday*, 1971 and *The Killing of Sister George*, 1969) or by demonstrating the psychological pain of coping with homosexual desires (*Tea and Sympathy*, 1956, and *Rachel, Rachel*, 1968). But these fell short of representation: 'gay' characters were only a site of struggle over social attitudes, not signs referring to members of a social reality with a culture, history and place of its own. Vito Russo argues rightly in the last line of the first edition of *The Celluloid Closet* (1981): 'There have never been lesbians or gay men in Hollywood films. Only homosexuals.'

But this would change in the 1980s with the mass-market release of 'gay films'. About a dozen such films attempted to show gay and lesbian life as it really is. These films were like manna from heaven for a community of people who had never seen themselves depicted as 'real people'. They included romance, cop films, and historical fictions – *Making Love, Lianna, Partners, Desert Hearts, Personal Best*. There had, of course, been much debate among gay and lesbian critics about these films – they're too stereotypical, they show too much sex, they don't show enough sex, too many upper-class gays, too many troubled gays, not enough of the problems faced by gays.

The films which featured entire plots about gay and lesbian life were important. Nevertheless, their plots were still structured around their characters' reactions to a homophobic world. Equally important was the introduction of a tiny number of characters whose homosexuality was not the 'problem' of the film, but was largely incidental to the narrative trajectories of the stories in which they appeared. The lesbian room mate in *Silkwood* (1984) and the gay male couple who are the club owners in *The Cotton Club* (1984) were some of the first articulated 'ordinary' gay or lesbian people who simply inhabited the world of a film.

In both cases, what enables the articulation of 'gay and lesbian' characters without raising them to signifiers of homosexuality or of homophobia are the existing class segmentation of gender stereotypes. In both cases, characters are just within the bounds of gender *conformity*, but only because they retain strong class markers. In *The Cotton Club*, the men are both 'masculine' publicly and privately – the 'gayness' is possible because they are older, gender-conforming, working-class men. Except for the fact that it occurs in a shared domestic space, their mutual affection is visually the same as that of their straight mafioso peers – awkward bear hugs and shoulder punching.

Karen Silkwood's girlfriend (Cher) is a working-class butch, still 'feminine' in comparison to the men of labouring class and because all the working women in Silkwood are more 'butch' than their middle-class counterparts. Although she is slightly *more* butch than her cosmetician girlfriend and than Meryl Streep, Cher evades the butch/femme stereotype because she and her clearly femme girlfriend apply makeup together and because Streep has already 'butched up' her heterosexuality through her political activism.

The Cotton Club and *Silkwood* shattered the closet, and with it the ultimate hermeneutic of suspicion: the desire to associate crucial plot elements with the appearance of homosexual characters. As counterpoints to the clearly gay or lesbian theme films, the representation of incidental lesbians and gay men meant that queer lives could cross the heterosexual stage but without demanding attention as a problem and without marking the boundaries of the bizarre. To some extent, cross-dressing – 1992's *Basic Instinct* and *The Crying Game* – would reestablish the closet, replacing homosexuality as the big screen's plot twist *par excellence*. Homosexuality continues to be implicated in both male and female cross-dressing, but the new presence of incidental lesbians and gay men means that while viewers might think they have detected homosexuals, they could not be sure that they had discovered the secret motivational scheme of the film.

Internal Affairs (1988) depended on gay and lesbian theme films to ensure that the intense relationship between the two male protagonists could distance itself from the unselfconscious homoeroticism of earlier cop films. The public articulation of gay men in media and films provided the basis for popularly held conceptions of gay men that made it possible to maintain that protagonists were *not* gay or wracked by repressed homosexual feelings. Similarly, *Internal Affairs* needed incidental gay men and lesbians in order to reverse the idea – intrinsic to Freudianism and to the generations of narrative film which emerged in relation to it – that sexuality

27

is the deep secret of the psyche and that the lack of secret equals adult heteromasculinity, the centre of normality. Stripped of any sexual secret, the incidental lesbian provides the vantage-point from which to observe the play of heteromasculine pathology. Heteromasculinity becomes the central pathology, an 'internal affair' with a language comprehensible only among heterosexual men. It is only because of her distance from heterosexuality that the dyke investigator (Lauri Metcalf) can suggest without irony or innuendo: 'Why don't you [Andy Garcia] and Dennis [Richard Gere] just take them both out and I'll judge which one is the biggest.'

GENDER AND GENRE: NEW AMERICAN GOTHIC, NEW AMERICAN OBSESSION

Internal Affairs starts out like an ordinary, if more than usually sophisticated and psychologically complete cop film. It has the requisite beautiful women and violent men: lies and corruption drive the plot's twists and turns. On the surface and palpable in the cheers and taunts of suburban teen audiences, the film is vicious towards its women and unrelenting in its displays of male–male violence and hatred of the cusp of homoeroticism. But crucial narrative supports for seamless misogyny and homophobia are missing and the film *can* also be effortlessly read as a scathing critique of masculinity and of heterosexuality.

The title is a partial clue to this twist, as is the visual style which locates this film as an urban cousin of New American Gothic, the hybrid genre established in films like *Blue Velvet, Drugstore Cowboy,* or *Track 29.* These new films are gothic because they deal with marriage/familial/ domestic psychology, but principally male versions of these. They revive and pastiche film noir cinematic techniques, and are made creepier by the substitution of the muted colour combinations associated with postmodern architecture for the black and white of 1950s noir. The wonderful Southern suburban architecture of the new film production facilities in coastal North Carolina provide the visual equivalent of the bad-seed narrative tropes associated with Southern fiction of the twentieth century.

Overwork and corruption – the two currencies of capitalism – emerge as the opposing symptoms of masculinity dangerously out of control. 'Internal affairs' is represented as the sissy, do-gooder division of the hypermasculine Los Angeles Police Department, where yuppy overachievers go to make the grade. 'Internal affairs' also marks the passionate obsessional death dance between two kinds of masculinity, embodied in Andy Garcia, the socially aware, sexually austere Latino yuppy whose work is his source of meaning, versus a distinctly unsexy Richard Gere, who plays the bigoted, middle-aged cop whose confused hypersexuality is itself a foreshadowing of Bill Clinton's play on 'family values'. With too many wives and a dozen children, Gere seems to use the family as a value or form of capital more than he values his families. The inscription of Gere's property scam on to his several 'families' suggests that the family itself is primarily a form of property consolidation, an intrinsic cog in a larger capitalist economy.

The film's plot is quite simple: good cop goes after bad cop and struggles to maintain their difference. The film replays this classic plot of masculine competition, but laughs at its own absurdity and retrogressive nature. Like a carefully detailed logic problem, the film proposes then evades the typical tropes that absolve heteromasculine pathology by blaming it on women or on the feminine underbelly of masculinity gone awry, previously represented as the oversensitivity of repressed homosexuality.

'WHEN THE GOODS GET TOGETHER'

Like Irigaray's punning conflation of women and property, the hetero-sexual women in *Internal Affairs* represent two forms of capital, but ones who inhabit a space which appears as a blank to the masculine eye. Garcia, the 'minority' cop who has traversed the class war from the barrio to the 'internal affairs' division of the LAPD, lacks cultural capital and is fitted out with an art-dealer wife. Her almost still-life world of form and aesthetics stands as a feminine counterpoint to the fast-paced and dirty world of police work.

Gere's women are conduits for his money laundering and real estate scam: he both possesses them under the rubric of paternity and familial obligation, and is possessed by them since they are 'the goods' who have the goods on him. Their psychological inscrutability marks the distance between the men's code of ethics and their feminine reality.

Garcia's cultural capital – the most beautiful and sexually faithful woman in the film – reveals the absence of sexuality at the heart of heteromasculinity. He is impotent, not because women's pathology destroys his sex, but because heteromasculine mutual obsession displaces sexuality. Gere's mistress, the powerful banker who has negotiated the legal but immoral mortgages, and his current (Latina) wife finally give up Gere, not out of moral duty but because he has jeopardized their economic capital by branching out into murder-for-hire.

Despite Gere's pathological, libidinal overdrive and high opinion of his sexual performance, the women are involved with him not from a reversed fatal attraction but for the money. The women are players, agents left undeveloped psychologically, not out of a misogynist impulse to deprive them of personhood but in order to avoid any suggestion that female desire elicits male pathology. Male psychosis arises within the psyche of men and needs no help from women.

BUDDIES AND BULLIES

Internal Affairs employs but reverses the typical buddy–bully relations, playing off abuse of buddies against obsessive bonding with bullies. Again, typical scenes establish the audience's familiarity with the cop genre, enabling the evasion of the usual psychological explanations for male behaviour. Early in the film, Gere visits a buddy who is strung out on cocaine. Gere caresses the face of the much larger man with the tenderness he had exhibited towards women leads in the 1980s films which established him as a sex idol. The homoeroticism and Gere's absolute sexual domination drip off the screen; Gere then has sex with his buddy's wife in a typical between-men displacement of homoerotic desire onto heterosexual sex.

But this rerouting of eroticism is *not* repeated: masculine mutual desire is cut loose because the principal women characters are place-holders in a Bourdieuesque economy of capital formation. They increasingly fail to read as women, and thus avoid serving as 'proper' (i.e., heterosexual) objects towards which men might reorient their desires. I emphasize the lack of triangulation because it suggests a move quite different than that proposed by Eve Sedgwick (1985) in her trenchant and highly influential discussion of earlier novelistic and poetic placement of women 'between men' to serve as a figural conduit for homoerotic desire. It may be that the establishment of lesbian and gay male cinematic *characters* – rather than signifiers of transient aspects of masculine and feminine psyches – makes it possible for heteromasculine mutual desire to be played directly, not as homoerotics or displaced heteroerotics.

The film knows that there is a fine line between heteromasculine mutual desire and homosexuality. Anal sex, which Sedgwick also establishes as a metonym for homosexuality, is not only invoked (not least in the title), but actually *heterosexualized*. Having convinced Garcia that he has not been sexually fulfilling his wife, Gere claims to have had sex with her. He corners Garcia in an elevator, shot Hitchcock-like from above (oh, Freud!) and, while beating him to a bloody pulp, tells Garcia that he has discovered the key to her sexual fulfillment: 'I fucked her in the ass', he screams, confounding the direction and gendering of anality as a sexual metonym. The same logic that separates women and men makes it impossible to equate Garcia and his wife: Gere doesn't want to fuck Garcia, he wants to outqueer him at the same time that he steals his property. The mutual inscription of the beating and the appropriation of butt-fucking at once reveal the violence of heteromasculine mutual desire (its sex must always be about domination, not desire) and liberates anality from its long role as a sign of or boundary-marker for male homosexual desire.

The competition between the men is not ultimately linked to homosexual desire repressed then unchained, but to a gambit of lies and deceptions that construct heteromasculinity as a blind rage. Thus the film's surface homo*erotics* refer us to deeper masculine pathology, not homosexual panic or homophobia but *andro*phobia, that will not be stabilized either by triangulation through a female or by designating one protagonist as a repressed homosexual entangled in the narcissism of a fully heterosexual male. Heteromasculinity has realized that a victory over a 'fag' is not much of a victory at all; the film is not afraid that some of heteromasculinity's actors might turn out to be homosexual, but that the aggressive masculinity may have been queer all along.

WHAT LESBIANS KNOW

The film is ultimately stabilized by one person, an investigator whose relation to the men is never sexually or domestically complicated and whose role as the 'normal' perspective on 'reality' is never in question. Freed from the necessity of linking homosexual desire to secrecy, the film has one person not racked by 'internal affairs': Garcia's lesbian partner whose sexuality is early stated and never problematized or produced as something-to-be-hidden. Like the later *Basic Instinct*, in which internal affairs investigators and lesbian knowledge once again collide, Metcalf – like Sharon Stone's lesbian author – is able to know something that men cannot. Not only is she Garcia's superior officer but she never mistakes his 'internal affairs' for investigative zeal: what lesbians and straight men know belong to epistemologically disjunct universes.

Again, the film must pretend to older tropes and then evacuate them. A smug audience thinks it knows Garcia's partner is a dyke. She has all the usual filmic markings: humourless, unpretty (though incredibly hot in her street clothes), oblivious or unresponsive to male attention. But where these signs would usually enter the viewer into a maze of closet queries – is she or isn't she?; are we supposed to think she is?; does the film know what it has done? – an early scene establishes her as an 'out' lesbian, or rather, outs her as lesbian in a way that is so stunningly dull that we are never allowed the self-satisfaction of having figured it out first. Both the buddy tropes and the homosexual as secret trope are shattered when Garcia is faced with betraying his 'buddy' by outing her in order to reestablish his loyalty to his wife, who fears that Garcia's passions are due to a sexual attraction to his 'new partner'. We know that his sexuality has been deflected into his obsessive relation to the object of his investigation: his desire is to 'nail' Gere not 'screw' his partner.

The phone rings in the middle of a marital spat, and Garcia's wife answers. Garcia, continuing their conversation, yells: 'I'm not having an affair with her, she's a dyke', which we hear echoed through the other end of the phone which is held by Metcalf. In this complex scene, the external truth of Metcalf's sexuality is announced not as a secret but as a reassurance. The non-secretness of Metcalf's sexuality functions in the film to

31

deflect the usual homoerotic buddy bond and foreclose the new possibility of the heteroerotic buddies which has developed as liberated women have emerged as partners in cop films. But simply making Metcalf not a buddy is insufficient. This could have been accomplished by desexing or desexualizing. The film has to permit her a sexuality, but make it unknowable and unavailable for masculine appropriation. She might simply have been given a girlfriend, but instead she is shot, not, as some might argue, because it is mandatory to punish gay or lesbian characters, but because this typical buddy-crisis scene serves to constitute her as a subject with a will, as the only cop free of psychotic drives.

She is shot in the front by Gere when she enters his house without exercising the proper police-assault precaution. She writhes in pain as Gere escapes. When Garcia finds her she apologizes. Garcia comes up to inspect her wound: 'You'll be okay', he reassures her, 'it went straight through'. His statement and the trajectory of the bullet obliquely describe her sexuality: she is penetrable, but not invaginated – the bullet goes right through. She can be taken, but not from 'behind'. Even in this most intimate signification of masculine violation, the bullet lodges nowhere, passes through, leaves only an aporia as its trace.

Her difference, and the film's final distance from buddy erotics, are reinforced while Garcia waits anxiously at the hospital in the now obligatory, if sadomasochistic scene of buddy domesticity. The doctor informs Garcia that whether she lives will depend on whether she is a 'fighter'. Traditionally, the erotically charged, verge-of-death scene serves to fuse the male buddies, diminishing their individual differences by producing a narcissistic relation in which the men's belief in and love of each other flows in a circuit of will and desire. The non-dying partner is capable of keeping his dying partner alive through the sheer force of his will. In *Internal Affairs*, this scene, though emotionally fraught, fails to achieve the necessary narcissism; Garcia is reduced to a plaintive child in the face of Metcalf's autonomous will to survive.

Giving her a sexuality but making it a non-issue leaves Metcalf unavailable for either maternal or heterosexual conversion; she is not so much asexualized as signifier of a space untouched by heteromasculine pathology. As the investigator who polices the police, the lesbian internal affairs cop is beyond the reach of the film's erotics. Like Wittig's non-woman lesbian she is beyond gender, beyond the long arm of the heterosexual regime.

LESBIAN SPACE VERSUS LESBIAN REPRESENTATION

The lesbian viewer, however, may be able to read off something about her life from Metcalf's character. For example, her changing from the stuffy 'dress-for-success' clothes she wears at the office to the jeans and jacket she wears to chase Gere is not only hot but symptomatic of the gender strictures placed on tough little butches in their professional roles. But Metcalf is barely legible as a lesbian person to the 'straight' viewer, and she is not meant to be. Instead, she is part of a representational calculus that means to critique the gendering of earlier genres of film. Metcalf's admittedly minimal role allows the plot to move forward not because her sexuality is a narrative problematic, but because she is the last kind of character left when the cop film goes politically correct and recognizes its prior dependence on misogyny and homophobia. Lesbian viewers who want to see themselves on screen may be disappointed by how little of Metcalf they actually get to see. But if there is spectatorial pleasure to be gained in deconstructing the politically regressive dimensions of long-standing genres, then a little bit of lesbian goes a long way.

REFERENCES

Dyer, Richard (1982) 'Don't look now: the instability of the male pin-up', *Screen* 23: 3/4: 61–73.

Kuhn, Annette (1987) *Cinema, Censorship, and Sexuality: 1909–1925*, London: Routledge.

Russo, Vito (1981) *The Celluloid Closet*, New York: Harper & Row.

Walsh, Andrea (1984) *Women's Film and Female Experience*, New York: Praeger.

Wittig, M. (1980) 'The straight mind', in M. Wittig (1992) *The Straight Mind and Other Essays*, Hemel Hempstead: Harvester Wheatsheaf.

Wong, Eugene Franklin (1978) *On Visual Racism*, New York: Arno.

2

THE MEANING OF TREUT?

Julia Knight

Within the space of a decade and on the basis of a relatively small body of work, the German director Monika Treut has made an indelible mark on lesbian and gay cinema. Her ground-breaking films of sexual exploration have, according to *Gay Times*, consistently challenged 'not only society's perceptions of lesbians and gay men but also our images of ourselves' (*Gay Times*, 23 March 1993). Her work has certainly attracted an enthusiastic following and excited discussion wherever it has been shown, and in recognition of her contribution to lesbian and gay film Treut was chosen as the winner of the 1993 *Gay Times* Jack Babuscio Award. Such an award is without doubt well deserved, in part precisely for the reasons cited by *Gay Times*, and is moreover very welcome since it accords the director critical acclaim in Britain that is long overdue.[1]

A LESBIAN FILM-MAKER?

At first glance, singling Treut out for her achievements *specifically* in lesbian and gay film appears highly appropriate. Several of her films, for instance, deal uncompromisingly with lesbian sexuality, often broaching highly controversial issues that other film-makers have studiously avoided. Her early short, *Bondage* (1983), is a frank documentary about Carol, a member of a lesbian S/M group, who talks about her predilection for bondage and the roles she likes to play: 'I identify as a top, but I'm switchable, so that sometimes I'm submissive. When I'm depressed . . . I have a friend put me into bondage and it makes me feel a lot better' (quoted in Treut 1984, p. 42). In her second feature film, *Virgin Machine* (1988), Treut uses the pretext of a journalist investigating romantic love and looking for her long-lost mother to give the audience a guided tour of San Francisco's lesbian sex industry. She recreates the city's long-since defunct Baybrick Club to stage an all-women strip show, and has her protagonist discover the pleasures offered by a lesbian call-girl service.[2]

On a personal level Treut's lesbian 'credentials' would also appear impeccable. She has consistently chosen to work with women who are established or prominent, well-known figures within the lesbian and gay community. She has, for example, collaborated extensively with film-maker and camera-woman Elfi Mikesch, with whom she codirected her first feature, *Seduction: The Cruel Woman* (1985) and whom she has used repeatedly as camera-woman on her later solo films. Although Mikesch's own films are often less overtly lesbian in content than Treut's, she is nevertheless renowned for her camerawork on the films of German gay directors such as Rosa von Praunheim and Werner Schroeter.[3] Treut has also incorporated into her film work such women as Susie Bright, editor of the lesbian sex magazine *On Our Backs*, and the outspoken academic Camille Paglia. Treut met Bright in 1986 when she visited the San Francisco Lesbian and Gay Film Festival with *Seduction* and, given Bright's extensive knowledge of the city's sexual subculture, invited her to play Susie Sexpert, the striptease aficionado and proud owner of an impressive dildo collection, in *Virgin Machine*. After encountering Paglia, Treut was so fascinated by the woman's energy and assertiveness that she was prompted to make a documentary portrait of her, *Dr Paglia* (1992), in which the so-called 'anti-feminist feminist' airs her views about herself and academia.

Treut is also among those who have spoken out in support of Ulrike Ottinger's provocative pirate film *Madame X – An Absolute Ruler* (1977)

Plate 1 Susie Sexpert enthuses over her dildo collection to Dorothee in *Virgin Machine*. (Courtesy of Out On A Limb film and video distributors.)

Treut (1981, pp. 15–21). Centred on a lesbian tyrant, Madame X, who sails a Chinese junk and entices women to join her on the promise of gold, love and adventure on the high seas, the film follows the fortunes of seven women who succumb to her offer. Rather than embarking upon new lives on Madame X's junk, however, the women are shown eventually and inevitably to reproduce the traditional power-relations and jealousies which the women's movement sought to challenge. Filmed in a highly stylized and anti-realist manner with an experimental soundtrack and obviously at odds with certain strands of feminist thinking, the film has repeatedly alienated many viewers.[4] According to Treut, however, this is precisely the film's appeal: its merit lies in the way it uses fantasy to 'break open' the narrow confines of certain lesbian lifestyles (Treut 1981, p. 15). And, although rarely shown, for some it has now become 'something of a lesbian cult classic' (Weiss 1992, p. 129).

It is unsurprising therefore that Monika Treut's work has circulated primarily and been discussed for the most part within a lesbian and gay milieu. Her films are always included in lesbian and gay film festivals, often programmed as a special feature. *Virgin Machine* (1988), for instance, received its British premiere in a special sneak preview at the 1988 Lesbian and Gay Film Festival in London, while *My Father is Coming* (1991) was screened as part of the opening night gala at the 1991 Frameline Film Festival in San Francisco. Treut's work is, of course, shown at other film festivals and in other contexts, but it is as if she has become almost *de rigueur* on the lesbian and gay circuit. And in Britain, only the lesbian and gay film distributor Out On A Limb has been prepared to bring her films into the cinemas.

Similarly, her work has on the whole received its most extensive coverage in the lesbian and gay press. *Gay Times*, for instance, ran two articles about her in the space of six months and this essay is included in a volume devoted to examining lesbianism and film. Where her films have been reviewed, they have also frequently been assessed largely in terms of their lesbian content. One reviewer observed that *Seduction: The Cruel Woman* 'reflects one way that lesbian-feminism discourse has changed over the past half dozen years: less talk about child custody, more about sadomasochism' (Carr 1986). And another reviewer described *Virgin Machine* as 'a joyous coming-out story, a fresh celebration of dykedom' (C. B. 1988).

Thus, to honour Treut for her achievements specifically in lesbian and gay film would seem entirely in keeping with the lesbian identity she and her work have projected and/or acquired in the course of the preceding decade. Yet, at the same time, her films have frequently angered members of the lesbian and gay community, eliciting criticisms on a number of different fronts. This is not to suggest that if a film is termed 'lesbian' it should necessarily appeal to all lesbians, nor that the term is or should be in any way prescriptive when applied to film-making. But these criticisms, when taken together with Treut's own public persona, start to make it problematic to try definitively to categorize her as a 'lesbian film-maker'.

With *Virgin Machine*, Treut was taken to task for 'enshrouding' the crucial sex scene between the film's central protagonist, Dorothee, and her escort agency date, Ramona, in 'filmic euphemisms' and 'visual rhetoric', rather than presenting 'what should be unequivocal fucking' (Harris, p. 23). Although some reviewers did applaud the film for its 'female eroticism' and 'raunch' (Harris, p. 23; see also *Square Peg* 1988, p. 8), anyone looking for something akin to the scenes of cunnilingus and orgasm in *Hungry Heart* and *Clips* made by the American group Fatale Videos would certainly be disappointed.[5]

According to Treut, however, for some *Virgin Machine* produced the expectation that her work was a guaranteed opportunity to see 'hot lesbian sex on screen' (Rosen 1992). Consequently, her next film, *My Father is Coming*, a gentle comedy with virtually no actual sex of any kind shown on screen, proved a disappointment to certain segments of the lesbian community. This, her third feature, annoyed for other reasons too. The American poster for the film presents Annie Sprinkle, who has a small cameo role in the film, in close-up, her pendulous breasts bared, leaning over the expectant face of a prostrate Alfred Edel who plays the eponymous father. Some members of the lesbian and gay community in New York considered the poster 'heterosexually themed' and Treut was castigated by *The Village Voice* for 'betraying the label of "lesbian filmmaker"' (Schwartzberg 1992).[6] And, as the 'unacceptability' or otherwise of female-to-male transsexuality has superseded similar debates around S/M lesbianism and pornography, the inclusion of a female–male transsexual character in the film also upset 'some politically correct lesbians' (cited in Warren 1992).

Furthermore, the director herself is not averse to giving interviews, introducing her films at film festivals and participating in after-screening discussions, and her own professed views on her work have done little to pacify those segments of the lesbian community she has angered. She has repeatedly voiced her rejection of 'exclusive lesbian politics', with its political correctness and insistence on so-called 'positive' images of lesbians (Guthmann 1991; Rosen 1992; Zeig 1991, p. 29). Instead, Treut has argued for the need to offer a full range of character types in lesbian films and has justified the possessive and bossy nature of the lesbian chef, Lisa, in *My Father is Coming*, by asserting: 'There are all kinds of lesbians. Lesbians are human beings and as troubled as anyone else in this world. . . . Why do we have to portray lesbians always as smart and beautiful and soft?' (cited in Rosen 1992).

She has also gone further and actively tried to resist the lesbian filmmaker label which has been bestowed upon her:

I identify myself in my work more closely as an artist than as a lesbian. The gay community expects from artists who are openly gay, like me, that our work cater to their needs. . . . I always had a hard time fulfilling these expectations. It is more than annoying that gay artists are supposed to promote a gay lifestyle. We are not advertisers, but people with visions, whose interests and obsessions are in constant change.[7]

(Zeig 1991)

And, as if to be deliberately provocative, she ended this last statement by referring to her fourth feature-film project based on Robert Merle's novel *The Virility Factor* and currently in preproduction, declaring: 'The main character in my next film will be a straight, "macho" guy. I wonder what lesbian audiences will say then.' Thus, in her own terms, the charge of betraying the label of 'lesbian film-maker' by using a 'heterosexually themed' poster for *My Father is Coming* would seem entirely inappropriate. Indeed, on more than one occasion Treut has maintained that she wishes to make films that appeal to and are accessible to a wide audience. With regard to *My Father is Coming*, for instance, she observed during one interview: 'I want to have different characters, make it an open film, an accessible film for different people, *not just the gay community*' (Schwartzberg 1992; my emphasis). This is not to assert that we, as viewers, have to understand or should only read Treut's films according to her own self-defined parameters. Rather, it is to argue that when considered alongside the aforementioned criticisms of her films, despite the apparent lesbian identity of Treut and her work, the director cannot be so straightforwardly or so completely integrated within lesbian and gay film culture as her winning of the Jack Babuscio award might at first suggest.

In this connection, it is interesting to note that since the release of *My Father is Coming*, perceptions of Treut have in fact started to change in some quarters. Given Treut's clearly provocative brand of film-making and self-promotion, one might have expected her to be included in discussions of the New Queer Cinema. But just as critics were in a position to reflect on the emergence of that cinema – barely a year after the release of *My Father is Coming* – Treut was already being dubbed 'post-queer'. In an article about New Queer Cinema in *Sight & Sound* B. Ruby Rich only mentions Treut in order to dismiss her precisely because 'by now [she] should probably be classified as post-queer' (Rich 1992, p. 32). Thus it would appear to be something of a paradox that the director be honoured for her contribution to lesbian and gay cinema just at a time when she is being excluded from what can be regarded as the latest stage in that cinema's history.

UNCLASSIFIABLE?

To a degree, however, her exclusion is unsurprising. *My Father is Coming* is a whimsical comedy about Vicky, an aspiring German actress living in New York and working as a waitress in between attending auditions. When her conservative, small-town father, Hans, arrives for a short vacation it precipitates a series of incidents which take both them and us, the audience, on a journey through a whole range of sexualities and sexual choices. As Vicky has told her father she is happily married, her gay flatmate, Ben, poses as her husband to try and maintain the pretence. When it comes to sharing a bedroom, however, Ben is more interested – much to Vicky's annoyance – in watching gay porn and talking about Latino men. After a disastrous audition for Annie Sprinkle's latest film, Vicky meets and is attracted to Joe, a female-to-male transsexual, and later also embarks on an affair with Lisa, the Puerto Rican lesbian cook at the restaurant where she works. Having accompanied Vicky to her audition, Hans, in contrast to his daughter, is charmed by Sprinkle who teaches him how to give his body up to sexual pleasure, but after finding Vicky in bed with Lisa he walks off in silent shock only to stumble across the Fakir Musafar who argues for the right to manipulate one's body in any way one wishes.

Although the film includes a lesbian relationship, it is not as central to the film as it is in Treut's two previous features: it would be impossible to review *My Father is Coming* in terms of its lesbian content. Indeed, the film is as much about the heterosexual Hans and his journey of sexual exploration as it is about Vicky and hers, and it is left unclear whether Vicky will choose to stay with Lisa or Joe, both or neither. Furthermore, while the film covers a range of sexualities, it steadfastly refuses to privilege or foreground one particular sexuality. So we see Hans responding positively to Sprinkle's highly individual, all-embracing attitude to sexual pleasure in a way Vicky cannot, while Vicky is shown as being open to homosexuality (among other things) in a way that Hans is not. When father and daughter meet up again at the end of the film, it is made clear that they have had time to reflect on their respective experiences and their attitudes towards each other have mellowed: they may not personally favour each other's choices, but they have come to accept that a range of options exist and have learnt to be tolerant of that which is 'different'. 'Different' *may* mean 'lesbian', but it may mean many other things too, depending on one's own preference; and the fact that the film does not celebrate one particular sexuality suggests that *what* it means is, in a sense, incidental. What is important, the film seems to suggest, is the need for tolerance.

In view of the conflicting perceptions of Treut's work, it is unsurprising that some film critics (including myself) have in fact commented on the difficulty of categorizing both her and her work – as anything, let alone as 'lesbian'. When I was invited to introduce *Virgin Machine* at Bristol Watershed in autumn 1992, I found myself almost at a loss to know how to start talking about her or her work. As Colin Richardson of Treut's British distributor Out On A Limb has observed: 'She is pre-, pre- *New Queer Cinema* but post just about everything else . . . her work is defiantly unclassifiable' (quoted in Rodgerson 1993, p. 78).

This 'unclassifiable' quality stems, at least in part, from Treut's eclectic brand of film-making which seems to display an irreverent disregard for all the established conventions of cinema, giving her films an unplanned, meandering feel which resists clear generic delineation. *Virgin Machine*, for instance, is narrative based, but the camerawork and editing during the first half, set in Hamburg, have more in common with avant-garde cinema. Filmed in black and white, there are moments where the lighting and framing of the actors' faces are also reminiscent of German silent cinema. However, in the second half of the film, set in San Francisco, Treut cuts quite abruptly from her fictional narrative to Susie Sexpert talking direct to camera, as if she is a presenter on a magazine-style television programme.

Furthermore, Treut enjoys incorporating real-life women into her fictional stories, blurring the distinctions between the two: the character of Susie Sexpert in *Virgin Machine* is based largely on Susie Bright's own persona, while *My Father is Coming* features Annie Sprinkle as herself. This overall style of film-making has resulted in writers using a bizarre array of adjectives whenever they try to describe what her films are actually like to look at and watch, ranging from quirky, off-beat and weird, through amateurish, conventional and intimate, to feminist New Age, sophisticated and radical. Indeed, one reviewer went so far as to suggest that with *My Father is Coming* Treut had invented an entirely new genre for the nineties: 'Capra-porn' (Scott).

CONTROVERSIAL?

Although it does little to convey any real sense of what her films are like or about, the one term that has been used repeatedly in reviews and discussions of Treut's work – and hence appears less open to dispute – is 'controversial'. The persistent use of this term could easily be attributed to her penchant for exploring those sexualities and areas of sexual practice that tend to be predominantly represented at the very least as transgressive, if not outrightly deviant or completely taboo: sadomasochism in *Bondage* and *Seduction: The Cruel Woman*, the lesbian sex industry in *Virgin Machine*, female-to-male transsexuality in *My Father is Coming* and a subsequent documentary *Max* (1992), and Annie Sprinkle's 'post-porn modernist art' in an earlier documentary, *Annie* (1989). In view of her preferred subject matter, the 'controversial' label has certainly functioned squarely to identify her as part of a sexual underground or subculture. And it is possible to argue that this – given that she is 'openly gay' and has addressed lesbianism in her films – has made the 'lesbian film-maker' label appear the most appropriate.

However, her reputation for being 'controversial' in fact stems principally from only one film, her first feature *Seduction: The Cruel Woman* (1985), rather than from her complete body of work. Moreover, the controversy has very little to do with any actual lesbian or sadomasochistic 'content' and much more to do with the film's production history and reception. Even before the film was made, Treut and her codirector Mikesch found themselves at the centre of a 'scandal'. Shortly after the project had been awarded funding, the German Minister of the Interior arbitrarily withdrew the production grant due to what he argued was an unacceptable combination of 'filth' and eroticism. He is reported to have objected to one scene in particular where a male masochist asks a professional dominatrix if he can be her toilet (Ripploh 1986, pp. 46–9; Saalfield 1989, pp. 40–3). After raising funds elsewhere the film was eventually premiered at the 1985 Berlin Film Festival and, as Treut recalls, it caused an outcry:

> That opening was like a riot. It's still a nightmare to me. . . . It was packed, sold out three days beforehand because in Germany the scandal was known about the Minister. . . . We didn't know what was going to happen. . . . In Berlin they have panel discussions after the films and the audience got so mad. They attacked us. Only people who hated the film talked. That was only men. They just went crazy: 'This is one of the worst movies I have ever seen in my life, blah, blah, blah.' I hate it when audiences act like this so I got pretty cruel myself. From the stage I was lecturing about masochism and saying, 'you don't have any idea what you're talking about'. The festival director said, 'Ms Treut calm down . . .'. Elfi was in major shock, she couldn't say a thing. The actors were frozen. The audience went crazy. So it was a big riot scene.
>
> (in Saalfield 1989, p. 42)

The film met with a similar kind of reception at its Canadian premiere in 1986 at Toronto's Festival of Festivals. Initially the film was banned by the Ontario Film Review Board on the basis that it was 'pornographic and injurious to the dignity of women' (Ripploh 1986, p. 47). But the festival appealed and the decision was reversed. However, after the screening members of the audience 'persisted in asking if the film was autobiographical', as Gillian Rodgerson relates: 'I remember Monika Treut being visibly frustrated at this refusal to discuss the film as a film; they were much more interested in her sex life than in her work' (Rodgerson 1992, p. 25).

41

Thus Treut and her work very quickly acquired a reputation for causing controversy, and the reception of *Seduction* has remained a 'talking point' in subsequent interviews with her and in articles about her (see, for instance, Saalfield 1989, pp. 40–3; Harvey 1991). But if we examine 'the film as a film', it quickly becomes apparent that while *Seduction* is about sadomasochism, or more accurately about S/M *desire*, and does revolve around a lesbian relationship it is much less (if at all) about lesbianism in particular or actual S/M sexual practices. Indeed, a textual analysis of the film suggests that the hostility with which the film was greeted in Berlin stems precisely from its refusal to show actual sadomasochistic activity, rather than from a genuine dislike or disapproval of that activity.

Loosely based on Leopold von Sacher-Masoch's *Venus in Furs*, the film is set in a pleasure palace run by Wanda, a professional tyrant, somewhere in the Hamburg docklands. Using a highly episodic narrative, the film follows Wanda through various encounters with her paying admirers and faithful servants. The film also charts the initiation of Wanda's 'innocent' American lover, Justine, into the sadomasochistic universe. On the night of her arrival at the beginning of the film she is given a guided tour of the pleasure palace and its 'toys'. Initially horrified, Justine gradually becomes fascinated and then begins to participate.

Although there are a few brief moments when the film shows either mental torture or physical pain being inflicted by one person on another, there is very little actual sex of any kind, or nudity, and no final act of total domination–submission. Instead the film constantly foregrounds the pleasure palace as a place where a paying public can go and act out their sexual fantasies or see them acted out. In one scene, for instance, a man and two women act out a scene of whipping in a room for a man who pays them to do so and then sits and watches. On several occasions Wanda and members of her entourage stage tableaux vivants while an audience watches. The acting in much of the film is also very theatrical, with the characters often consciously posing as if deliberately to create a particular image for someone else's gratification, and some sequences are more like filmed performance pieces than scenes from a feature film.

Consequently, rather than offering what one reviewer termed 'hard-core action' (Carr 1986), *Seduction* explores sadomasochism as a form of role-playing or theatre. Although S/M is often regarded as a form of sexual violence – like rape, for instance – Treut maintains that to reduce S/M to the practice of sexual violence against an unwilling victim is to misunderstand the sadomasochistic universe. According to the director, this neglects the possibility of sexual pleasure and personal expression that can arise from *playing* with feelings of power and helplessness. Having studied the writings of both de Sade and Sacher-Masoch, Treut argues: 'For me it's not about real brutality. . . . I'm interested in the liberating possibility of a game which appropriates images and projections of cruel women in order to draw pleasure and sovereignty from them' (Treut 1984, p. 35). In this context, Treut (and others) view sadomasochism as more of an art form which, like other art forms, offers the possibility of personal expression.

By showing the theatrical nature of the practices indulged in at Wanda's pleasure palace, *Seduction* constructs the participants as consenting individuals. As such, they are motivated by their own desire and Justine's initiation can be regarded as representing an 'awakening' of her sexual desires – and in a sense the specific nature of those desires is relatively unimportant. By highlighting the need for consent and sexual desire to be present if sadomasochistic practices are to be pleasurable, the film represents sadomasochism as a means of realizing a self-determined sexuality, of exercising control over one's own body. Thus, at the time of its original release, one reviewer asserted: '*Seduction: The Cruel Woman* offers what is probably the only intelligent inside view of consensual sadomasochism ever put on film' (C. B. 1988).

As if to support this reading of the film, Treut herself has pointed to the actual experience of viewing the film. She asserts that the film itself functions like classic masochist desire. By refusing to show the 'hardcore action' one might expect to see in a film about sadomasochism, *Seduction* arouses a desire in its audience and then indefinitely postpones its fulfilment (Ripploh 1986, p. 49). As a result we, the film's audience, not only watch but – whether we like it or not (and the Berlin reaction would suggest many viewers do not) – are drawn into and experience the sadomasochistic universe. And if we remain to watch the film we can also be said to participate in that universe of our own volition and thus remain in control of our situation.

THE PROMOTION OF SEXUAL CHOICE

Although *Seduction* revolves largely around the lesbian relationship between Wanda and Justine and explores S/M desire, it is possible to assert that the notions of exercising sexual choice and assuming control of one's own body/sexuality are equally if not more central to the film. Furthermore, these notions, together with toleration for sexualities different to our own – as opposed to the exploration and promotion of one particular sexuality – are arguably the overall structuring principles of Treut's narratives.

She brings these notions together most clearly and perhaps most successfully in *Virgin Machine* (1988), the humorous story of Dorothee, a Hamburg journalist who is investigating romantic love. Dorothee watches and photographs couples sitting on the river bank, interviews various 'specialists', but fails to find romantic love with boyfriend Hans. Dissatisfied, she starts to look elsewhere and the film hints at a sexual relationship with her half-brother. Eventually she leaves Germany for San Francisco, where she meets Susie Sexpert who introduces her to the city's lesbian sex industry and subculture. As Dorothee's curiosity is aroused, she also spies on a couple living in her hotel as they act out S/M rituals.

Although fascinated by this strange new world, Dorothee persists in her search for romantic love, believing herself to have found it when she meets Ramona, a lesbian sex therapist, with whom she enjoys a romantic date that culminates in a night of sex. But it turns out that, for Ramona, Dorothee is just another client, and she charges Dorothee for both her time and her expenses. This brings about a sexual 'awakening' for Dorothee which dispels her dreams of romance. It is as if she realizes that romantic love is a myth which, by encapsulating the promise of happiness, prevents women from pursuing their own sexual pleasure. Although Dorothee fails to find love with Ramona, she does experience sexual desire, and this permits her to start pursuing her own sexual pleasure by participating in the lesbian sex industry. The final scenes show Dorothee on stage at the recreated Baybrick Club and, afterwards, symbolically casting off her old life by throwing the photos she took in Hamburg – images of romance – into the sea.

The women Dorothee meets in San Francisco can be viewed as having clearly placed themselves in control of their own lives by creating their own lesbian sex industry. Not only do they bar men from their clubs, they also actively enjoy their own self-determined sexual activities. In one scene, for instance, Ramona, dressed in a man's suit, skilfully mimics the act of male masturbation with the aid of a beer bottle while doing a semi-strip for a highly appreciative female audience. In another, Susie proudly shows Dorothee her collection of dildoes and sex toys, taking great pleasure in detailing where she gets them and how she uses them. Thus the film suggests that it is not so much that women object to the sex industry itself, but rather to the fact that traditionally they have had little or no say in it.

Consequently, although the film does focus primarily on lesbian sexuality, it also clearly highlights the need for women to have the freedom to choose with regard to their sexuality. Treut emphasizes the idea of sexual choice, and hence promotes the recognition of a diverse range of sexualities by making Dorothee a journalist: rather than representing her as making a simple transition from one sexuality to another, Dorothee is shown investigating and assessing various possible options. The resolution of the film can therefore be read as the product of a conscious choice made from a range of possibilities, rather than as the only alternative available or the spontaneous emerging of a previously repressed sexuality. And if we accept this reading of the film, it is possible to argue that *what* Dorothee chooses is – as with Justine in *Seduction*, and Hans and Vicky in *My Father is Coming* – almost incidental. What is important is having the freedom to choose.

A PLEA FOR TOLERANCE

This tolerance for a whole range of sexualities that structures Treut's films is reinforced by her use of humour and by the way she roots her characters in the everyday. Much of the humour emanates from the director's predilection for 'showing very outrageous female characters',[8] which, when combined with the way she represents them as openly enjoying their sexualities, creates a strong sense of fun. This sense of fun allows us, as viewers, to share – and hence to some extent to identify with – the characters' enthusiasm and pleasure in their choices. This does not mean that we also necessarily share the character's actual sexual preference (although, of course, that may be the case); rather it is to suggest that since these characters are located within narratives that are structured around the notion of sexual choice, the humour helps construct a spectator position which makes it difficult to be judgemental about sexual preferences different to our own. Thus, irrespective of sexuality or politics, it is difficult to respond unfavourably to images such as Susie Sexpert discussing her dildo collection with Dorothee in *Virgin Machine* or Annie Sprinkle rendering Hans speechless during their encounter in a public toilet in *My Father is Coming*. As Treut recalls of *Virgin Machine*'s premiere at the 1988 Toronto Film Festival: 'Some really hard-boiled feminists came to see the film, ready to be angry; by the end, they were laughing and could not hold an anti-porn stance with regard to the film.'[9]

Although Treut is drawn to the 'outrageous', at the same time she avoids representing her characters as exotic or 'other' by rooting them in the everyday. In *My Father is Coming*, for instance, although we see Ben, Vicky's gay flatmate, watching his porn videos and posing at the local night club, we also see him doing his ironing. Similarly, while the film includes two short scenes of Annie Sprinkle 'performing', she is also shown packing up various sex toys in a cardboard box after a day's work auditioning for her next film. Even in *Seduction: The Cruel Woman*, Justine may be drawn into the sadomasochistic universe at Wanda's pleasure palace, but at one point she also complains like a sullen child about having to role-play a nurse because she hates wearing white! And just before Wanda's pleasure palace is due to open, another lover complains to a secretary: 'Do you expect the photos to hang themselves up? Everything is always left to the last minute.'

This 'everyday' quality is even evident in her documentary work. In 1992 Treut made *Dr Paglia* and *Max*, two of the four documentary portraits that comprise her documentary compilation, *Female Misbehaviour* (1992). As the umbrella title suggests, neither Paglia nor Max conform to dominant models of female (and/or feminine) behaviour – Paglia due to her aggressive brand of feminism and Max because of her/his transsexuality, yet Treut chose to film them both in very mundane settings: the plain living room of a very ordinary apartment or simply walking along a street. Moreover, in marked contrast to the distinctive camerawork of her feature films, both documentaries have been filmed in a highly conventional manner.

This is not to suggest that her films are or can be thought of as 'realistic'. Although she likes to use non-actors wherever possible – she found Mary Lou Graulau who plays Lisa in *My Father is Coming* 'on the street' and David Bronstein who plays Ben had been working as a secretary in her distributor's office (Warren 1992) – Treut has been quick to point out that the characters in her films would never meet in real life.[10] Rather, it is to assert that, in direct contrast to films like Jonathan Demme's *The Silence of the Lambs* (1990) and Paul Verhoeven's *Basic Instinct* (1992), Treut challenges prejudices about sexuality by representing as ordinary those people all too often constructed as deviant because of their sexual preference.

TARGETING AND CREATING AN AUDIENCE

The fact that Treut's films in fact encompass a range of sexualities, together with her use of humour and the way she constructs her characters as ordinary people, give her films the potential to appeal to a very wide audience. Indeed, since they deal with the notion of sexual choice and can be read as pleas for tolerance, it suggests they are actually consciously aimed at as wide an audience as possible. As Treut herself has asserted with regard to *My Father is Coming*: 'I would really like that straight people can see the film and enjoy a lesbian, a gay man, a transsexual person. I don't like to make all these divisions between people; I'd like to get beyond that' (cited in Guthmann 1991). She has also maintained that she made the move from documentary to feature-film directing precisely in order to gain access to wider audiences (Knight 1990, p. 21). This is not to assert that her films are necessarily specifically targeting a mainstream or mass audience, nor is it intended to deny the fact that her films may have specific appeal for some lesbian audiences, but rather that her films are not addressing a *purely* lesbian and gay audience; and thus to categorize Treut as a 'lesbian film-maker' is to deny the broader appeal and, more importantly, the wider relevance of her work.

However, despite the address and potential appeal of her films to a wider audience and despite the far more light-hearted tone of *My Father is Coming*, the labelling of Treut as 'controversial' has persisted. Indeed, it has almost become a 'talking-point' in itself in articles about her and interviews with her. Thus she is often asked if she considers herself a controversial director, or it becomes a convenient hook or starting-point for a discussion of her work (see, for instance, Zeig 1991, p. 29; Knight 1992, pp. 30–1; Harvey 1991). Although Treut has on occasion tried to distance herself from the label, stressing, for instance, that she just wants viewers of her films 'to have a good time' (cited in Rosen 1992), or simply acknowledging that her films get 'mixed reactions' (quoted in Zeig 1991), she has at the same time actively courted a 'controversial' image. As she observed in one interview: 'Maybe it's an old-fashioned European concept, that creating controversy is the most important thing for an artist' (Harvey 1991).

She has, for instance, issued or authorized publicity photos of herself which quite consciously and deliberately position her as someone who is very much part of a sexual underground. In one photo she appears clad in leather, very much the dominatrix figure, with an eroticizing back light; while in another she has slicked back her shoulder-length hair and donned a fake moustache to suggest her own possible leanings towards transsexuality. And she has been reported as having once considered having a sex change since she thought she would have an easier time as a film-maker if she were a man. However, she maintains she quickly dismissed the idea when she started to research precisely what was involved (see, for instance, Schwartzberg 1992; Rosen 1992).

She has also openly professed her support for other controversial figures, such as Camille Paglia and Annie Sprinkle. At a time when it was fashionable to be critical of – if not to completely dismiss – Paglia, Treut found much to say in her favour: 'What fascinated me in particular about Camille

Plate 2 Monika Treut and her masculine 'other'. (Courtesy of Out On A Limb film and video distributors.)

Paglia is that she comes over as a very aggressive, bossy woman. Her energy is amazing and a lot of people . . . cannot deal with her. She seems to talk at 360 words a minute, like a machine gun, she's extremely assertive, but also extremely interesting as a woman and as a female academic.'[11] At times she has been positively effusive in her praise: 'I think women need these kinds of role models. Camille is absolutely fearless, very smart, and a good scientist' (Schwartzberg 1992; see also Harkness 1992). Like Paglia, Treut has also risked the wrath of certain branches of feminism by suggesting that, in the struggle for equality, women have tried to deny the role hormones and their natural biology play in their emotional make-up.[12]

It could be argued, however, that by playing up to her controversial image Treut has simply attempted to utilize an age-old marketing tool to help create that wider audience for her films while using her eclectic brand of film-making to try to create a niche for herself in the marketplace. Controversy has always proved to be a big box office draw, and Treut has in fact demonstrated a keen interest in the promotion, distribution and exhibition of her work. She liaises closely with her distributors and, as already mentioned, is more than willing to be interviewed and to attend panel discussions. Her choice of titles and posters for her films has also served to fuel the fire: she has usually chosen sexually suggestive titles and some of the promotional posters for her films depict sexual encounters. In addition to the US poster for *My Father is Coming*, described above, the poster for *Virgin Machine* used the image of Shelly Mars's naked torso (Ramona) with Ina Blum (Dorothee) gazing longingly at her breasts. But, as already demonstrated, most of her films contain very little, if any, of the actual sexual activity that the titles and posters seem to promise.

AND SO TO CONCLUDE: A LESBIAN DIRECTOR?

As already stressed, Monika Treut undoubtedly deserved to win the Jack Babuscio Award in 1993, since her films certainly challenge perceptions and images of lesbians and gays. But it is possible to argue that her work also does much more than that. By persistently promoting the right to sexual choice and by representing as ordinary those people all too often constructed within popular culture as deviant because of their sexual preference, Treut can be viewed as having consistently argued for tolerance of different sexualities – *whatever* those sexualities may be. That argument means, however, that the relevance of her films extends far beyond the boundaries of the lesbian and gay community, and needs to be seen by a far wider audience – and Treut's self-promotion as a 'controversial' director can be regarded as one possible means of trying to achieve that end. If this is the case – and it is my contention that it is – then honouring Treut for her contribution to lesbian and gay cinema may be entirely understandable, but

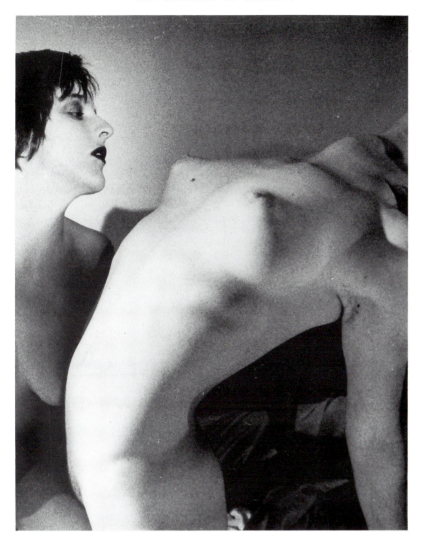

Plate 3 Sexual desire: the image from *Virgin Machine* used for the film's poster. (Courtesy of Out On A Limb film and video distributors.)

the labelling of her as a 'lesbian film-maker' is not only problematic, but seriously diminishes her potential to reach that wider audience.

ACKNOWLEDGEMENTS

My thanks to Val Martin, Monika Treut, Margaret Deriaz and Ulrike Sieglohr.

49

NOTES

1 The relative neglect of Monika Treut in Britain has been largely due to her lack, until recently, of a distributor.
2 An increasing number of film-makers have now begun to address these areas and sensibilities have changed to a degree, but for a sense of the controversial nature of such issues in the 1980s, see 'Lesbian Summer School', *Square Peg* 21 (October 1988): 22–3.
3 Mikesch has been noted in particular for her camerawork on von Praunheim's *Anita: Dances of Vice* (1987) and Schroeter's *The Rose King* (1984).
4 In her 1981 article, in *Frauen und Film*, Treut notes that when the film was shown at the women's media centre in Hamburg the audience was divided between stunned fascination and outright aggressive rejection of the film. When the film was shown at London's NFT in 1992 as part of a season to launch Andrea Weiss's book *Vampires and Violets*, it precipitated a similar reaction, with half the audience walking out.
5 However, Treut is currently working on an erotic short.
6 It is also pertinent to note that Treut's British distributor, Out On A Limb, chose an entirely different and less provocative image for the UK poster.
7 This is very similar to arguments made by feminist film-makers, especially in Germany, who found themselves expected to make films that dealt only wih what were deemed to be 'women's issues'.
8 From an interview with Monika Treut, conducted by the writer on 6 November 1988 in London.
9 Ibid.
10 From the same 1988 London interview, at which time she also explained that several of the women who appear in *Virgin Machine* were not actors, but simply people she met while in San Francisco for the 1986 Lesbian and Gay Film Festival.
11 From an interview with Monika Treut, conducted by the writer on 9 April 1992.
12 For Paglia's views see, for instance, S. Moore, 'The genda agenda', *Weekend Guardian*, 30–1 May, pp. 20–1, 31. Treut echoed Paglia's view during an after screening discussion at the Goethe Institute, London, on 9 June 1992.

REFERENCES

C. B. (1988) Untitled review, *Now Magazine*, 8–14 September 1988.
Carr, C. (1986) Untitled review, *The Village Voice*, 14 January 1986.
Gay Times (1993) 'Invitation to the presentation of the Jack Babuscio Award', London, 23 March 1993.
Guthmann, E. (1991) ' "Pansexual Comedy" opens film festival', *San Francisco Chronicle*, 21 June 1991.
Harkness, J. (1992) 'Treut film journeys through subculture', *Now Magazine*, 20 February 1992.
Harris, D. (undated) 'Thrilling ride through underground S.F.', *Calendar Magazine* (review supplied by Hyena Films).
Harvey, D. (1991) 'German director's latest controversial work', *San Francisco Chronicle*, 29 December 1991.
Knight, J. (1990) 'Vestal vision', *Independent Media* 95, January 1990.
——— (1992) 'Off our backs', *Sight & Sound* 2, 2: 30–1.
Moore, S. (1992) 'The gender agenda', *Weekend Guardian*, 30–1 May 1992.
Rich, B. Ruby (1992) 'New Queer Cinema', *Sight & Sound* 2, 5: 31–4.

Ripploh, F. (1986) 'Die Wahl der Qual', *Tip* 3, 86: 46–9.

Rodgerson, G. (1992) 'Playing it dangerous', *Gay Times*, September 1992.

—————— (1993) 'Film – winning ways', *Gay Times*, March 1993.

Rosen, S. (1992) 'Filmmaker Monika Treut in candid interview', *Quota*, March 1992.

Saalfield, C. (1989) 'The seduction of Monika', *Outweek*, 12 November 1989, pp. 40–3.

Schwartzberg, S. (1992) 'Treut films the outer edges of sexuality', *Eye Weekly*, 20 February 1992.

Scott, J. (undated) 'A gender-bending genre for the 90s', source uncredited (review supplied by Out On A Limb).

Treut, M. (1981) 'Ein Nachtrag zu Ulrike Ottingers Film *Madame X*', *Frauen und Film* 28, June 1981.

—————— (1984) 'Die Zeremonie der blutenden Rose. Vorueberlegungen zu einem Filmprojekt', *Frauen und Film* 36, February 1984.

Uncredited (1988) 'Movies', *Square Peg* 21 (October 1988).

Warren, S. (1992) 'Monika Treut, woman of the world', *Our Paper (San José)*, 12 February 1992.

Weiss, A. (1992) *Vampires and Violets*, London: Jonathan Cape.

Zeig, S. (1991) 'Monika Treut's dominant eye', *Off Hollywood Report*, Summer 1991.

3

ORANGES ARE NOT THE ONLY FRUIT

Reaching audiences other lesbian texts cannot reach

Hilary Hinds

Jeanette Winterson's first novel, *Oranges Are Not The Only Fruit*, is one of those success stories of which feminists feel proud. From its small-scale beginnings as a risky undertaking by the newly formed Pandora Press in 1985, through the winning of the Whitbread Prize for a First Novel later the same year, to its much lauded adaptation for BBC television by Winterson herself in January 1990, the work's reputation, like that of its author, has grown and prospered. Winterson itself is now unquestionably treated as a 'serious' author, highly praised by other 'serious' authors such as Gore Vidal and Muriel Spark; yet she is also a popular success, appearing on Clive James's chat show on TV and being sympathetically profiled in the popular press. The 'serious' side of the success story, her qualification as a representative of high culture, is largely dependent on her literary output: *Oranges*, and, more especially, her third novel, *The Passion*; her popular success and high media exposure can be dated to the TV adaptation of *Oranges*. That an author who is a lesbian and a feminist should be so successful in such contrasting contexts is seen as something to celebrate by other lesbians and feminists. Whatever misgivings may be felt about the traps and pitfalls of the mainstream, the sight of 'one of us' being given so much approval by the pillars of the establishment, whence usually comes opprobium, is a source of enormous pleasure.

This article examines the meanings of the ambiguous cultural status of *Oranges*, a text which cuts across the high/popular culture divide with its success as a BBC2 'quality' drama, and its acclaim from the popular press, lesbian audiences and serious critics alike. Through an analysis of its reception, I shall examine what it meant for an avowedly lesbian novel to be fêted by the mainstream media and press as well as being so successful within a subcultural context. Did the reviewers in the lesbian, feminist and radical press read it differently from those in the mainstream? Was the text's 'literariness', its high-cultural status, apparent from the outset, and how important was this to the acceptability of its unambiguous affirmation of lesbianism?

'FIRST FRUIT': *ORANGES* THE NOVEL[1]

Oranges Are Not The Only Fruit was published on 21 March 1985 by Pandora Press, the feminist imprint of Routledge & Kegan Paul. Usually described by reviewers as a 'semi-autobiographical novel', it focusses on the childhood and adolescence of 'Jeanette', and her relationship with her evangelical-Christian mother. Her mother's plans for Jeanette to become a missionary are thwarted when she discovers that she is having a sexual relationship with her best friend, Melanie; the rest of the narrative is concerned with Jeanette's resolution of the divergent pulls of church and sexuality on her life. Interspersing this narrative are short fables or fairy tales, commenting on the principal action, and direct interventions by an authorial voice.

Most reviewers agreed that *Oranges* was a notable first novel. In the mainstream and alternative presses, words like 'brilliant', 'beautifully written', 'decidedly imposing in [its] originality', and 'moving' recur. Critics delighted in its humour, decided it was 'quirky' and 'eccentric', and proclaimed Winterson a 'talent to watch'. A few reviewers, admittedly, were not unequivocal in their praise, complaining of 'utterly routine moments', that the novel became 'shrill', had 'the superficially modern pace of a pop video', or veered 'dangerously close to indulgent high-school diary entries'.[2] First impressions, however, were generally extremely positive.

There was general agreement, too, about the source of this novel's distinction: its decidedly 'literary' quality. *Time Out* identified 'an encyclo-paedic depth of knowledge [which] will appeal to literary magpies, with strange facts and unusual references popped in here and there' (March 1985). Others adopted the tone of the professional literary critic. John Clute in the *New Statesman* wrote of: 'the dense, polychromatic clarity of its rendering of the circumstances in which the protagonist and her mother pass their days, pixillated, obsessed with a revivalist God and His fallible Pastors, insanely blinkered but joyful' (12 April 1985). Marsha Rowe suggested that 'a narrative stance of bravado and sharp style plays with the idea that history is only storytelling';[3] Zoe Fairbairns discussed the functions of the three different viewpoints in the novel (*Spare Rib*, July 1985); *Ms* magazine compared Winterson with the established authors Flannery O'Connor and Rita Mae Brown, and the *New Statesman* com-pared the novel with a painting by L. S. Lowry. This initial acclamation of *Oranges* as a 'literary' text by the radical press was later taken up by the mainstream reviewers, particularly once the novel had won the Whitbread Prize for a First Novel. The prize became an increasingly important part of

Winterson's pedigree, particularly once she adapted the novel for television. This combined with the notion of *Oranges* as a 'quality' text, and both became central to how the TV adaptation was previewed and reviewed. 'Quality' is a key word to which I shall return later, but it is important to note that this concept was in play from the outset, not resulting from the Whitbread, but certainly greatly augmented by it.

The consensus amongst the different presses as to the 'brilliance' of the book, however, was not straightforwardly extended to their assessments of its themes. They generally agreed that the novel was 'about a Lancashire girl growing up on the Evangelist lunatic fringe' (*Time Out*, March 1985), or concerned the:

> early life and times of our heroine with her adopted mum, self-styled Missionary on the Home Front among north country heathen. Bible quizzes, distributing tracts and laying out the dead are all normal routine until adolescence sows the seeds of temptation. A delightfully quirky and original first novel.
>
> (*Sunday Times*, 1 December 1985)

Characteristically, a light-hearted, even flippant, tone was adopted, at times the reviewers even seeming to be trying to mimic the novel's narrative tone. Humour, then, a childhood within the context of an evangelical sect were seen as being at the heart of *Oranges*.

What marks out the 'mainstream' critics, however, is their contentment with this highly individualized account of the novel, its meaning discussed in the classic literary terms of character, narrative and authorial expertise. Critics who assessed the novel on grounds other than these were to be found within the 'alternative' presses. Zoe Fairbairns located the novel specifically in relation to feminism and religious ideologies: it showed 'the flourishing and development of some religious women's strength in spite of a patriarchal concept of god' (*Spare Rib*, July 1985). Few other reviews saw feminism as of any significance, *Time Out* even taking pleasure in distancing Winterson from the whole idea: 'Jeanette describes herself as a "post-feminist" and refuses to be allied to the oppressed women faction' (*Time Out*, March 1985). Most interesting, perhaps, is Liz Barker's review in the *Liberator*, which took the political significance of the novel for granted in a way few of the others had:

> The first [major point of interest] is in watching the power of institution unleashed when a challenge is presented. In this case it's the author's homosexuality which the church views as the work of a demon. . . .
> The second is that . . . the writer goes through the process of feeling rejected by the church but manages to leave behind the intolerance and illiberalism of it.
>
> (*Liberator*, date unknown)

This assumption that the novel had a political dimension, and could be read as a case study of the power of institutions (the church and the family), rather than simply being about a girl growing up with an evangelical mother, was exceptional, and did not recur in subsequent reviews of either the novel or the TV adaptation.

Most interesting, perhaps, in the light of critical developments in relation to the TV adaptation, were the assessments made of the theme of lesbianism in the novel. Most reviews, mainstream and alternative, mentioned it; they saw it, however, more as an element of the 'quirkiness' and humour than anything else: 'Jeanette, out shopping with Mother, discovers lesbianism while watching Melanie boning kippers on her fishstall' (*Observer*, 22 December 1985). Lesbianism was thus constructed as one more comic device, useful in moving on the action of the novel, marking the shift from childhood to adolescence, and effecting the break from the domestic status quo that the narrative demands. Other critics seemed to regret the lesbian theme as an untimely intervention into an otherwise 'highly enjoyable first novel': 'with the daughter's discovery that she loves other women . . . the novel shifts in tone – becoming more serious, but also more shrill and less self-assured' (*Publisher's Weekly*, 12 April 1985). Few, other than the *Liberator* reviewer quoted above, saw the lesbianism as symptomatic of anything other than the next stage in this *Bildungsroman*. It was not until later, when Winterson herself had come to be treated more as an 'author', that lesbianism became the subject of prurience and intrigue; then, much more familiar stereotypes of lesbianism began to appear:

> the Winterson legends which float around literary London would make a Bournemouth colonel gasp and stretch his eyes. Lock up your wives and daughters – rumour has it that many a well-heeled lady cared no more for the marital goosefeather bed when this gipsy came to her door.
>
> (*Evening Standard*, 7 September 1989)

The text alone had not seemed to offer the possibility of sexual intrigue and titillation to reviewers. It was only once it became identified with its author that the potential for 'lesbianism' to equal 'scandal' began to be realized.

By the mainstream press particularly, then, *Oranges* was not seen principally as a lesbian text: Jeanette's lesbianism was seen merely as a suitable foil to her mother's evangelicalism, its significance assessed in terms of humour, narrative and 'character'. Far from confirming Winterson's own assertion that lesbianism is at the centre of the story, on the basis of the reviews one would think it were, as one reviewer put it, one of 'countless novels on the stands about families, separation, and the emotional spaces people create or don't create for one another' (*Ms*, October 1985). By suggesting that Jeannette is a character with whom we can all sympathize, because lesbianism is just another human experience, these critics aspire to a universal reading. Whilst this liberal humanist reading has the advantage of being accepting and inclusive of lesbian experience, it does deny all sense of the novel having any *specificity*, whether to lesbian experience or to northern working-class experience. Lesbian oppression, whether in the form of violence, repression, stereotyping or denial, has no part in such a depoliticized reading, and thus remains unacknowledged.

'THE YEAR OF THE FRUIT': THE TELEVISION ADAPTATION IN CONTEXT

At the end of December 1989, the television and newspapers were suddenly full of a forthcoming television serial, Winterson's adaptation of her novel *Oranges Are Not The Only Fruit*, to be shown in January 1990. A good deal of media publicity and excitement, in the form of extracts, previews and interviews with Winterson herself, heralded the first episode. However, the screening of *Oranges* was also subject to a degree of pre-broadcast nervousness: what would a television audience make of the uncompromising lesbianism of the text? The BBC took precautions, many of the previews making clear that there could be scenes of an 'explicitly' lesbian nature. Despite the producer, director and writer predicting that controversy 'was as likely to result from the satirical treatment of evangelical religion as the sexual content' (*Guardian*, 3 January 1990), the newpapers focussed unerringly on the 'explicit nude lesbianism' (*Today*, 10 January 1990) in their build-up to the screening. Its lesbianism was seen to be the text's defining characteristic, and was the prime focus of the pre-broadcast press excitement.

Elsewhere, however, Winterson also suggested that the lesbianism would indeed be the focus for any controversy generated amongst viewers, because of the way that the protagonist, Jess (Jeanette in the novel), was represented:

> What will make people most angry is a feeling that they have been manipulated because it is very difficult *not* to be sympathetic with Jess. You want her to win out and it is very difficult to sympathise with the other side which is where most people would normally place themselves. . . . Finding themselves in complete sympathy with Jess (rather than family or church) is what some will find most difficult.
>
> (*Lancashire Evening Telegraph*, 9 January 1990).

Being 'manipulated' into identifying with a lesbian character, she predicts, will be the source of this hostility. But it did not work out this way; instead, reviewers in tabloids and broadsheets alike applauded long and loud.

What happened, then, to this expected rumpus, the outrage at 'explicit' lesbian sex scenes? In order to investigate this question, two factors contributing to the context in which the text was produced are worth exploring further, before turning to the press responses: first, the specifically historical and political context of the production, and second, the context formed by the history of television drama itself.

Particularly significant for the reception of *Oranges* were the repercussions from the arguments that had circulated in relation to two events of 1988 and 1989 respectively: the passing of Section 28 of the Local Government Act, which aimed to ban the 'promotion of homosexuality' by any bodies funded by local authorities, and the death threat made against Salman Rushdie on the publication of his novel *The Satanic Verses*. These two events had elements in common, most significantly in the responses and opposition that they elicited: the liberal arts establishment saw each as undermining the principle of free speech. One of the most successful counterarguments made in opposition to Section 28 was that posed by the arts lobby, who saw 'great works', either by lesbian and gay writers or concerning lesbian and gay issues, as being under threat from this legislation.[4] This argument carried the implication that lesbianism and homosexuality were to be understood differently in this context: they necessitated a response in keeping with their status as art, rather than in relation to their sexual/political status. Concerning Rushdie, the arguments were similar: the novel may be offensive to Islam, nevertheless the artist should not be silenced but allowed to function free from outside political or religious constraints. In both instances, then, the issue of 'art' was seen to be paramount: a text's status as art should protect it from the crudities of political critique. Thus *Oranges* was read in a cultural context where high-cultural 'art' had been established as having a meaning separable from questions of politics, sexual or otherwise.

Significant, too, in relation to Rushdie and to *Oranges*, is the way that religious fundamentalism was represented in the media: freedom of speech was being threatened by religious extremists, who were characterized as repressive, violent and alien to the liberal traditions of their 'host' country. Although this related specifically to the Muslim faith, it fed into and fortified a preexisting climate of opinion regarding so-called fundamentalism fuelled by news stories from the USA exposing financial corruption and sexual intrigues within the ranks of high-profile evangelical groups. 'Fundamentalism', then, came to be characterized as both a violent threat (*viz* Rushdie) and an object for our superior laughter, as its essential hypocrisy was exposed (*viz* US groups).[5] Both these elements can be seen to have played their part in the TV representation and media reception of the evangelical group so central to Jess's childhood in *Oranges*.

Also important for the reception of *Oranges* was the specifically television context: the traditions of drama and literary adaptations which have formed such a significant part of (particularly) the BBC's output. One line of the heritage can be traced from the *Wednesday Play* in the 1960s, through *Play for Today* to the current Wednesday night positioning, dubbed by the press the 'controversy slot'; these all have a reputation of presenting high quality work, although the subjects they treat and their modes of visual representation have also earned them the reputation of being 'difficult' or controversial. The other line of the heritage is traceable through the long tradition of literary adaptations on television, initially of nineteenth-century 'classics' by Dickens, Austen, Trollope and so on; and latterly of more contemporary novels such as *Brideshead Revisited* and *Jewel in the Crown*, until, as with the instances of David Lodge's *Nice Work* and Winterson herself, adaptations followed very swiftly on the publication of the novel. *Oranges* was able to draw on these two traditions, the drama and the literary adaptation, for it both occupied a drama slot, associated with such prestigious writers as Dennis Potter whose *The Singing Detective* is still used as a benchmark of 'quality' television drama, and yet it was also a literary adaptation and thus took advantage of the preexisting status of the novel and the author.[6] *Oranges*, then, was able to benefit from the institutional significance of the television drama and the literary adaptation even before the first episode was screened.

'HIGH QUALITY DRAMA TO SILENCE THE PRUDES': LESBIANISM AND ART TELEVISION

The traditions of television drama and the literary adaptation, then, have strong associations of 'quality' and 'high culture', and are traditions on which, by virtue of its scheduling and publicity, *Oranges* was able to draw. 'Quality' was a watchword from the start, both for author – 'whatever else *Oranges* is, it is very high quality television' (Winterson in *Spare Rib*, February 1990) – and for the previewers and reviewers: 'We *are* discussing art in the case of *Oranges Are Not The Only Fruit*' (*Sunday Times*, 21 January 1990). One of the ways it was identified as 'art' was to mark it out as different from the everyday output of television: 'This series may not be the "safe" kind which automatically delivers huge audiences, but it undeniably provides some of the most moving and humorous scenes seen on television for a long time' (*Television Today*, 18 January 1990).

The programme's quality was widely expected to result in formal recognition through TV awards: many joined with Tom Bussmann in predicting that 'there's a whiff of BAFTA in the air' (*Guardian*, 11 January 1990), and suggested that this was the natural sequel to the novel having won the Whitbread. Only Louise Chunn, writing in the *Guardian*, wondered if Winterson was not straying away from the pinnacles of high culture in adapting her work for the small screen: 'But this is the woman Gore Vidal called "the most interesting young writer I have read in 20 years", she's a Whitbread prize winner, a *serious* writer. Surely she's a novelist above all else?' (*Guardian*, 3 January 1990).

Although Chunn wondered if Winterson's literary credentials were not being compromised by this dallying with a mass medium, and thus with popular culture, other reviewers were more confident that she was simply translating her talents from one area of high culture into another: from 'literature' into a television equivalent of 'art cinema': namely, 'art television'.[7] *Oranges*, placed as it was in the 'serious' Wednesday night slot, can be seen to share a number of characteristics with what film critics have identified as 'art cinema'. With its high-cultural overtones of European seriousness and the avant-garde, 'art cinema' has come to hold an almost revered place in some circles, in contrast to other more popular cultural forms such as Hollywood cinema or television. Thus *Oranges* was able to retain its high-cultural status despite its translation into television, usually ascribed as a low-cultural form. However, the question remains as to how a *lesbian* text was able to occupy this high-cultural space so successfully.

Mandy Merck, in her article '*Lianna* and the lesbians of art cinema' (1986), has suggested that there is a particular relationship between art cinema and the representation of lesbianism: as she aphoristically puts it, 'if lesbianism hadn't existed, art cinema might have invented it' (ibid., p. 166). By this, she means that the representation of lesbianism in art cinema is sufficiently 'different' from dominant (more popular) cinematic representations of sex and sexuality to be seen as courageous and challenging, and yet at the same time it simply offers more of the same: that is, it works with the familiar equation 'woman=sexuality' (ibid.). Merck concludes that 'it is the legitimisation of the female spectacle which makes lesbianism such a gift to art cinema' (ibid., p. 173). Thus what is at stake is not only *what* is represented, but *where* it is represented: the underlying equation of women with sexuality may be the same in all kinds of representation, but none the less lesbianism is read as 'meaning' something different in art cinema than in other contexts; similarly, it was read as meaning something different in 'art television', the context in which *Oranges* was read, than it would have done elsewhere on television.

The 'controversy slot'

As with other 'quality' dramas, the controversy of *Oranges* was seen to arise primarily from the explicit representation of sex. Certain of these productions acted as sexual reference-points for *Oranges*:

> A lesbian love scene between two adolescent girls on BBC2 next week could mark a new stage in the passage of television from the kitchen sink to the boudoir.
>
> This new challenge to viewers comes after the explicit straight sex of David Lodge's *Nice Work* and Dennis Potter's *Blackeyes*.
>
> (*Sunday Times*, 7 January 1990)

The representation of sex in *Oranges* then, was seen as an advance on the work of Potter and Lodge in two ways: first, it showed lesbian rather than 'straight sex', which of necessity represented something more challenging, risky and 'adult'. This seems to confirm that for 'art television', as for art cinema, there is a strong association with and expectation of 'adult' and 'realistic' representations of sex. The sexualized context of this position in the schedule was of significance for the serial's reception: the representation of sex in *Oranges* could be seen as risky and challenging, rather than merely titillating. Secondly, the 'quality' of Winterson's drama was better: *Blackeyes* was repeatedly berated as 'that over-publicised, overrated Dennis Potter effort' (*Lancashire Evening Telegraph*, 9 January 1990) or as 'exploitative nonsense' (*Today*, 10 January 1990). Its 'quality' was a guard against 'those dreary public outbursts of British prudishness' (*Birmingham Post*, 18 January 1990). Together, then, these two elements worked to produce a context in which lesbianism could be read as something positive.

Decentring lesbianism

A second possible reason for the acceptability of the lesbianism in *Oranges* follows from Merck's claim that another of the features of art cinema is that it 'characteristically solicits essential humanist readings' (1986, p. 170). If this were also the case in relation to *Oranges*, then, it would imply that the adaptation's success rested on the critics' ability to read it as being *really* about something other than its lesbianism. If this was so, then it would confound Winterson's own stated hopes, for she asserted quite clearly that she framed the whole text as a challenge:

> I know that *Oranges* challenges the virtues of the home, the power of the church and the supposed normality of heterosexuality. I was always clear that it would do. I would rather not have embarked on the project than see it toned down in any way. That all this should be the case and that it should still have been so overwhelmingly well received cheers me up.
>
> (Winterson 1990, p. xvii)

The critics, in the mainstream press at least, signally failed to pick up the gauntlet that Winterson had thrown down. As with the novel, the lesbianism is decentred and the critics present us with a drama 'about' all sorts of other things. The three-part series, we are told, 'is fundamentally about a young person looking for love' (*Today*, 10 January 1990); it is 'a wonderfully witty, bitter-sweet celebration of the miracle that more children do not murder their parents' (*Observer*, 14 January 1990); it 'follows Jess in a voyage of self-discovery from her intense religious background, via a friendship with another girl' (*Todmorden News*, 18 August 1989); it is 'a vengeful satire on Protestant fundamentalism' (*Listener*, 18 January 1990). Although *Time Out* complains about 'the author's own use of that hoary liberal cop-out about *Oranges* being about "two people in love" – who wants to see that tedious story again?' (*Time Out*, 18 January 1990), most critics welcomed the opportunity to read *Oranges* as essentially about *all* human relationships, rather than specifically about lesbianism.

As with the novel, the decentring of the lesbianism does not involve its denial: in most accounts of the storyline it is mentioned, but nearly always in relation to something else, generally the ensuing rejection and exorcism of Jess by members of the evangelical group. In this context, lesbianism is seen either as comic comeuppance for her mother's repressive childrearing methods – 'Warned off boys by this hell-fire freak, Jess turns instead to girls' (*Financial Times*, 10 January 1990) – or as a source of pathos: 'a bitter-sweet tragedy, the tale of how a young woman tries and fails to reconcile her religion with her lesbianism' (?2, 11 January 1990). Lesbianism, then, is always seen in relation to other issues, be they religion, the family or simply 'growing up'.

'Unsafe sects'

However, this humanist perspective on the text is only one element in this decentring of lesbianism; another is the emphasis that is placed on the representation of religion. This is important not only as an example of this decentring, but also because, contrary to what most previewers predicted, it was this that became the focus for viewers' and reviewers' anger, rather than the representation of lesbianism itself. So, as well as the evangelical group being seen as one of the main sources of the humour of the series, its members are also written about as ridiculous ('prattling, eye-rolling, God-fearing women', *Daily Express*, 11 January 1990), and as a potentially violent threat ('each and every one . . . looked as though she could kill with a blow of her nose', *The Times*, 11 January 1990). Class stereotypes of small-minded working-class women here reinforce the ridiculousness of the evangelicals. Furthermore, their Christian fundamentalism is explicitly linked to Muslim fundamentalism, by now associated with repression and violence in the press reviews: Jess is brought up 'in a provincial family whose fundamentalist religious beliefs make the Ayatollah Khomeini, by contrast, seem a model of polite tolerance' (*Evening Standard*, 22 January 1990). This association of the two fundamentalisms, Christian and Muslim, with repression is further strengthened when *Television Today* expresses the hope that the 'small, if vocal, number of objectors' to the serial will not 'turn writer Jeanette Winterson into the nineties Salman Rushdie' (*Television Today*, 18 January 1990).

Subject to the most anger, however, was the exorcism of Jess carried out by the pastor and assorted members of the congregation when her sexual relationship with Melanie is discovered. Critics commented on the 'brutal' nature of this scene, noted that it is 'sexually charged', and Steve Clarke suggested that: 'if anybody was disturbed by the scene in which the pastor – armed with rope, gag and pulsating neck – straddled the young Jess to exorcise the demon of illicit love, then so they should have been' (*Sunday Times*, 21 January 1990). Hilary Kingsley in the *Mirror* concurred: the headline announced that the scene was 'Brutal, Shocking, Horrifying. But You Mustn't Miss It' (*Daily Mirror*, 15 January 1990). Anger and disgust were not only legitimate – they were to be actively sought as the 'correct' response; thus emotions that many expected to be directed towards the lesbian scenes were actually located instead with the representation of this repressive religious group. Perhaps it was possible for so much sympathy to be shown to the plight of Jess and Melanie not only because of the way their relationship was interpreted, but also because of the brutality of the punishment that they underwent. Their persecutors had already been established as outmoded, repressive and anti-sex, and it was a small step to add violence to this list by drawing on preexisting connotations of fundamentalism: 'Jess . . . is promptly subjected by her mother's fundamentalist sect to the sort of persecution and torture so dear to the hearts of religious fanatics throughout the ages' (*Financial Times*, 10 January 1990).

This clearly suggests that the punishment tells us more about religious fundamentalists than it does about the status of lesbianism in our society. The liberal viewer can feel distanced from the punishment meted out to Jess because these people, after all, are not 'normal' members of our society. This sympathy, then, can be seen to rest on two mutually reinforcing bases: first, it is a response to the punitive, anti-sex attitudes of the evangelical group – and even gay and lesbian sexual rights had increasingly become the objects of liberal championing since the passing of Section 28; and second, it is responding to the representation of fundamentalism, which had become a prominent liberal target in the wake of the Rushdie affair. Thus it appears that the yoking of the lesbianism with the fundamentalism was itself crucial for the favourable mainstream liberal response: lesbianism became an otherness preferable to the unacceptable otherness of fundamentalism.

'Unnatural passions': the role of the sex scene

If the representation of the evangelical group is a crucial factor in determining critical response to the series, this raises the question of what place *was* ascribed to lesbian sexuality by the reviewers. In relation to art cinema, Merck suggests that the lesbian love scene carries a particularly heavy burden of meaning: because of the tendency to allegorize these films, to read them as essentially about something other than the overt narrative, these scenes have taken on a particular symbolic function, namely 'the ability to represent "lesbian experience"' (1986, p. 169), to encapsulate the entire range of meanings of lesbianism, whether sexual, social or political. What meanings, then, were ascribed to *Oranges'* long-awaited sex scene, 'arguably the most explicit female love scene yet broadcast on British television' (*Sunday Times*, 7 January 1990)?

The makers of the series declared that their intention with this scene was 'to avoid the kind of romantic idealism with which lesbian scenes were portrayed in the 1988 BBC production of D. H. Lawrence's *The Rainbow*' (*Sunday Times*, 7 January 1990). The producer, Phillipa Giles, told the *Daily Mirror*: 'We decided to make it obvious that the girls were having a sexual relationship, not a wishy-washy thing. . . . We wanted to face the question everyone asks – *What do lesbians DO?*' (*Daily Mirror*, 15 January 1990). Most reviewers, however, read it with the kind of romantic idealism the makers were trying to eschew. It is 'romantic, innocent and beautiful', wrote Christopher Dunkley (*Financial Times*, 10 January 1990); the erotic relationship is portrayed in a way 'which maintains its essential innocence' (*7 Days*, 11 January 1990). Steve Clarke, in the *Sunday Times*, surpassed the others in his breathless enthusiasm for the scene: 'the two girls' tentative exploration of each other's bodies was almost Disneyesque in its innocent wonderment' (*Sunday Times*, 21 January 1990); anybody who objected to these scenes would simply be 'dreary' (*Today*, 10 January 1990). There is scant evidence, then, that these reviewers were shocked by this representation of lesbianism. Not only did the manifest youth of Jess and Melanie allow them to define and praise the relationship in terms of its tenderness and innocence, it also implicitly allowed the lesbianism to be understood as an adolescent phase, a naive exploration that would be outgrown. Moreover, the fact that the critics ignored any other scenes that might modify, or even contradict, this reading of tenderness and innocence meant that this characterization of the sex scene alone was allowed to represent the text's 'lesbianism', avoiding any broader or more challenging meaning of lesbianism.

Significantly few of the mainstream reviewers commented on *Oranges* as in any way erotic. Whilst most talked only of Jess's first relationship, with Melanie, in the 'quality' press only Mark Steyn allowed Jess's relationship with Katy, her second lover, to contribute to his assessment of the text:

> More shocking than any nudity was the parallel between religious salvation and sexual discovery, subtly drawn in scenes which were nevertheless masterpieces of suppressed eroticism. 'You were going to tell me about Jesus,' said Katy. 'Well, what is it you wanted to *know*?' asked Jess. 'Why don't you tell me,' Katy replied, lolling against the caravan, '*gradually*'.
>
> (*Independent*, 25 January 1990)

Steyn alone showed a willingness to go beyond the feeling that for lesbianism to be acceptable it had to be tender, innocent, essentially asexual.

Critics elsewhere, however, were more willing to contemplate an active erotic reading of the text. In the alternative publications, on the one hand, and in some of the tabloids, on the other, there is a marked contrast to this predominantly liberal mainstream interpretation of the sexuality in *Oranges*. Some of the tabloids, for example, made a concerted effort to construct a pornographic reading of the text. They anticipated the 'fruitiest lesbian love scenes ever on British TV' (?2, 11 January 1990), employing words like 'steamy' or 'torrid', and concentrated on the actresses' feelings about the sex scene to try and enhance this sense of the illicit and risky. Most notable of these attempts was one that appeared in *Today*:

> According to a male friend, the lesbian love scenes in this drama are not nearly fruity enough. In order to fully fulfil the 'ultimate male fantasy' he says the actresses should have had bigger breasts.
>
> What we need, he adds, is a lot more tits. Samantha Fox and Maria Whitaker would be ideal.
>
> Had this transpired, I would have had to suggest a slightly different title for this excellent serial: Melons Are Not The Only Fruit . . .
>
> (*Today*, 25 January 1990)

By referring to perhaps the two most famous 'Page 3' models as potential participants in this drama, there is a clear – perhaps even rather desperate – attempt to recruit what had looked as if it was going to be 'the ultimate male fantasy' for that function. The serial had evidently fallen short of what might be expected of something that included 'explicit nude lesbianism'. Since it was not close enough to the ethos of 'Page 3', it was necessary both to force this reading on to the text by means of such epithets as 'torrid' and 'steamy', and to reconstruct it as a tabloid ideal by recasting and renaming it, both of which would emphasize more strongly its pornographic possibilities. Whilst, then, the 'eroticism' of the text was acknowledged as central here, this review makes clear that the text did not lend itself easily to the expected and desired pornographic understanding of lesbianism: it was seen as having a meaning independent of, or separate from, dominant male fantasy, and was thus in need of reworking in line with such conventions.

In the alternative presses, by contrast, this separateness both from male fantasy and from 'Disneyesque' tenderness was seen as one of the serial's strengths: Jonathan Sanders in *Gay Times* noted that 'Jess and Melanie's fireside coupling steered a fine course between eroticism and the straight male prurience consideration' (*Gay Times*, March 1990). Cherry Smyth's assessment of the sex scene, in *Spare Rib*, identified it as 'radical' and different from more usual representations of lesbianism on TV:

Although a little pre-Raphaelite in style, the scene is uncomplicated and unapologetic. Their refreshing lack of embarrassment and shame is a breakthrough for a mainstream TV drama slot. Is BBC2 stealing the radical remit from Channel 4? Jess is too knowing and sure of her desire for the scene to collapse into pre-pubescent coyness and 'innocent' caressing.

(*Spare Rib*, February 1990)

The very quality of innocence which the mainstream reviewers identified is denied here, and is instead replaced by its opposite: the assertion that Jess is 'knowing' and 'sure of her desire'. Sanders, similarly, had found 'heartening' the 'uniform moral ease and technical skill with which the teenage lesbians expressed their desires' (*Gay Times*, March 1990). Although Rosalind Brunt identified one of the main themes of *Oranges* as 'passionate erotic friendship between young women' (*New Statesman and Society*, 12 January 1990), it was only the lesbian and gay critics who situated the text firmly within a discourse of desire. Not only was 'innocence' countered in these reviews, but also, in *Spare Rib* in particular, there was an emphasis on the subtlety of the sexual references employed: 'Jess introduces Melanie to church and leads the congregation in "When I was sleeping, somebody touched me", a delightful innuendo that prefigures the scene where the young women make love' (*Spare Rib*, February 1990). This interpretation and emphasis from Smyth suggests that perhaps the text operated rather differently for lesbian and gay audiences: used to relying on the subtleties of innuendo and veiled meanings, they read the text through a specific set of codes apparently undiscerned by other audiences.[8]

The politics of the lesbian text

As well as discussing the sex scene, Smyth also broadened out the political focus of her review by stressing the radical possibilities of the representation of lesbianism in *Oranges*: 'At the point where the fate of many a dramatic lesbian character is firmly sealed, Jess continues to convert young women to her way of loving' (*Spare Rib*, February 1990); Jess thus retains her position as agent and heroine throughout. This review is notable, too, for referring outside the series, to a 'lived experience' of lesbianism, in order to measure the 'quality' of the drama: 'The awkward milkshakes and doorways she shares with Katy, her young Asian lover, convey the desperately unhappy courtship of adolescents who haven't "somewhere proper to go"' (ibid.).

It was not only the alternative publications that hinted at the political significance of the drama. Kate Battersby, in *Today*, hinted at a feminist reading of the text when she suggested that 'many women will identify with the adolescent Jess's bid for freedom and self-expression' (*Today*, 10 January 1990). Another very favourable piece, also by a woman, Hilary Kingsley, says that *Oranges* is:

an important milestone for women.

Male homosexuality has been represented in television drama frequently over the years.

But to television, as to Queen Victoria, lesbians do not exist – except in an Australian jail.

No wonder the late night soap *Prisoner: Cell Block H* has a high following among gay women.

(*Daily Mirror*, 15 January 1990)

Despite historical inaccuracies (lesbianism clearly *had* been represented on television before),[9] Kingsley was identifying something important by suggesting that *Oranges* was an exceptional text in making lesbianism its central concern.

Lesbian viewers seemed to agree that *Oranges* was a milestone, staying at home in droves on Wednesday nights to watch it. This enthusiasm was in part, no doubt, because it made lesbianism a visible presence on television where, with the exceptions of *Prisoner*, *Out On Tuesday* and some documentaries and films, it was usually invisible. Moreover, it became visible in a mainstream slot, rather than in the furtive late-night positions of most representations of lesbian and gay issues on television. The way that the lesbianism was represented was also unusual: rather than becoming either villain or victim, the lesbian protagonist remained a heroine throughout. The screening of *Oranges* on BBC2 also represented the infiltration of that bastion of television high-cultural respectability by a programme directed and produced by women, scripted by a lesbian, and one whose main themes was lesbianism; this, too, added a certain edge to the pleasure of *Oranges* for a lesbian audience. Furthermore, whatever debates may rage about the dangers or desirability of being accepted by dominant culture, here, at last, was a programme about lesbianism that, far from being run down or ignored by the reviewers, was praised to the skies. From many perspectives, then, *Oranges* signified something pleasurable and exceptional for lesbian viewers.

CONCLUSION: *ORANGES* TO EVERYONE'S TASTE

BBC's *Oranges Are Not The Only Fruit* . . . had the capacity to make us laugh and cry, to shock us with its brutal exorcism scene, to move us with its compassion for youthful lesbian love and to leave us – as at the end of a good book – silently grieving the loss of a friend.

Oranges is a book, of course. And how delighted author Jeanette Winterson must have been. Seldom can a fine novel have been transported with such skill and with such little disruption to the small screen.

(Daily Express, 25 January 1990)

In many ways Peter Tory's review summarizes some of the complexities of what *Oranges* represented for viewers, as well as suggesting some of the reasons why it met with the success that it did. To begin with, it confirms the text as an example of high status 'art': the prestige lent to the whole enterprise by the presence of the original novel; the 'faithfulness' of the adaptation, avoiding what Mark Steyn had called 'the coarsening effects' of translation into a mass medium (*Independent*, 25 January 1990); the text's capacity to appeal to our common humanity and provoke the great and enduring human emotions and responses of joy, sadness, anger and compassion – all these confirm the text's relationship to high culture.

And yet this review did not appear in a 'quality' newpaper, where we might expect to find support for such a cultural product, but in the popular press, endorsing a serial whose precursors, such as Potter's *Blackeyes*, had often been roundly condemned as pretentious nonsense. Moreover, it appeared in the *Daily Express*, a newspaper not usually noted for its sympathy for 'do-gooding' liberal causes. Tory's 'compassion for youthful lesbian love' may not be the response which many lesbians would seek, but it is none the less an unequivocally and uncharacteristically welcoming reading of the production's representation of lesbianism.

These complexities and ambiguities demonstrate the need to consider the validity of the terms of the high/popular culture divide, for *Oranges*, as a complete cultural product – author, novel, television drama – seems consistently to elude and collapse these categories. Central to this elusiveness seems to be the text's lesbianism. Although it may be true to say that the lesbianism is defused by the text's associations with high culture and its consequent openness to a liberal interpretation, it is also true that *Oranges* has retained, and increased, its lesbian audience and its subcultural consumption, and has also been praised by a tabloid press usually hostile to lesbian and gay issues.

Not all lesbian texts, of course, operate as *Oranges* does. However, the remarkable, if rather confusing, popularity of this text highlights some of the general complexities that emerge when one introduces the category of the 'lesbian text' into cultural analysis. Whilst it is possible to think of several lesbian texts that come within the category of high culture, such as those of Gertrude Stein or Radclyffe Hall, and others, such as those by Sarah Dreher and Anne Bannon, that would be considered lesbian pulp fiction, many lesbian texts defy such categorizations. Indeed, even the examples mentioned above pose problems: some critics happily claim *The Well of Loneliness* for the canon whilst still conceding that it is 'bad writing'. Moreover, the readership of much recent lesbian pulp fiction is

67

arguably more diverse than its heterosexual equivalent. Precisely because of the lack of representations of lesbianism within mainstream culture, lesbian texts which are available take on a particular significance. Lesbian readers and viewers do not divide neatly into consumers of high or popular culture, since their prime interest here is often the representation of a lifestyle, an identity or a sexuality which is marked by its absence elsewhere within the media or literature. This, then, raises the question of whether the introduction of the question of lesbianism confounds many of the assumptions about texts and readers which have informed debates about high and popular culture in much criticism in recent years.

And what, finally, of *Oranges* itself? Having asserted its fluidity, its ability to cut across so many critical and cultural categories and positions, its refusal to be pigeonholed as one sort of text or another, its appeal for a diversity of audiences, it is impossible to arrive at a conclusive statement about it. Perhaps it is enough to suggest that any text that can transgress so many barriers deserves all the critical attention – from whatever source and from whatever perspective – that it can get.

ACKNOWLEDGEMENTS

I would like to thank the following people for their help, and for their perceptive and encouraging comments on earlier drafts of this article: Richard Dyer, Lynne Pearce, Martin Pumphrey, Margaret Reynolds, Fiona Terry and, especially, Jackie Stacey.

NOTES

1 Subtitles appearing in inverted commas are borrowed from newspaper reviews of *Oranges*.

2 These comments are drawn from reviews of *Oranges* published in, amongst others, the *New Statesman*, *Publishers Weekly*, *Everywoman*, the *Times Literary Supplement*, the *Sunday Times*, *Ms*, the *Observer*, and *Time Out*.

3 Extracts that are referenced ?1 and ?2 are from uncredited reviews kindly sent to me by Pandora Press.

4 For further exploration of the terms of the challenges presented to Section 28, see Jackie Stacey, 'Promoting normality: Section 28 and the regulation of sexuality', in S. Franklin, C. Lury and J. Stacey (eds), *Off Centre: Feminism and Cultural Studies*, London: Harper Collins Academic Routledge, 1991.

5 For a discussion of western charactizations of Islam, see Edward Said, *Orientalism*, London: Routledge & Kegan Paul 1978. For a discussion of the impact of the Gulf War on such notions, see Kevin Robbins, 'The mirror of unreason', *Marxism Today* March 1991, pp. 42–4.

6 For discussions of the notion of 'quality' television, see Paul Kerr (1982) 'Classic serials – To Be Continued', *Screen* 23, 1: 6–19, and Charlotte Brunsdon, 'Problems with quality', *Screen* 31, 1 (Spring 1990): 67–90.

7 'Art television' remains a rather tentative concept within critical work; John Caughie, however, provides a useful discussion of it in 'Rhetoric, pleasure and "Art television" – dreams of leaving', *Screen* 22, 4 (1981): 9–31.

8 For examples of studies which have moved away from textual analysis and investigated audiences and readers of popular texts, see Ien Ang, *Watching Dallas: Soap Opera and the Melodramatic Imagination*, London: Methuen, 1985, and Janice A. Radway, *Reading the Romance: Women, Patriarchy and Popular Literature*, Chapel Hill: University of North Carolina Press, 1984.

9 Previous representations of lesbianism on television are few and far between. They include isolated episodes in serials and soap operas such as *Brookside*, *Eastenders, St Elsewhere, The Golden Girls*, and the 1988 dramatization of D. H. Lawrence's *The Rainbow*; or, more unusually, TV movies such as *The Ice Palace* and *A Question of Love*, which dealt more centrally with lesbianism.

REFERENCES

Ang, I. (1985) *Watching Dallas: Soap Opera and the Melodramatic Imagination*, London: Methuen.

Brunsdon, C. (1990) 'Problems with quality', *Screen* 31, 1: 67–90.

Caughie, J. (1981) 'Rhetoric, pleasure and "Art television" – dreams of leaving', *Screen* 22, 4: 9–31.

———— (1984) 'Television criticism: "A discourse in search of an object"', *Screen* 25, 4–5; 109–20.

———— (1986) 'Popular culture: notes and revisions', in C. McCabe (ed.), *High Theory/Low Culture: Analysing Popular Television and Film*, Manchester: Manchester University Press.

Franklin, S., Lury, C. and Stacey, J. (eds), (1991) *Off Centre:Feminism and Cultural Studies*, London: HarperCollins Academic.

Kerr, P. (1982) 'Classic serials – To Be Continued', *Screen* 23, 1: 6–19.

McCabe, C. (1986) 'Defining popular culture', in C. McCabe (ed.), *High Theory/ Low Culture: Analysing Popular Television and Film*, Manchester: Manchester University Press.

Merck, M. (1986) '*Lianna* and the lesbians of art cinema', in C. Brunsdon (ed.), *Films for Women*, London: BFI Publishing.

Modleski, T. (1982) *Loving with a Vengeance: Mass-Produced Fantasies for Women*, London: Methuen.

Myers, K. (1984) 'Television previewers: no critical comment', in L. Masterman (ed.), *Television Mythologies:Stars, Shows and Signs*, London: Comedia.

Pearce, L. (1994) '"Written on tablets of stone"? Roland Barthes, Jeanette Winterson and the discourse of romantic love', in S. Raitt (ed.), *Volcanoes and Pearl Divers: Essays in Lesbian Feminist Studies*, London: Onlywomen Press.

Poole, M. (1984) 'The cult of the generalist: British television criticism 1936–1983', *Screen* 25, 2: 41–61.

Radway, J. A. (1984) *Reading the Romance: Women, Patriarchy and Popular Literature*, Chapel Hill: University of North Carolina Press.

Robbins, K. (1991) 'The mirror of unreason', *Marxism Today*, March 1991.

Said, E. (1978) *Orientalism*, London: Routledge & Kegan Paul.

Winterson, J. (1985) *Oranges Are Not The Only Fruit*, London: Pandora.

———— (1990) *Oranges Are Not The Only Fruit – The Script*, London: Pandora.

4

SALMONBERRIES
Consuming kd lang
Louise Allen

At first it appears that *Salmonberries* (1991), starring kd lang as Kotzebue
and Rosel Zech as Roswitha, is concerned with the development of lesbian
identity. The film hints at biological determinism, as it appears that kd
lang's character may well have been 'born that way'. With no lesbian role
models in 'sight', kd lang trudges through the snow in this small Alaskan
town 'looking' as if she has just walked out of a lesbian bar in any western
metropolis – as indeed she probably has. Clearly kd lang's status as a
lesbian idol is important to an analysis of this film and its consumption by
lesbian audiences. In particular, it is necessary to assertain what *kinds* of
identifications are being (re)constructed in the relationship between the text
and the audience in this context of intertextual lesbian stardom.

In *Salmonberries*, Kotzebue's developing lesbian identity is coupled
with her search for her racial identity. In terms of how both sexual and
racial identity are represented in the narrative, it is possible to argue that an
'ethnic' plot (Kotzebue's search for her Native American identity) is
employed as a vehicle to 'carry' a more significant and, I shall argue,
more *desirable*, lesbian identity. Subsequently it is plausible to suggest that
in this film racial differences between Kotzebue and Roswitha, along with
differences of gender/sexuality between 'butch' Kotzebue and 'femme'
Roswitha, are interwoven in an attempt to reinforce racial privileges and
hierarchies within contemporary western lesbian culture. This essay examines how lang's lesbian idol status and her following of dedicated lesbian
fans informs readings of this film, and how this process of consumption is
articulated within the representation of racial identity.

Salmonberries is set in a small Alaskan town called Kotzebue, which kd
lang's character is named after, as she was abandoned at birth nearby. The
film centres around Kotzebue's search for her ancestry, and Roswitha's, the
town librarian, search through her past, particularly her escape from East
Berlin with her husband who was killed in the escape. Throughout the
narrative a close friendship develops between the two women, and subsequently it becomes clear that Kotzebue's search is also a search for a
lesbian identity.

Early in the narrative the 'common' lesbian experience of 'passing' is referenced through the scene in the library when Roswitha mistakes Kotzebue for a young man. Kotzebue has already been into the library for information about her ancestral heritage (she believes she is related to the Russian founders of the town). However, she had begun to throw books around in her frustration and Roswitha had threatened to call the sheriff. When Kotzebue returns, Roswitha refers to her as a young man. This is of central significance because it appears to reference the common experience of gender confusion among 'butch' or 'visible' lesbians. Several camera angles are used to film this 'moment' of gender confusion. This moment and their 'look' is also accompanied by periodic flashes of light seeming to come from inside the building. The room is illuminated several times which serves to emphasize the gender mistake by clarifying, through light and visibility, the 'look' operating between the two characters. The flashes of light have a similar effect to that of a torch lighting up a darkened scene, except that the effect in the film has a symbolic function. Roswitha was *wrong* about Kotzebue's gender and the light flashing on and off seems to invite Roswitha to *see* the *truth*. Consequently, the mistake becomes articulated as a form of challenge – a challenge to Kotzebue to 'show' her 'true' gender; subsequently Kotzebue takes up this challenge by stripping naked in the library and proving her identity.

That difference between the two women is articulated in terms of gender is exemplified by the gender mistake at the beginning of the narrative. However, difference is also articulated between Roswitha and Kotzebue in terms of race, but symbolically, through the use of light and dark imagery. Racial differences between Roswitha and Kotzebue are articulated through the dance-hall scene. This is the point in the narrative where Kotzebue has given Roswitha a lift in her snowmobile. After taking a detour, the machine breaks down and Kotzebue has to drag Roswitha back to town through the snow in a sledge. When Roswitha arrives back in town and storms in to the local community centre, where a Native American dance class is in progress, Kotzebue follows her. Roswitha partially joins in the dancing while staring at Kotzebue who backs away behind a door. Again a light source is employed to illuminate Roswitha's face and her 'look'. The light falls on Roswitha's face in the way that a singular spotlight may fall on a star. Kotzebue's face, by contrast, is in darkness as she stands behind an unlit doorway.

The symbolic rearticulation of racial differences between the two characters in the dance-hall scene is compounded by the scene in the Berlin hotel room where Kotzebue's racial identity is parallelled with her lesbian identity. Roswitha's is not a search for racial identity but rather for peace of mind concerning her husband. Her trip to Berlin with Kotzebue brings aspects of her past to a close, and perhaps this can be taken to mean that her heterosexual identity is also facing closure in the light of her new found friendship with Kotzebue. At another level, Roswitha's search through her past reflects Kotzebue's search for her parents. While they are in Berlin Roswitha notices that a pendant worn by Kotzebue (which she claims was with her when she was found at birth) is identical to one worn by a Native American woman in their home town. They realize that Kotzebue is Native American, and the daughter of a local white man who, many years ago, gave such pendants to a number of his Native American girlfriends. Shortly after this discovery Kotzebue proclaims love and desire for Roswitha in their hotel in Berlin. Kotzebue's discovery of her racial identity corresponds to the discovery of her lesbian identity (desire for Roswitha) because signs and symbols are often used to evoke mutual recognition in lesbian culture. Pink and black triangles, for example, are used in lesbian culture to provoke mutual recognition between lesbians in order to sustain a shared cultural identity, and this is important in relation to the significance of the necklace in the narrative. Although Kotzebue's desire for Roswitha is not wholeheartedly reciprocated, and at the end of the film we are left wondering how their relationship will develop, the erotic significance of differences between them is successfully employed as a powerful narrative focus.

In *Salmonberries* differences are foregrounded between Kotzebue and Roswitha in terms of race, and also in terms of gender identity: Kotzebue is a 'visible' or 'butch' lesbian and Roswitha is a 'femme' (heterosexual?)/ bisexual woman. Ideas relating to visibility inform both of these articulations of difference. The narrative does indeed refer to 'common' lesbian experiences such as the gender confusion which is entailed in a 'visible' lesbian 'look', and a developing self-awareness of lesbian identity. Nevertheless, it is important to understand how the performance of racial identities in the narrative's framework of butch and femme identities present the desirability of a 'white' lesbian identity.

PRODUCTIVE READINGS

It is perhaps possible to see how a specifically 'white' lesbian experience is referenced in *Salmonberries* through an analysis of kd lang's significance in lesbian culture. The consumption of kd lang by her lesbian fans occurs within multiple practices and sites of cultural consumption, and also significantly within a white-dominated lesbian 'scene'. The emergence of a lesbian country and western style is also a site of consumption of kd lang as a country singer. The practice of cinematic production, then, is itself not an isolated cultural event but relies for significance and social coherence on a diversity of popular cultural practices and forms and mediated constructions of identity.

Angela Partington (1991) has examined how consumption of 1950s melodrama by working-class women occurred in respect of the relationship of this specific audience to the consumer culture of that time. She claims:

> working class women's consumption of film melodrama was a form of appropriation, and . . . their enjoyment of melodrama was in terms of 'masquerade', an acting out of the repertoire of femininities produced within consumer culture, and therefore a form of resistance against those who were attempting to socialize them into housewives.
>
> (Partington 1991, p. 50)

Clearly, then, the meanings constructed through the consumption of films rely on specific forms of identity and audience knowledges and experiences which are brought to the films of the moment, or moments, of consumption.

Adlon's 'avant-garde' direction in *Salmonberries*, also witnessed in his *Bagdad Café* (1987), could be argued to delimit audiences in relation to their respective degrees of accumulation of 'cultural capital' (Bourdieu 1980a). Bourdieu's notion of cultural capital relies on the idea that tastes exist within a social hierarchy in relation to the accumulation of *education* but also in relation to *class*. At one level the avant-garde or 'arty' direction utilized by Adlon in his films requires audiences to be in possession of high-cultural taste in order to read the significance of cinematic techniques which lie outside the normative codes of Hollywood romance. Jackie Stacey (this volume) has pointed out how mainstream cinematic techniques in *Desert Hearts* (1985), and the appropriation in this film of country music love tunes with 'heterosexual' themes, facilitate audience participation while simultaneously perverting the usual heterosexual narrative in Hollywood romances. Pleasures experienced in viewing these two films, therefore, are delimited according to the specific (and hierarchical) differences in the audience. Consequently, then, it is not necessarily the case that a lesbian audience constitutes a unity of experience. Stacey illustrates this in relation to 'lesbian film':

> This question of *the* lesbian spectator, or *the* lesbian look, may be reified and oversimplistic. Indeed there is likely to be a whole set of desires and identifications with differing configurations at stake, which cannot necessarily be fixed according to the conscious sexual identities of the cinema spectators.
>
> (Stacey 1988, p. 114)

Readings brought to *Salmonberries* by lesbians, with regard to kd lang's significance as a lesbian idol and within the context of the cultural consumption of kd lang 'products' at a wider level (albums, posters, t-shirts, magazine articles, videos and also country and western culture), refer to a specificity of cultural practices of identity formation within the framework of a white-dominated lesbian scene, and particularly to the performative identities of butch and femme and race which are played out on that scene. Judith Butler (1990) describes the gendered body as 'performative', by which she means that social acts constitute the gendered body. She argues:

> that the gendered body is performative suggests that it has no onto-
> logical status apart from the various acts which constitute its reality.
> This also suggests that if that reality is fabricated as an interior essence,
> that very interiority is an effect and function of a decidedly public and
> social discourse, the public regulation of fantasy through the surface
> politics of the body, the gender border control that differentiates inner
> from outer, and so institutes the 'integrity' of the subject.
>
> (Butler 1990, p. 136)

Butler's analysis of performative identities is significant in terms of discourses of butch and femme and race which pervade the narrative of *Salmonberries*. Such identities, of gender and race, are used in the narrative in performative ways in order to create a dialogue between race and sexuality for the purposes of (re)producing racial and gender (in terms of butch and femme) hierarchies.

RACE, GENDER AND PERFORMANCE

The representation of lesbian identity in this film is effectively deployed through the discourse of race, as a developing lesbian identity is carried by an 'ethnic' backdrop in the narrative. This controversial relationship is debated in current lesbian theory concerning how racial differences are symbolically rearticulated in discourses of butch and femme. Lisa M. Walker (1992) claims that the femme occupies a similar position to the 'woman of colour' who passes as white with regard to how visibility is prioritized in cultural politics. To this end, Walker critiques the earlier arguments of Sue Ellen Case (1989) and bell hooks (1989).

Walker maintains that Case authenticates working-class butch and femme lesbians, in relation to constricting tendencies in 'orthodox femin-ism'. According to Walker, Case's challenge to orthodox middle-class feminism parallels the ways in which the cigar-store Indian represents how dominant discourse represents racial identity as 'masquerade'. This is described by Case as denying the 'social reality' of the Native American. Case argues that feminism has negated butch and femme histories, butch and femme 'social reality', through an emphasis on the performative function of these identities. Feminism, she claims, has represented butch and femme as a 'sign' of lesbianism thus eliding the historical and cultural development of these identities.

In much contemporary lesbian theory butch and femme lesbian identities are paralleled – at the level of performance – with racial identities. Case cites theatre company Split Britches' stage production of *Beauty and the*

Beast, where the butch Beast desires the femme Beauty, and where subsequently meanings and identities constructed around racial difference in popular culture are re-presented. Walker, in her essay, notices how Judy Grahn (1984) celebrates the butch as a mythical shaman figure. Walker argues, and I would agree, that 'Grahn's attribution of tribal roots to the butch constructs racial difference as a matter of the butch's authenticity' (Walker 1992, p. 887). Walker also argues that Case employs a metaphor of the cigar-store Indian – a reference to the cultural appropriation of Native American identity, to gain control over the colonized – in order to reinvest in 'social reality' for the butch/femme couple. Walker, however, constructs the commendable argument:

> In describing the operations of classism, the essay sets up an opposition between middle-class and working-class lesbians that subtly bestows the working-class lesbian with an aura of authenticity that is withheld from lesbians of the middle and upper classes. The construction of this authenticity can be traced through discourses of sexuality and race that, while they are not fully articulated together, intertwine to locate the subject position 'butch-femme'.
>
> (Walker 1992, p. 876)

Walker's point is important because she articulates how racial signifiers are used to develop a theory of lesbian butch and femme identities, and she also problematizes the split in Case's account between 'social reality' and 'masquerade'.

Walker continues her examination of how the discourse of race is employed to enable theoretical articulations of butch and femme. On Case's use of the cigar-store Indian to illustrate how identity becomes the 'property' of the dominant class, just as butch and femme identities are negated by orthodox feminism, Walker goes on to argue:

> The cigar-store Indian represents the caricature of cultural difference on which . . . colonization is based by emphasizing the symbols of 'Indianness' we learn from popular culture – most likely feathers, war paint, and brown skin. The Native American's visual signification of both cultural imperialism and authenticity is then carried by comparison to the butch and femme couple.
>
> (ibid., p. 877)

Walker argues that Case renaturalizes working-class butch and femme lesbian identities, along with black identities.[1] Case's conclusion presumably infers that white and middle-class identities have at hand the potential to locate 'other' identities in culture. We have learned, for example through Partington's analysis of film audiences (1991), that 'dominated' groups are able to form resistances to 'dominant' culture through active readership practices, for the benefit of empowerment; however what is at stake in a reading of *Salmonberries* is how discourses presenting lesbian butch and femme as 'subversive' of normative gender roles can be seen to employ racial signifiers (similar to those referenced in *Beauty and the Beast* (1992)) in order to articulate a 'subversion'. Therefore in attempting to 'subvert' one set of normative and hierarchical practices (heterosexuality) it is possible to reaffirm further hierarchical relations of (racial) difference.

Walker also argues that bell hooks 'conceives of racial difference too narrowly in terms of the visible' (ibid., p. 878). hooks argues that, while not identifying as gay is an apparatus of protection for white gay men and lesbians, most black people do not have the choice of such protection. Walker suggests, however, that this does not adequately explain the position of black people who 'pass' for white, and that also hooks' analysis overlooks the discrimination that some members of the gay (and straight) community suffer for not conforming to normative visible codes of gender identity. Walker claims that 'some men are perceived as femme and some women are perceived as butch no matter how hard they try to conform' (ibid., p. 879). Walker is right to challenge authenticating theories which do not account for the fact that *all* roles are superficial to the effect that 'straight' women along with lesbian femmes are also *performing* 'feminine' identities; although the effects of these two performances are differentiated, because of the way in which 'femme' lesbians can, at one level, be seen to problematize the relationship between gender identity and sexuality. White people, along with black people 'passing' as white can also, then, be said to be *performing* white identities, but similarly 'passing' in this sense can be seen to exemplify how the visible signification of skin colour cannot be unproblematically attached to racial identity.

Walker, however, in one sense is confused as to how 'non-visibility' can be understood. Some women, she says, are 'perceived as butch', although she does not exemplify how this happens outside the discourse of 'visibility', leaving us to speculate which forms of cultural identification occur 'invisibly', and how these forms relate to the more 'visible' codes of skin colour and dress. Admittedly, then, cultural identification is conferred through dress codes and skin colour (Walker's 'visibility') but it is also conferred through language (use of patois, Asian languages, gay and lesbian language such as parlare and 'code names' in lesbian and gay culture), accent, sentence construction, badges, signs, walk, pose, mannerisms, 'the look', etc. Black people 'white' enough to 'pass' have all these forms of identification to employ in order to identify as black, and so do lesbian femmes in order to identify as lesbians. What happens much of the time is that some black people passing as white and some lesbian femmes also use these other (non-visible?) strategies in order to invest in privileges of whiteness and heterosexuality respectively. Although at a conceptual level the lesbian femme identity can be seen to dislocate gender identity from sexuality (dressing in a certain way does not indicate a particular sexual identity), at another more insidious level the femme position, as it is located within the butch/femme dichotomy, may also replicate the reactionary politics of straight culture by positioning the butch identity as outmoded, unfashionable or even merely undesirable; which can refer to dominant discourses on sexuality that locate lesbianism at a wider level as a 'deviance'. Therefore Walker's understanding of 'the visible' is at one level constrained through a definition of visibility relating to dress codes and skin colour, and, at another level, dissipated to deflect importance from the social contexts and frameworks within which privileging relations of difference are redeployed and re-presented.

A critique of Walker can help to explain how a dichotomizing view of 'dominant' versus 'sub'culture can neglect how cultures which are supposedly unitarily 'sub'cultural can employ 'dominant' dicourses selectively in relation to race, class and gender/sexuality (gender/sexuality with regard to the cultural politics of butch and femme identities). Subsequently it should be possible to develop a critique of *Salmonberries* on these grounds. Although authenticating theories described by Walker elide the significance of the performative strategies of *all* identities (Butler 1990), what is critical to understand in readings of *Salmonberries* is how racial identities can be utilized in lesbian culture in a performative way, through butch and femme, to rearticulate and re-represent racial hierarchies.

WHITENESS AND LESBIAN IDENTITY

Differences between Roswitha and Kotzebue in *Salmonberries* can be read in a number of different ways in relation to the debates outlined above. Kotzebue, the Native American, 'visible' and 'butch', lesbian desires Roswitha, the white, blonde, Native European 'femme' (heterosexual?). The eroticization of these differences throughout the film is important in respect of discourses of race and butch and femme identities. In his article 'White' (1988) Richard Dyer develops a critique of cinema concerning how photography and lighting techniques are used to represent the sexuality of the 'White Goddess' in film. He argues: 'In the elaboration of light and dark imagery the blonde woman comes to represent not only the most desired of women but also the most womanly of women' (Dyer 1988, p. 48).

In this film, Roswitha represents ultimate whiteness. Being blonde, feminine and 'heterosexual' (for at least part of the film) she personifies an idealized image of the white woman in contemporary western culture (significant in terms of the popularization of Marilyn Monroe as such an icon). More pertinently, the contrast of light and dark imagery throughout the film emphasizes Roswitha's whiteness: she wears a white coat, the film is set in the snow – which is so expansive as to dominate the *mise-en-scène* of every outdoor shot. Roswitha's whiteness is developed particularly

Plate 4 Roswitha's whiteness is visually compounded by her white coat and the white snow. (Courtesy of the British Film Institute Stills Department.)

effectively through the scene in the dance hall, where her face is illuminated by a mysterious light source which falls on no other dancers; it is reminiscent of how in Hollywood a spotlight falls on a star, while the rest of the scene is in darkness. It is the point in the narrative where Kotzebue has dragged Roswitha through miles of snow in a sledge. As Roswitha begins to dance in the Native American dance class already in progress, Kotzebue backs away through an unlit doorway. They watch each other for a few moments: Roswitha's lit white face in stark contrast to Kotzebue's darkened image. Throughout the film, in contrast to Roswitha, Kotzebue is represented as anarchic and unruly (throwing books in the library, stripping naked), and this relates to representations in popular culture constructing black people as violent and unpredictable and representations of black sexuality as anarchic and boundless.

Kotzebue's identity in the film is of course Native American; however, her character is also able to 'pass for white', and has been doing so successfully (if not intentionally) for many years; this is especially significant in relation to the fact that the part was written especially for kd lang. In an interview in *Vanity Fair* (1993) kd lang describes her identity as, among other things, 'part Sioux' (Bennetts 1993, p. 50). Therefore the idea of 'passing as white' takes on special significance in terms of lang's popularity in lesbian culture among predominantly white lesbians. This is not to argue, however, that kd lang has no black fans, but rather to suggest that pleasures involved in 'consuming kd lang' are mediated through cultural discourses of race which operate to benefit white lesbian stars but also white lesbians on a white dominated scene. (It is significant that black lesbian singers without the option of 'passing', such as Tracey Chapman and Joan Armatrading, never 'came out' publicly, and never became significant role models in lesbian culture.)

It is possible to see how racial identity in this film is transposed on to gender/sexual identity (butch and femme) examining how the acquisition of Native American identity in the narrative is analogous in several ways to the acquisition of lesbian identity. As it turns out Kotzebue has a white father (still living in the town) and Roswitha helps her discover this by identifying Kotzebue's necklace which is identical to one worn by the Native American woman with whom her father is currently living – and which he has given to many of his girlfriends. This method of identification through the use of symbols displayed on jewellery is analogous to lesbian mutual recognition through the symbolic display of badges, earrings and so on (for example, pink and black triangles and the labyris). Kotzebue also investigates her identity while forming a close relationship with another woman (sounds familiar?). Subsequently in the narrative, Kotzebue's realization of her racial identity collides with the realization of her lesbian identity, when she declares her love for Roswitha in the hotel room in Berlin. Desire for Roswitha, however, is imbued with ideas of racial difference. At the moment of seduction (which in fact is several hours long) Kotzebue proclaims: 'I was in the dark, Swita you're bright.'

Dyer has exemplified how, in popular culture, the ideal woman is white and blonde, and we can see how Roswitha is desired because she is just this. It also appears that Kotzebue's desire for Roswitha is bound up with a desire for white identity, and more specifically white *lesbian* identity. Kotzebue's revelation of how she had been in the 'dark' before she found 'bright' Roswitha may refer at one level to how Roswitha helped her discover her 'true' identity; however the light/dark connotations in this statement suggests that a Native American identity (indeed any black lesbian identity) is undesired and that whiteness and brightness (a white lesbian identity) is more desirable – perhaps some of Roswitha's white face powder will rub off onto Kotzebue, making her less 'dark'

If indeed a 'white' lesbian identity 'wins out' for Kotzebue (and lang) over a Native American identity, this is significant in relation to a diversity of lesbian audience experiences. White lesbian audiences may find it

Plate 5 During the seduction, the difference between Roswitha and Kotzebue is articulated within the discourse of race: 'I was in the dark, Swita you're bright.' (Courtesy of the British Film Institute Stills Department.)

convenient that Kotzebue can 'pass' for white, if they do indeed choose to identify with the character. The film's weak portrayal of Native American identity enables white lesbian images to be consumed unproblematically. However, the viewing of *Salmonberries* is only *one* mode of 'consuming kd lang'. The popularity of lang, in relation to country and western lesbian styles, and the rearticulations of butch and femme identities in, for example, kd lang's *Vanity Fair* photo shoot with Cindy Crawford, are also important in understanding the particular hierarchical identifications which are reconstructed through a reading of *Salmonberries*. Clearly kd lang's appearance in *Vanity Fair*, sitting in a barber's chair in a 'manly' suit getting shaved (molested?) by Cindy Crawford in a woman's swimming costume, is an example of how lesbianism is being popularized in the mainstream media through the eroticization of butch and femme identities. These photographs, and *Salmonberries*, reinvest in the principle both that 'every butch wants a femme' and, specifically in the case of Cindy, that 'every (heterosexual) woman can have a dyke to play with'. It is important to examine, therefore, how far a diversity of sites of consumption of kd lang may contribute to specific readings of *Salmonberries* by lesbian audiences.

THE SINGER OR THE SONG?

In order to understand how racial identities are utilized performatively in lesbian culture, I shall now move on to examine how kd lang's fame as a country singer has helped to popularize a country and western lesbian style. Lesbian country and western takes the form of shared dress codes (for example, chaps, cowboy boots and hats, waistjackets and so on) and women-only club nights (for example at Venus Rising and The Powerhaus in London) where line dance instruction is often offered. There has also been a repopularization among lesbians of musicians such as Patsy Cline and Tammy Wynette. This country and western explosion within the context of a predominantly 'white' lesbian scene has arguably developed because of the influence of the genre of the western film and TV shows (such as *Zorro* and *The Lone Ranger*) on a specific generation of 'young lesbians' growing up in the 1970s *vis-à-vis* an identification with male characters, similar, perhaps, to the way in which James Dean has become something of a lesbian idol.[2]

Recently there has been a form of embourgeoisement of American popular culture through more 'polished' representations of cowboys, for example in *Dallas*, and also through a general popularization of the 'taste' or 'style' of the American mid-West. This is apparent in the interior design and fashion in *Twin Peaks*, and specifically within gay and lesbian cultural production in *Desert Hearts* (1985) and *My Own Private Idaho* (1991). In *Idaho* River Phoenix plays a character similar to James Dean's character in *Rebel Without a Cause* (1955), and at certain points in the narrative Phoenix's acting style directly references Dean's in *Rebel*; in particular the Phoenix character's narcolepsy references the opening scene in *Rebel*, where Dean curls up asleep on the street next to a clockwork toy. Phoenix's similarity to Dean is now, of course, further compounded by the fact that they both died young.

At one level a lesbian country and western style can operate as a challenge to gay male 'camp' and also theories on 'camp', as it critiques 'camp' for an approach to gender subversion which excludes lesbian appropriation.[3] However, at another level, lesbian country and western can be said to reproduce performative discourses of race which invest in the 'frontiers' culture of the 'Wild West' through a reliance on the popular cultural codes of the western film which re-present/reinforce hierarchical racial differences between 'cowboys' and 'Indians'. It is clearly not the case, however, that lesbian cowboys and girls are all *white*, but what is certain is that all pleasures taken within this appropriation are mediated through prevailing discourses of racial hierarchy and the performative strategies therein. For example, how are Native American, and black lesbians generally, located within this style? With regard to butch and femme identities, power imbalances are multiplied when considering a white lesbian in the peformative role of a 'butch' (Cassidy?) 'cowboy' and a black lesbian in the performative role of a 'femme' 'Indian'.

In an analysis of lesbian cultural forms (*Salmonberries*, the *Vanity Fair* article, lesbian country and western, and kd lang as lesbian idol), racial and gender (butch and femme) identities need to be understood in relation to how butch and femme identities may or may not be 'subversive' of a unitary heterosexuality (what about black heterosexual identities?). Furthermore the performance of racial identities in *Salmonberries*, particularly apparent in the dance-hall scene, and particularly elucidated *as* performance through Kotzebue's ability to 'pass', is inextricable from the performative gender identities of butch and femme within the narrative. This must be borne in mind when attempting to understand how lesbian readings of the film are constructed in respect of differing subject positions. In cultural studies it has been understood that 'subordinate' groups have been able to produce and sustain strategically empowering forms of identity through the construction of 'alternative' or 'subcultural' readings of 'dominant' cultural forms.[4] However, it must be remembered that 'domination' and 'subordination' are not unitary *or* discrete categories of experience, and the ability to 'reclaim' one set of 'dominant' experiences through active participation in readership practices (the western film, heterosexual role play) is always in danger of operating to reinscribe certain subjective identificatory forms *as* dominant – on the grounds of race, class and gender/sexuality.

BLACK BUTCH, WHITE FEMME?

Performative racial identities in *Salmonberries* are interconnected with performative roles of butch and femme which position the femme as a version of ideal white womanhood and the butch as the 'other' – as in the discourse of racial difference. However, we can begin to negotiate problems around how a white butch signifies in this transposition when it becomes apparent that a 'white' lesbian identity is favoured by Kotzebue over a Native American identity (in fact black lesbian butch and femme positions operate to problematize white butch and femme *as* ideal lesbian identities). The narrative of *Salmonberries* can then be seen, in one sense, to normalize white lesbian experience. Here two 'white' lesbian characters are seen to play with racial signifiers. Blackness can be read in the film as undesirable, and this exemplifies how white butch and femme identities can, in certain cultural articulations, serve to devalue black lesbian experiences in popular lesbian representations of lesbian sexuality. Therefore, it has been argued that – through the use of butch and femme subject positions which have been constructed within the discourse of racial difference in *Salmonberries*, the use of an 'ethnic' backdrop as a vehicle to carry a 'lesbian' plot, Kotzebue's desire for Roswitha's 'brightness', the pictoral framework of *white* snow, and the fame of kd lang within country and western lesbian culture – the emergence of lesbian identity in this film seems to be a white one.

The story is an old one in lesbian romance, and is similar to that in *Desert Hearts*. Instead of 'boy meets girl' we see 'butch meets femme', unruly meets respectable, sexually self-assured meets sexually vulnerable. Within the context of these butch and femme codes of difference, perhaps we can see how white lesbian experience is represented in the film as desirable through the way it mystifies itself out of the picture (and the film) as *specifically* white through an emphasis on the dialogue between butch and femme subject positions. Bourdieu has argued: 'There is no way out of the game of culture; and one's only chance of objectifying the nature of the game is to objectify as fully as possible the very operations which one is obliged to use in order to achieve that objectification' (1980b, p. 225).

What is apparent is that 'the game' has no clear-cut set of rules that can be seen to rest, for example, on gender alone. Within *Salmonberries*, and other cultural forms discussed here, the discourse of white privilege attempts to mask its own operations through reinstating 'dominance' and 'subordination' as unitary and discrete categories. However what must be realized (through examining how the narrative of *Salmonberries* plays with the *idea* of Native American identity only to reinscribe white lesbian identity as ideal) is that only when categories of race, class and gender are seen to be indelibly interrelated in every site of struggle (and when meanings constructed through readership practices are seen to be conferred in these terms), can we move towards a critique of white lesbian culture/theory in terms of its investments in class, racial and gender privileges.

NOTES

1 In this chapter the category 'black' includes anyone who is, in descent, African, Asian, Native American or Kouri. This definition is not meant to elide the importance of racial or cultural differences, nor to position white experiences as unitary, and certainly there are theoretical and material problems involved with categorizations of 'black', 'white' and 'race'.

2 Sue Golding discusses James Dean's idol status in lesbian culture in 'James Dean: the almost-perfect lesbian hermaphrodite', in T. Boffin and J. Fraser (eds), *Stolen Glances: Lesbians Take Photographs*, London: Pandora, 1991.

3 See L. Allen, ' "Annie get your dental dams". Lesbian country and western. Is it Camp? Do we Care? ', unpublished paper, Lancaster University, 1994.

4 See A. Partington (1991) 'Melodrama's gendered audience', in S. Franklin, C. Lury and J. Stacey (eds), *Off Centre: Feminism and Cultural Studies*, Harper Collins Academic/Routledge.

REFERENCES

Allen, L. (1994) ' "Annie get your dental dams": lesbian country and western. Is it camp? Do we care?', unpublished paper, Lancaster University.

Bennetts, L. (1993) 'kd lang cuts it close', *Vanity Fair*, August 1993.

Bourdieu, P. (1980a, 1980b) 'The production of belief: contribution to an economy of symbolic goods', and 'The aristocracy of culture', *Media, Culture and Society* 2, 3: 261–93, 225–54.

Butler, J. (1990) *Gender Trouble*, London: Routledge.

Case, S. E. (1989) 'Toward a butch-femme aesthetic', in L. Hart (ed.), *Making A Spectacle, Feminist Essays On Contemporary Women's Theatre*, University of Michigan Press.

Dyer, R. (1988) 'White', in *Screen*, 29, 4: 44–64.

Golding, S. (1991), 'James Dean: the almost-perfect lesbian hermaphrodite', in T. Boffin and J. Fraser (eds), *Stolen Glances: Lesbians Take Photographs*, London: Pandora.

Grahn, J. (1984) *Another Mother Tongue: Gay Words, Gay Worlds*, Boston: Beacon Press.

hooks, b. (1989) Talking Back, Thinking Feminist, Thinking Black, Boston: South End Press.

Partington, A. (1991) 'Melodrama's gendered audience', in S. Franklin, C. Lury, and J. Stacey (eds) *Off Centre: Feminism and Cultural Studies*, Harper Collins Academic/Routledge.

Stacey, J. (1988) 'Desperately seeking difference', in L. Gamman and M. Marshment (eds), *The Female Gaze, Women As Viewers Of Popular Culture*, London: Women's Press.

Walker, L. M. (1992) 'How to recognise a lesbian: the cultural politics of looking like what you are' *Signs* 18, 4: 866–900.

5

SEX IN THE SUMMER OF '88

Susan Ardill and Sue O'Sullivan

After a couple of years of quietude, events took place in London during the summer of 1988 which indicate new shifts in struggles around lesbian sexuality. In this short article we will give a résumé of those events and speculate on the new map of sexual politics which seems to be emerging.

Although many lesbians had been active, some for the first time, in the campaign against Section 28 in the half year prior to this summer, these campaigns were primarily pragmatic and did not necessarily engage with theoretical issues. (Section 28 of the 1988 Local Government Act prohibits local authorities from the 'intentional promotion of homosexuality' and forbids the teaching of the 'acceptability of homosexuality as a pretended family relationship'.) Yet in defending ourselves against what has so far remained largely an intimidating ideological attack, lesbians and gay men did have to negotiate some fundamental theoretical questions, such as whether or not we are born or made this way. (A surprising level of acceptance of essentialist notions, as in 'we've always been here and we don't harm you, so why not leave us alone', was manifest throughout the wave of activism.) Also, having our sexual identities become the focus of such an attack inevitably meant that collective underlying anxieties and unresolved political conflicts were stirred up. And Section 28 gave rise to a new urgency propelling us towards each other – the search for emotional and political solidarity had an edge that was not present before. (Were we correct in sensing a grudging element to this solidarity, as though we were forced together out of need rather than desire – was this characteristic of Thatcherite Britain?)

We feel that all of this contributed to the particular atmosphere of the events that summer: there was a groundswell of enthusiasm for discussing ambiguities and confusions: a desire to reappraise the old questions in the light of new conditions; and at the same time a sense of unease caused perhaps by the fact that realignments and new alignments had occurred (including coalitions between differing lesbian politics and with gay men) which had not yet been synthesized.

85

SHE MUST BE SEEING THINGS

Events often arbitrarily signal beginnings or ends, and we are not suggesting that the Lesbian Summer School which took place in London in July 1988 was the start of something new – but we will start there with the notorious *She Must Be Seeing Things* scandal. Accounts were often contradictory, but it is clear that this American lesbian film and what it was reported to contain (brutal scenes of lesbian sadomasochism (S/M), heterosexual rape, mindless role-playing: in fact one article said 'the entire film consists of violence against women') became the focus of an angry and emotional clash. The handful of women who saw it as a pornographic film physically attempted to prevent long extracts from it being screened in an open evening session about lesbian representation in film. They also condemned outright the session organizers and members of the Lesbian Archive who defended their right to show the film.

It seems clear that a small minority of women at the Summer School wanted an outright ban of the film; it seems equally clear that some women who stayed to watch were upset by what they saw and walked out. What did they see, and were they seeing things? Many of the issues around lesbian sexuality which have been simmering and occasionally boiling over for a few years previous to 1988 – butch/femme; domination and submission; who's a real lesbian (or feminist) and who isn't; and a relatively new entry to the rostrum, the relationship of heterosexuality to the sexuality of committed lesbians – were sparked off again in lesbian discussion of Sheila McLaughlin's film. The other thorny subjects of jealousy, obsession, religion, guilt, repression and voyeurism which *Seeing Things* raises have received scant attention. Huge questions around 'race' (the 'butch' woman, Agatha, is black while Jo, her 'femme' lover suspected of infidelity with a man, is white) were also initially largely overlooked.

It was abundantly clear therefore that the conflicts at the Summer School, and later during the film's cinema run, only peripherally engaged with the film itself. Instead, the focus of the debate was *whether or not the film should be shown and watched*, thus crystallizing the main strands of lesbian feminist discourse then current: shock, righteousness and prohibitiveness versus the urge, even if very tentative, to explore sexual issues. Polarization is inherent in this scenario. For us, the question arises as to why all these debates around lesbian sexuality are always posed in terms of issues like S/M, which are on the whole of marginal concern to most lesbians. It is apparent that this sadomasochistic game, where some women flaunt 'shocking' words and dress and others exhibit shocked reactions, constantly requires the ante to be raised. Extremity is the keynote: the extremity of the subject matter means that both sides, and certainly all in between, get to avoid talking about those problems which really dominate our personal lives, like frustration, loneliness, jealousy and obsessive dependencies; the extremity of the emotional display at these public events and on paper seems to be a displacement of the intensity with which we as women live out our sexual selves.

Yet perhaps the Summer School represented a significant shift in this dynamic, because the women arguing in favour of screening the film were not 'extremists' and did not meet the intensity of the arguments for restriction with any similar emotiveness. The unilateralism of their opponents was thus illuminated in a way which seems to have had considerable impact at grass-roots level.

WE'RE OLD ENOUGH TO MAKE UP OUR OWN MINDS

Repercussions and ripples were immediate. The grapevine buzzed with differing tales of what had happened at the Summer School and in our experience most women's reactions were out of synch with the small group of women who had set up a 'safe space for lesbians to come to if they were distressed by the film' after they had failed to stop it being shown. A significant number of women whose political sympathies have been much closer to revolutionary feminism than to socialist feminism, women who have been committed radical feminists for years, women new to the arguments as well as those who may well have been actively opposed to lesbian sadomasochism, were fed up with how the prohibitionists went about their business and the lengths to which they would go to pressure women into following their line. Revolutionary feminists' continual refusal to take real account of race and class has increasingly alienated even those women who have sympathy with other aspects of their politics. At the Summer School this was underscored by the fact that one of the *Seeing Things* organizers was a strong black lesbian who stood her ground as a *black feminist* in the face of all the sound and fury. School mistresses may have some purchase on our psyches but rebellion was in the air.

One of the failures of the politics which takes no account of our ongoing struggles with ambiguity, nuance, contradiction and difference is that no one except the elite can sustain it forever. In the end, sustaining a vision of a better future, committing oneself to change, is done while standing in smelly but possibly fertile muck. The summer of 88 signalled a groundswell of openness, an urge to have difficult, knotty discussions. Many women wanted to make up their own minds, draw their own distinctions, find their own place in lesbian feminist politics. The rarified purists were experiencing a backlash. To us it seemed as if they were stuck somewhere back in the 1970s, oblivious to new realities.

The Summer School set off a newly articulated move away from past political styles. It had some part in setting the tone of the rest of the summer's lesbian discussions focussing on sexuality and sexual practice.

A WAVE OF TOLERANCE

Shortly after the School, attention shifted to American lesbian feminist writer Joan Nestle, here on a speaking tour to mark the British publication of her book *A Restricted Country* (1988). Nestle is that rare creature in America, a committed socialist as well as a sexual radical. She cofounded New York's ground-breaking Lesbian Herstory Archive, and first came to prominence through an article about her own participation in butch/femme bar culture of the 1950s in the notable sex issue of *Heresies* (1981).

Most of Joan Nestle's events were packed out. Nestle is a charming and articulate figure, who speaks openly about her own sexuality, always attempting to link personal experience into wider collective concerns. The events were remarkable for the spirit of exchange apparent between the wide variety of women who attended them. It is ironic that less than a month after the furore about *She Must Be Seeing Things*, exactly the same issues and words (if not more) could be aired so freely. Because Nestle is genuinely concerned with the content of lesbian sexual lives and, importantly, able to talk about it (an upfront American, after all) her frankness deconstructed the discourse of prohibition London had been accustomed to. The motivation for her disclosures is not to polarize or create conflict, but is marked by a willingness to listen to other women without fearfulness, to pull things from the margins to the centre. That such a controversial woman, straight from the 'enemy camp', received such a good hearing and generated so much obviously heartfelt participation indicated how strong the tide for exploration is.

Cross-currents abound, however. It is as though politicized lesbians in London are still reacting against the internal agenda of 'shoulds' and 'shouldn'ts', at the same time as having to respond to external demands and attacks. A lot of energy is being spent in rejecting and defending and not much in paying attention to the substance and direction of the 'new tolerance'.

This seems to have resulted in a stalemate of sorts, nowhere more apparent than at the panel discussion 'Putting the sex back into sexual politics', held at the end of the Joan Nestle tour. An audience of 300 men and women (mainly women) listened to 6 speakers putting their contrasting views of the 'where to now?' of sexual politics.

There was a definite buzz of anticipation on the evening. No one could remember such large numbers of women and men getting together to talk about sex and politics in years, even taking into account the mixed gay and lesbian actions protesting Section 28 during 1988. Here was a gathering of people across a wide political spectrum: radical feminists, socialist feminists, S/M dykes, deconstructionists, gay men of good will, a small but significant number of black gay men and lesbians, oldies and youngies, the curious, the sceptical, the hopeful. Yet hardly any sparks flew on the night. It was almost as if getting ourselves to such an occasion was as far as we could go with any confidence.

PUTTING THE SEX BACK INTO WHAT POLITICS?

It was interesting to note the way in which the politics of representation – which here focussed on the issues of pornography and censorship – had such a firm hold on the panel and the audience. It's true that two women on the panel presented complex radical feminist positions which addressed the state of the world, but it was the discussions around images, meanings of images, symbols, words – *representations* – which dominated the evening. The irony is that this focus on representation is as true for the lesbian feminist anti-pornographers as it is for those gay men and lesbians attempting to open up discussions around ambiguity, who tend to be in the 'sex radicals' camp. The difference in their politics is then played out around how they believe individuals are affected by different representations.

On this occasion, going through all the predictable refrains in the pornography discussion seemed clearly a time-killing exercise. There was an uneasy sense that there were other things to talk about, but no one quite knew what they were. Better stick to the lines we knew by heart in this particular debate. At no time did anyone address the theme question by asking 'which politics can we put sex back into?'; there was hardly any reference to the real work and campaigns and personal struggles we were involved in. It's as though there was a collective blank-out when it came to articulating anything about the hard times we were (and are) living through. No longer are we sloganizing, no longer are we mindlessly sectarian, no longer are we particularly cynical; perhaps what we are is stupefied.

What struck us most on that evening was the difficulty everyone seemed to have in imagining how a different set of affairs could work. The willingness to open up possibilities was certainly present, but willingness tempered with past experiences was not enough. It seems as if many women and men were holding back, as if the usual patterns of attack and confrontation were not considered suitable behaviour, but what was there to replace them with? The combination of openness, lack of any radical new political visions *and* the particular constellation of gender and racial dynamics, seemed to confound many.

It was significant that of those present, black gay men and women were the most provocative and disclosing around sex and sexual politics, speaking from their own experience of the necessity of tussling with contradictions and not relying on simplistic notions of difference. Most white lesbians (in the majority at the event), who previously might have leapt in with both feet, appeared subdued and cautious in response to this. Many white gay men seemed equally at a loss as to how to handle gender differences. So here was a significant event at which nothing particularly significant was said – an indicator of how far things have moved, but how much further there is to go.

AND THERE WAS MORE

Other events took place within this period which added to the sense that talking about sex was the only thing to do as the summer of '88 drew to a close. Initiatives came from all sorts of disparate angles, including a Saturday afternoon video debate on S/M for lesbians. Again anticipation ran high and the mood was one of willingness to explore and understand. Several hundred women packed the hall to listen to a pro and con debate, which didn't eventuate as planned, as a last-minute withdrawal by the anti-S/M position left the line unbalanced.

The audience discussion which followed turned into a Chain Reaction Gang question and answer session (Chain Reaction Co-op organizes a disco for lesbian 'sex radicals' and is heavily associated with lesbian S/M. This was not so much an exploration of the meaning and practice of S/M, as revelations from a very particular group of lesbians with a generally recognized dress style, almost all white and quite young, pleased as punch to be the centre of such curiosity, which was fine but left uncovered vast areas of experience and analysis. Again the urge to talk was evident but the results were disappointing.

WHAT'S IT ALL ABOUT?

So the summer of 1988 was marked by a turn away from self-policing and attempts to block others but, particularly for lesbian feminists, there was uncertainty as to what to put in its place. There also seems to be some danger that the reaction against restriction will take on an uncritical momentum of its own – so that 'listening to and respecting each other' becomes an end in itself. Already there are signs of a fetishistic tolerance which avoids asking questions as much as the old regime did.

A new blocking mechanism may be set up, where previously forbidden 'words' are more freely used, such as dildo, sex toy, S/M, butch/femme, fucking etc., but we still don't know the relationship of these words to what we actually do sexually, let alone how we negotiate these objects and acts and integrate them into the rest of our lives, physically, emotionally or politically. The thrill or breakdown of fear about saying these words or even being willing to hear other lesbians say them, could set up a new hierarchy more centred on a discourse of prohibition/tolerance than on the content of these words.

Many 'old' problems were evident in the summer's organized events, which no amount of openness could make disappear. The lesbians who flocked to the Summer School, to Joan Nestle's talks, to the panel, the S/M debate and the screening of *She Must Be Seeing Things* were overwhelmingly white and relatively young. The questions this raises are certainly not new, but they emphasize yet again the specificity of the current 'we' of any lesbian discussion around sexuality.

DOES ANYONE KNOW THE WAY?

Pornography, censorship, violence against women, and so on, are among the array of preexisting concerns for feminist sexual politics which are neither outdated nor without resonance for many lesbian feminists. However, we believe that we have reached the state where our experiences, our analysis and the conditions imposed upon us by the state make possible the critical formation of a fresh sexual politics. Can we shake off the hold of limiting prohibitions and realize that openness to talking about experiences considered frightening, 'bad' or of no interest is not going to kill us? Can we then go on to ask critical questions without killing the lesbian we question and then go further to revitalize and create a sexual politics which engages many lesbians across acknowledged differences and understood inequalities? We too are caught with the will and the belief but not the formulation.

AFTERTHOUGHT

It's significant that we can talk about *lesbian* sexuality and sexual practice – even if with uncertainty and with an awareness of how the intersections of class, race, age and disability structure our lesbian sexualities differently. In some ways our lesbianism does set us apart from 'women', whoever they are. It makes us different and forces us to reflect on our sexuality. This is commonly accepted and understood by both lesbian feminists and most heterosexual feminists. But we're still waiting for individual heterosexual feminists to come out of the closet and discuss and reveal the intricacies of their sexuality and sexual practice, to stop generalizing and get specific, even if it focusses on individuals or small groupings. Is domination and subordination a clear-cut issue in heterosexual sex? Do heterosexual feminists have thoughts on S/M? Has anyone sighted a butch het woman and femme het man together? Is *Cosmopolitan* correct in telling us that strong, assertive (feminist?) heterosexual women can't bear 'new men' in bed and long to be swept off their feet by machos in the sheets, 'new men' in the streets? Answers on a postcard please!

6

'IF YOU DON'T PLAY, YOU CAN'T WIN'

Desert Hearts and the lesbian romance film

Jackie Stacey

What is most surprising, looking back at *Desert Hearts* (1985) from the vantage-point of the 1990s, is that it did not prove to be the first in a long line of popular lesbian romance films with 'happy endings'. Instead, sadly for some, it continues to stand out in significant isolation as practically the first and, so far, the last film of its kind in contemporary American cinema.

When I first began to think about the film for a lecture on lesbian romance at a lesbian and gay film festival in 1987, I, for one, fully expected it to be followed by other films reworking this popular genre. Indeed, at this time Richard Dyer displayed tentative optimism when he announced:

> It may just be that lesbian and gay cinema is at last coming of age. In part this is a matter of quantity – there are now enough films made by and about lesbians and gay men to begin to discuss them properly. *Beautiful Laundrette*, *Desert Hearts* and *Parting Glances* prove that lesbian and gay feature films can be made without vast budgets and still be good box office.
>
> (Dyer, 1987, p. 18)

Had someone asked me then what I would write about the film in 1993, some six years later, I would have predicted a comparative piece: how had those lesbian romance feature films following *Desert Hearts* fared in relation to their founding model? After all, it was a popular film in both senses of the term: it used Hollywood conventions and it had also been a box office success (see Florence, forthcoming). However, instead I now find myself returning to the film, not with material for comparison, but with some serious questions about the whereabouts of its 'descendents' (or even its sequel – surely *Desert Hearts II* was signalled by the final train departure, transporting the couple to a new beginning?) and the consequent need to examine critically the category of the popular lesbian romance.

This is not to suggest that lesbian film-making has not continued in the meantime, or that in the US and Britain it has in some way been totally repressed by the attempted New Right 'backlash'. Far from it; in Britain at least, a greater and greater visibility of lesbians in the media has developed recently. As I have suggested elsewhere, legislation such as Section 28 of the Local Government Act had the effect of *producing* rather than *repressing* lesbian and gay visibility in British culture.[1] There has never, for example, been such a presence of lesbian characters and storylines on British television: the post-Section 28 climate saw the production of *Oranges Are Not The Only Fruit*, *Portrait of a Marriage*, the Channel 4 series *Out on Tuesday*, *Out*, and *Summer's Out* and BBC2's *Saturday Night Out*; similarly British soaps such as *Brookside* and even *Emmerdale* (one of the more traditional British rural soaps) have recently developed lesbian storylines in the early 1990s. Neither is this visibility restricted to television: independent lesbian productions continue (see Weiss 1992), and regular lesbian and gay film festivals in New York, Amsterdam, Sydney, Turin, San Francisco and London, to name only the most famous (Dyer 1987), testify to the lesbian enthusiasm to see new material.

Feature films about lesbians, however, have remained almost exclusively the prerogative of Hollywood. Recently, lesbians in mainstream cinema have been represented as psychopaths or potential murderers, as in *Single White Female* (1992) and *Basic Instinct* (1992). There are some exceptions such as *The Color Purple* (1985) and *Fried Green Tomatoes* (1991) in which female admiration and solidarity becomes the acceptable face of lesbianism on the Hollywood screen.[2] The only lesbian romance feature in the cinema to have been released in the 1990s is *Claire of the Moon* (1992). This film tells a romantic story similar to *Desert Hearts*, but was distributed on the independent circuit only and has had nothing like comparable audiences. Similarly, *I've Heard The Mermaids Singing* (1987), which might arguably be included within the category of 'lesbian romance', though it is certainly not a classic 'girl meets girl' narrative, received widespread acclaim (probably partly because it did not conform to this formula) but remained more firmly within the art house network than *Desert Hearts*.

There is a fashionable view in this age of *queer cinema* that the absence of Hollywood-style, happy-ending romances should not be lamented, since we should not be striving to produce *acceptable images* of homosexuality; far more desirable are those films which risk exploring the hidden side of queer lifestyles.[3] Sheila McLaughlin's *She Must Be Seeing Things* (1987), for example, investigates jealousy and power games in a lesbian relationship, and *Swoon* (1991) tells the story of Richard Loeb and Nathan Leopold, two homosexuals who kidnapped and murdered a young boy 'for kicks'. Such films have been celebrated for their refusal to present the acceptable face of queer culture to the straight world. Indignant indifference is articulated towards what 'others might think' in the face of the present desire to explore all sides of trangression.[4]

Indeed, in such a context it is hard to begin a chapter on *Desert Hearts*, the Hollywood-styled fantasy of transformative and successful lesbian romance. If Ruby Rich could write that it was 'risky to be romantic' and 'downright retrograde to be lesbian' in the postmodernist 1980s (Rich 1985), then one can hardly begin to predict how she might preface her enthusiasm for the film in the queer theory 1990s. However, despite the shift from 'lesbian and gay' to 'queer' cultures, with all that accompanied it, the fact remains that *Desert Hearts* was the most popular lesbian film with British lesbian audiences in a survey carried out for the feature *We've Been Framed*, shown as part of the Channel 4 *Out* Series in 1992.[5] And, of course, it was a box office hit and a financial success: '*Desert Hearts* . . . is still one of the highest-grossing independent features right now. When we opened in New York, we came within tickets of breaking the house record for the cinema – and that was previously held by *Rocky III*' (Deitch, quoted in Root 1986, p. 229).

Desert Hearts was Donna Deitch's first feature. Initially a photographer, Deitch had previously made avant-garde, non-narrative films and documentaries funded by agencies such as the National Endowment for the Arts, the American Film Institute and the Jerome Foundation.[6] It took six years from the initial idea to make the movie of Jane Rule's 1964 novel *Desert of the Heart*, which Deitch first read in 1979. Having obtained the film rights, Deitch then spent two-and-a-half years fund raising for the project:

> My inspiration was the way Broadway shows are put together, with investors buying units or shares. And that's what I did: I sold shares in *Desert Hearts* at a thousand dollars a go.
>
> All sorts of people bought the shares. Some were motivated purely financially – they thought it was a good and timely investment. Others were politically interested: they wanted to see a positive film about a relationship between two women. Some were motivated emotionally by the same issue.
>
> (Deitch, cited in Root 1986, p. 229)

> In San Francisco I sold it as politics. In New York as Art. In LA I convinced them it would be a box office hit.
>
> (Deitch, cited in Mackenzie 1991, p. 45)

Deitch is said to have raised every cent of the money for the production herself; the sum quoted ranges from $850,000 (Deitch, cited in Root 1986, p. 229) to the $1.5 million (Deitch, cited in Finch, 1986, p. 45). However, all accounts are unanimous in stressing Deitch's achievement in raising the money through sponsorship parties and adverts herself. The budget then limited the ways the film could be made: some scenes could not be filmed, and 'period art direction is more basic than Deitch wanted because of lack of money' (Florence, forthcoming) The film was shot in thirty-one days, and few repeat takes were affordable. The film was then sold to Goldwyn, who marketed and distributed the film. As Penny Florence points out, the 'political economy' of lesbian film-making is fundamental to the kinds of films produced, and yet is rarely discussed by critics and theorists, and invariably ignored by lesbian audiences. In the light of Florence's account of such funding difficulties, the absence of *Desert Hearts* 'look-a-likes' is hardly surprising. The lengths to which Deitch was forced to go to keep control of the product, in the making at least, are remarkable. Thus, although the film was shown on the commercial circuit and this, together with its 'highly commercial filmmaking techniques' (Koenig Quart 1990, p. 114), means that it is usually considered a 'mainstream' feature film, it is nevertheless important to remember that its production took place within a self-funded, independent context; indeed, more unusually, the funding was collected 'piecemeal' by the director over a period of several years and to a substantial degree came from within lesbian and gay communities.

As well as the lack of mainstream lesbian romances produced in the last seven years, what is perhaps also surprising is that lesbian film theorists have had so little to say about the film. Neither Teresa de Lauretis (1990; 1991) nor Andrea Weiss in her survey of representations of lesbians in the cinema, *Vampires and Violets* (1992), nor indeed Mandy Merck in her book *Perversions: Deviant Readings* (1993) have much, if anything, to say about the film.[7] Perhaps, despite its claims to have the 'hottest sex scene on the screen', it was seen as simply too tame – in contrast to the 'riskier' role-plays of something like *She Must Be Seeing Things*, which has been debated much more widely (see de Lauretis 1991; Weiss 1992). Whatever the reason, the lack of critical attention the film has received indicates a worrying discrepancy between lesbian audiences in general, for whom this was their favourite film, and lesbian academics, whose relative silence on the film's success is striking.

Set in 1950s Nevada, *Desert Hearts* tells the story of Vivian (Helen Shaver), a stiff, nervous English Literature Professor at Columbia University, New York, who arrives in Reno to obtain a 'quick' divorce. Met by Frances (Audra Lindley), the owner of the ranch where she is to stay for the six-week duration of her visit, Vivian is introduced to Cay (Patricia Charbonneau), Frances's 'step-daughter', a wild, bohemian, self-assured lesbian who supports her artistic interests by working in the local casino. Reno, the place of life-changing events, such as divorces or the making and losing of fortunes, offers the perfect location for a questioning of the past and for experimentation with new possibilities for the future. The scene is thus set for risk-taking, gambling and self-exploration, as Cay gradually introduces Vivian to adventures new in this desert context, accompanied by country and western classics such as *Leavin' on Your Mind*, *Get Rhythm* and *Blue Moon*. Unlike so many previous lesbian romance films, *Desert Hearts* has a happy if somewhat open-ended resolution.

When the film was first screened in Birmingham, where I was living at the time, it seemed to me that two very different responses characterized its reception by lesbian audiences. On the one hand, many shared Ruby B. Rich's sense that, *at last*, a feature film in mainstream distribution to be seen by millions had been made by a lesbian director, offering lesbian audiences the pleasures of a successful romance between two women. To quote Rich fully:

> In the postmodernist '80s, it is risky to be romantic, unfashionable to be direct, and downright retrograde to be lesbian. Enter *Desert Hearts*, the debut feature by Donna Deitch that dares to risk social ignominy and deliver what some of us, growing up in the culturally bereft 1950s and 1960s, have always been waiting for.
>
> (Rich, 1985, p. 9)

Many women savoured the delights of explicit lesbian sex on screen, felt uplifted by the romance between two women that does not end in disaster or punishment, and enjoyed, with relief, the attractive and inspiring image of lesbianism *Desert Hearts* delivered (a stark contrast to the usual depictions of lesbians as mannish, neurotic, criminal, unnatural, and by the end of the film, often dead).[8] On the other hand, there was also some sense of disappointment after screenings. Why had the film failed to move or grip the audience in the way they expected a romance film to do? A repeated sentiment was that, had this not been a lesbian film, there would have been little of interest in it; the film just built up to the sex scene and that was that. In other words, the audience had not felt the usual emotions associated with romance films, such as fear of loss, desire for a union under threat, or an elation at the union of the couple.[9]

The rest of this chapter considers *Desert Hearts* in the light of these two very different responses to the film by lesbian audiences. The enthusiasm and the disappointment seem to contradict each other on preliminary examination; however, my argument will suggest that far from being entirely incongruous, they stem, in fact, from the same problem – a problem which exists more generally in the reworking of the traditional romance genre for the cinematic representation of lesbianism.

ROMANTIC CONVENTIONS

Before considering *Desert Hearts* as a romance film, I want first to examine the conventions of romance films more generally in order to situate it within the context of its generic history. Typically, Hollywood romance films deal with the so-called private sphere of love and relationships. To talk of the romance film as a separate genre is unusual, as romances tend to be more frequently found embedded in another genre. However, whether a love story, a comedy or a thriller, romances in films are constructed around particular formulae which, although they vary over time, nevertheless display certain enduring patterns (see Stacey 1990).

Romantic narratives are usually concerned with a potential heterosexual love relationship whose fulfilment is threatened by a series of problems. The obstacles which stand in the way of 'true love' are many and varied. They include the 'other lover or spouse': *Brief Encounter* (1945) and *Falling In Love* (1984); a haunting past: *Rebecca* (1940) and *Frankie and Johnny* (1991); an illness or death: *Love Story* (1970), *Ghost* (1990) and *Truly Madly Deeply* (1991); geographical separation: *Out Of Africa* (1985) and *Sleepless in Seattle* (1993); class, race or national difference: *Pretty Woman* (1990), *Made in America* (1993) and *Mississippi Masala* (1991); the attraction at first not being mutual: *Calamity Jane* (1953), *Strictly Ballroom* (1992) and *Much Ado About Nothing* (1993); or indeed almost all of the above: *Camille* (1936). Whatever the barrier to the romantic union, the question which must sustain the narrative tension is: will they (and importantly, how will they) or won't they overcome it? The emotional intensity for the audience experienced through desire and loss/ fulfilment is dependent upon the cinematic achievement of sufficient interest in this central narrative question. During the move towards closure it is typically, although not exclusively, the heroine who suffers pain, loss, denial, self-sacrifice and punishment. The narrative resolution offers either the pain of loss or the satisfaction of fulfilment if the couple stay together in either literal or symbolic heterosexual marriage. The function of these barriers is to produce narrative tension and to encourage audience involvement in a particular set of intense emotions. The pleasures of romances, then, involve audience participation in the desire for love to win out over these obstacles.[10]

Despite the obvious differences from these heterosexual formulae, lesbian romance films share some of their narrative structures. In particular, the reliance on the use of obstacles to provide narrative desire and tension is striking.[11] However, rather different obstacles structure lesbian romance films: heterosexual men, suicide, murder, neurosis, isolation, depression, homophobia and fear of discovery are among the favourites – not a very appealing line-up. The most frequent obstacle to lesbian love in film romances is the figure of the heterosexual man: in *Another Way* (1982) and *Coup de Foudre/At First Sight* (*Entre Nous*, US) (1983), jealous husbands attempt to destroy the lesbian relationships; in *Personal Best* (1982) one of the athletes, Chris, leaves the lesbian relationship and begins a new one with a man. Death comes a close second: Martha commits suicide in *The Children's Hour* (1961); and Livia is shot at the end of

Another Way (1982). In *Lianna* (1982) the unusual factor of another woman is one barrier, and Ruth's fear of losing her job when Lianna leaves her husband and moves in with her uninvited provides further tensions. The final image of Lianna, lonely and rejected, is perhaps preferable to the deaths of the lesbians in *Another Way* and *The Children's Hour*, the nervous breakdown in *At First Sight* or the rejection of lesbianism for heterosexual normality in *Personal Best* (see Pally 1986). However, the shift from the construction of lesbianism as masculine, sick, neurotic or dangerous to one in which it is simply sad and depressing offers little comfort to audiences seeking a more rewarding, affirming or even inspiring lesbian image.

These obstacles in the lesbian romance film are all phenomena which have contributed to the definition of lesbianism as the negative other of heterosexual culture. Indeed, they are part of the way in which lesbians have been perceived as unnatural and undesirable. It is thus precisely the negative 'qualities' ascribed to lesbianism within heterosexual culture which have been externalized as obstacles to the romance in the film narratives. The sources of oppression, one might argue, have been used as the symbolic barriers to lesbian desire and have typically not been overcome through forms of closure. Lesbian romance, then, has been defeated by problems too great to resolve in narrative terms. The legacy which *Desert Hearts* inherited, then, as a lesbian romance narrative, presented something of a double-bind: the traditional forms of dramatic interest and emotional suspense in this genre had been produced through obstacles which reinforced definitions of lesbianism as a negative category.

'THE SORT OF MOVIE YOU CAN TAKE YOUR MOTHER TO'?[12]

In relation to these 'lesbian disaster movies', *Desert Hearts* might at first seem to have all the conventional ingredients: heterosexual competition, marriage, other lovers, familial pressure, social disapproval, public humiliation, depression, loneliness and fear of discovery. However, one by one they are rapidly and effectively eliminated. Given that the whole context of the film is Vivian's divorce from a marriage that 'drowned in still waters', as she describes it to Cay, certainly her marriage is no threat to their potential relationship.

Similarly, there are heterosexual men who enter into competition, who might come between the two female characters but they, too, present only potential problems which are easily overcome. The character of Darrell (Dean Butler), for example, falls for the 'wrong woman'; conventionally he should have gone for the one on the brink of conversion who is tempted back into heterosexuality, not the 'dyke'. Despite his liberal offer to turn a blind eye to Cay's lesbian desires, the audience knows that he stands no chance from the beginning. Whilst apparently grateful for his protective paternalism against other men's sexual harassment at the casino, Cay nevertheless makes it clear on more than one occasion that his feelings for her are not in the least reciprocated. Indeed, in the scene at the bar where Darrell tries to intervene and humiliate Cay in front of Vivian and Silver, all three female characters dismiss him in different ways. Cay speaks for them and the cinema audience when she says 'whatever you set out to do, you achieved just the opposite'. The other heterosexual male character who might be in competition is Walter (Alex McArthur), Cay's half-brother, who comments enviously of Cay, 'how you get all that traffic with no equipment beats me'. A mildly flirtatious relationship is established between him and Vivian, but it is one which resembles that of an admiring student for the sophisticated professor from out of town, rather than one suggesting any serious engagement. Walter even seems willing to facilitate the development of Vivian and Cay's relationship when he escorts her to the party after which we see their first kiss.

Furthermore, the traditional pressure from outside the lesbian relationship, from friends and family, is also relatively easily overcome. Very early on in the narrative Cay asserts her disdain for traditional stigmas around her sexuality. When Silver (Andra Akers), her best friend, announces her own engagement (see Plate 6) and encourages her to pursue a relationship with Darrell so they can make up 'a four', Cay confidently refuses to be intimidated by Silver's warnings about her reputation. Her defiance about

Plate 6 Cay admires Silver's engagement ring. (Courtesy of the British Film Institute Stills Department.)

her own sexuality remains firm. Even Vivian, who clearly comes from an environment where reputation matters very much, academia, is not intimidated by gossip and other people's disapproval. In the 'riding scene', for example, Lucille (Kati Labourdette), fellow divorcee at the ranch, declares herself 'out to lunch when it comes to queers', to which Vivian replies that she doubts either of them 'will be sorely missed'. Her confident refusal to condone such homophobia, however, may have as much to do with her class superiority as with her apparently liberal attitudes towards homosexuality.

The biggest *external* threat to the lesbian romance in *Desert Hearts* is the familial pressure, which comes from Frances. In several scenes she succeeds in coming between Cay and Vivian, both visually and narratively: on their first meeting, for example, although the sequence of alternate close-ups of the two women dominate the scene, excluding Frances, she is nevertheless positioned in between them, in the driving seat, almost protecting the newcomer from the reckless Cay who drives at top speed in reverse and charms Vivian through the car window, until an oncoming truck forces her to drive on; in the midnight-feast scene in the unlit kitchen, the intimacy of Cay and Vivian's secret, whispered exchange is interrupted by Frances' request for a drink; and finally, after the engagement party, Frances literally throws Vivian off the ranch, having packed her bags and booked her into a hotel in town.

Frances' disapproval of Cay's lesbianism is represented as a complex, symbolic, mother–daughter possessiveness, combined with a focus on her longing for Cay's dead father, Glen, her lover for many years, whom Cay resembles. This very 1980s Oedipal scenario (no blood ties, but rather lesbian daughter and unmarried step-mother figure) connects lesbian sexuality and motherhood through the gradual depiction of Frances' anxieties about her own desire for intimacy with Cay. This is then echoed in Cay's relationship with Vivian who is also the 'older woman' (see Merck 1994). The physicality of their relationship is foregrounded in a number of scenes. The interruption to the kitchen scene between Cay and Vivian is followed by one in which the mother–daughter roles are symbolically reversed: Cay brings Frances a coke, attempts to calm Frances' night-time anxieties about the future, cuddles her and then tucks her in for the night. Cay, dressed more for seduction than mothering, in only underpants, an open denim shirt and cowboy boots, puts Frances back into bed, and first sits on the bed next to her, then astride her, and finally falls over onto the far side of the bed next to her. At this point the camera is positioned above 'the couple', conventionally a shot reserved for scenes of sexual intimacy, and a medium close-up shot shows their faces next to each other on the pillow with Frances twirling Cay's hair between her fingers as she suggests they move into a new house together. A cut to a medium shot shows Frances buttoning Cay's shirt up and slapping her bare legs, reproaching her for being improperly dressed in front of the 'professor'. As Cay tries to swing herself back over Frances and off the bed, Frances grabs her and pulls her back down again for a hug. The roles are then reversed as Frances chastises Cay for her deviant sexuality and becomes the disapproving (heterosexual) mother once again. In this symbolic mother–daughter relationship the power constantly shifts from one character to the other, as does the mood of their exchanges, which moves from the terrain of mothering to that of sexuality and back again.

The intimacy between Cay and Frances is further established at the engagement party and at the wedding, in other words against the backdrop of the public rituals of heterosexuality (see Plate 7). In contrast to the other male–female couples on the dance floor at the party, Frances dances with Cay, as she reminisces about Glen and explains to Cay why he was so special to her: 'he just reached in and put a string of lights around my heart' (a metaphor which Cay later uses in her attempt to make Frances understand and accept her feelings for Vivian). After Silver's wedding, Cay, who has by now left the ranch and moved into town, runs after Frances in an attempt at a reconciliation. She stops Frances in her tracks when she tells her she loves her and begs for her to be happy for someone else for once in her life. They embrace and Frances cries in Cay's arms. Frances' anxiety about public opinion (and about her own sexuality?) is shown in a close-up shot of her tear-stained face when she declares: 'look at us . . . standing in the middle of the street . . . next thing you know they'll be talking about me . . . '

Plate 7 . . . against the backdrop of the public rituals of heterosexuality. (Courtesy of the British Film Institute Stills Department.)

The rivalry between Frances and Vivian for Cay's affection is represented throughout the film. Notably, after the very public humiliation of Vivian when she is thrown off the ranch, Cay explodes at Frances in anger and reproaches her for interfering in her life. Frances reveals her competitiveness with Vivian when she regretfully acknowledges 'she broke your heart, more than I could ever do'. Frances' homophobic disapproval is thus increasingly shown as jealousy, and her desire to keep Cay for herself brings into question the nature of her own desires.

However, despite the strength of feeling between Frances and Cay, and the obvious rivalry with Vivian, Frances' refusal to accept Cay's lesbianism never feels like a real threat to the romance. When Cay warns Frances not to stand in her way at the end of the bedroom scene, she is full of conviction, and the narrative events which follow confirm her sincerity. Thus, the most convincing *external* barrier to the development of a relationship between Cay and Vivian is relatively easily overcome and provides little narrative tension for the audience. One by one, then, all the usual problems for the central female characters in a lesbian romance are solved. The film thus affirms the lesbian desire and condemns with varied, but consistent vehemence the prejudice and disapproval coming from external factors such as heterosexual men, friends and family. Yet, ironically, to return to the point with which I began talking about the filmic conventions of lesbian romance, it is precisely because these characters do not present convincing problems for Cay and Vivian that there is a lack of narrative involvement and the sense of emotional flatness about which many lesbian spectators complained. The absence of 'gripping moments' and 'exciting tension' might, then, be read as an outcome of the affirmation of the lesbianism which nonetheless enthused lesbian audiences everywhere.

THROWING CAUTION TO THE WIND

If all the obstacles conventionally put in the way of lesbian romances are relatively easily overcome, what are the major barriers to the relationship between Cay and Vivian in *Desert Hearts*? After all, narratives always demand problems to resolve, otherwise there would be no story. In fact, two factors are introduced into the narrative which function as the conventional barriers to the romance. What is significant about them, however, in contrast to those discussed above, is that they are located not in external characters or factors, but in the two female characters themselves. The first is the differences between the two women, and the second, connected, problem is Vivian's internalized homophobia.

The differences between Cay and Vivian provide a source of fascination, but, in accordance with the conventions of classic heterosexual romance, they also produce something of a barrier, since the characters come from different worlds, both geographically and culturally. As Mandy Merck (1994) has suggested, their inscription within such symbolic dichotomies is written into the film adaptation, in contrast to the novel, and could be seen as its attempt to conform to the popular conventions of the romance film. Throughout the film the two characters are contrasted within a set of familiar stereotypes.[13] Vivian is portrayed as the intellectual who desires order and control and relies on her mind to solve problems. For example, her response to having been thrown off the ranch by Frances, she tells Cay, will be to write a short story for her revenge. Cay, on the other hand, is constructed through her love of physicality, her emotional outbursts and her spontaneity: she loves horses, fast cars and ceramics. On their very first meeting on the desert highway they are both in cars which are, significantly, going in opposite directions, not simply to or from town, but one is travelling forwards and the other is in reverse.

This mind/body dualism is then further elaborated through the East/West stereotypes each character represents: Vivian is the uptight, repressed New Yorker teaching Literature, Cay the dyke from the dude ranch in Nevada who hands out money to gamblers in a casino. 'The West' has traditionally been constructed within white American culture as the place to go to make one's fortune, to try one's luck. In leaving the safety of 'civilization' on the East coast and venturing 'out West', Vivian is following a well-trodden path: 'morally it's the Wild West and anything goes' (Deitch, quoted in Lipman 1986, p. 16). The desert functions as a *transformative space*, a place where the miles and miles of wide-open landscape can absorb the past and new possibilities can be found. Mythically, it is the place of adventure and self-determination. This is Cay's territory. To complete the picture, Cay works in a casino: encouraging and facilitating *other people's* gambling is her business. Thus she introduces Vivian to a whole new world of risk-taking, first for money and for fun, then for love (and for life?). Vivian is clearly looking for change, since Nevada promises quick divorces and thus possible new paths for the future. Although her world is absent from the screen visually, she brings with her a strong image of the academy on the East coast: it is structured, predictable and respectable. She and her husband had been 'a professional couple' who had conformed to the expectations and tastes of their bourgeois milieu. They were high on form, low on passion. Vivian has a reputation to maintain and takes her responsibilities seriously: she misses parties to prepare classes. Thus the luck and chance of the casino are contrasted with the structure and stability of the academy. Their tastes also bespeak different cultures and educations: in the scene in the open-top car where Vivian is seated between Cay and her 'casual' lover Gwen (Gwen Welles), a memorable medium close-up from in front of the three women is accompanied by changes in radio programme from *Be Bop a Lula* sung by Gene Vincent to Prokoviev's *A Suite for Three Oranges* and back again. Their clothes also symbolize their differences:

Vivian wears classical, and thus not very revealing, styles, whereas Cay appears in casual clothes worn in a way which emphasises bodily display. Thus 'the scene is set: the East is the world of the mind and its repression of the body, the West is the desert and the heat that frees the body from its restraints' (Rich 1985, p. 9).

These differences are also (to some extent anyway) mapped on to the lesbian stereotypes of 'butch' and 'femme': Vivian is passive, blonde, wears skirts and a pink dressing-gown and is on the verge of conversion; Cay, on the other hand, actively pursues, has short dark hair, wears denim shirts with collar turned up and has always 'made it with women' (see Merck 1994). This difference is exaggerated in the publicity poster (see Plate 8) in which Vivian is ascribed the feminine position as object of the gaze, and Cay vies for the masculine prerogative of bearer of the look (see Roof 1991). Cay's butchness defines her as doubly deviant, since she not only refuses heterosexuality but also 'real womanhood' through her 'masculine' love of fast cars, feminine women and cowboy clothes. Thus, although Patricia Charbonneau would hardly be called butch in some lesbian contexts, in *Desert Hearts* her representation of Cay is coded as such in contrast to the other female characters in the film. Indeed, Cay seems positively surrounded by an excess of femininity.

Moreover, this 'hyperfemininity' and its 'butch' counterpart are constituted through a set of 'colour codings' which connote wider discourses of

Plate 8 Image used in the poster for *Desert Hearts*. (Courtesy of the British Film Institute Stills Department.)

racial difference.[14] Reinforcing associations of 'darkness' with emotionality and physicality, Cay's 'dark colouring' is contrasted with the blondeness of Frances and Silver, as well as of Vivian (see Plates 6, 7 and 9). In the case of Frances, her otherwise rather unconvincing bid for femininity is perhaps 'rescued' by virtue of her blondeness; Silver, on the other hand, lives up to her name and in her performance at the engagement party positively radiates glistening heterosexual femininity. Vivian is untouchable, on a pedestal both as distant, learned, professor and as sexually pure (a virgin lesbian); her femininity might thus be understood in relation to the cinematic discourse of the 'blonde goddess' which Dyer has argued figures gender through constructions of racial differences (Dyer 1988). As Dyer suggests, whiteness can be seen as central to representations of certain kinds of femininity, especially in relation to notions of sexual purity and desirability. This argument might be extended to an analysis of how 'femme' stereotypes in lesbian romances, such as Vivian, are linked to norms of femininity through blondeness and, by extension, whiteness. Thus it could be argued that these butch/femme images 'play' with categories of difference in terms of 'whiteness' and 'darkness' in order to stage the lesbian desire between two white female characters.[15] Indeed, their desire is constructed across a positive proliferation of differences (geographical, generational, cultural, sexual, 'colour' and so on), so much so that their shared 'whiteness' is practically invisibleized.

It is important that the differences between these two characters are not merely significant in relation to each other, but that others use them to cast doubt over their suitability or compatibility. Frances, for example, takes every opportunity to draw attention to Vivian's otherness in the dude ranch context, representing her as 'too deep for us to understand'. She warns Vivian, as they sit in front of the movie screen in silhouette, that she should be wary of Cay since she does not have anything in common 'with a person of your calibre'. Vivian's 'outsider' qualities, which at first elicit admiration and respect from Frances, soon become the object of her contempt: 'it'll be a cold day in August before I take in another educated type', she declares bitterly. In the casino bar scene, Darrell similarly comments that Cay is 'stepping way out of her range with that women'.

To some extent, then, the possibility of romance between these two characters is threatened by the literal and symbolic distance between their two worlds. However, the potential fluidity of their identities is increasingly realized as roles are reversed, images transformed and new pleasures explored. Vivian gradually gives up her books (and her reading glasses) in favour of horses and the desert sun. Willing also to be the pupil rather than the teacher, she entrusts herself to Cay's tutelage in the ways of casino culture and attire. Having already appeared in trousers and shirt for the 'riding' scene, she then agrees to throw caution to the wind and get decked out in country-and-western-style embroidered shirt and jeans. In the shopping scene Vivian rather coyly pulls back the curtain with a flourish to display her new 'western' outfit. Cay looks on admiringly, lifting the oversized shirt in an attempt to tuck it into the jeans, conveniently revealing Vivian's stomach. Both women are then on display side by side, Vivian framed in the changing-room doorway and Cay reflected in the mirror, as they gaze flirtatiously at each other, becoming both looker and looked-at, whilst simultaneously being on display for the spectator's gaze (see Roof 1991).

As well as a new image, Vivian also acquires an ease in her movement and a growing sensuality. Two scenes in particular establish the emergence of Vivian's sense of physicality and pleasure in her own body. To the tune of *Crazy* (for being so lonely), sung by Patsy Cline, Vivian watches as the sleek dark horses canter by her in the paddock, leaving a cloud of dust behind them. As she admires the movement of the animals, she removes her wedding ring and hides it in her other hand. The image then dissolves to show Cay driving to work in her convertible, running her fingers through her hair and accompanied by the same music. Vivian's connection to Cay has thus begun, as has her gradual 'discovery' of the physical side of life. Her potential enjoyment of her own body and thus, by implication, her sexuality, is shown most explicitly in the shower scene. Unlike many more famous shower scenes in the movies, this one definitely represents pleasure rather than danger. Shot in slow motion to Jim Reeves's *He'll Have to Go* on the soundtrack, Vivian closes her eyes as the water cascades down on to her face and shoulders wetting her hair which, for the second significant time in the film, is not tied up. As she washes away the humiliation of her dismissal from the ranch by Frances, and her embarrassment at the pleasure in her first kiss with Cay, she nevertheless moves closer to the romance in so far as the scene connects back again to that first kiss in the rain and anticipates her future sensuality. As Jim Reeves sings 'let's pretend that we're together all alone', the ironic combination of our voyeurism and Vivian's autoeroticism is underscored. The use of music thus once again both reinforces the image but simultaneously encourages a critical distance on it, and draws attention to the narrative structure of Hollywood romance as *convention*. The exclusion of lesbianism from the discourse of romance, and yet the aim of this film to offer Hollywood romantic clichés for a lesbian audience, is thus foregrounded through the 'camp' play of the image–music dialogue throughout the film. Again the continuation of the same non-diegetic music as a dissolve replaces Vivian with a shot of Cay at work, linking the two characters across their separation.

Far from inhibiting the progress of their romance, then, Cay and Vivian's differences offer the possibility of imagining new identities which they find through each other. Vivian especially undergoes a transformation and begins to discover the physical side to life; as the publicity poster puts it, 'the most surprising person she met was herself'. It is through her exploration of lesbianism, then, that the mind/body dichotomy is broken down and the boundaries (or some of them) mapped out at the beginning of the film are shown to be mutable.

However, one final problem remains, and to some extent this is the most convincing threat to their successful 'consummation': Vivian's homophobia. Despite her apparently liberal attitudes towards Cay's lesbianism in discussions with other characters (such as Lucille and Frances), Vivian nevertheless appears filled with terror when she finds herself kissing Cay passionately in the lakeside scene. She thereafter cuts off contact with Cay and refuses to answer the hotel door when Cay, inevitably, comes knocking. In the conversation which follows, when Cay is finally allowed in, Vivian rationalizes her behaviour first as 'innocent', then as 'a moment's indiscretion, a fleeting lapse in judgement', and reassures herself that such inappropriate feelings will not resurface to disturb the foundations of her ordered life as a 'respected scholar', to which she plans to return. Cay, as unconvinced as the audience by this speech, continues the seduction. Thus, when a close-up shot of Vivian alone drinking and monologuing shows her declaring that all she remembers is arriving, 'the rest is a blur', we, like Cay, do not accept her story. The cut to a shot of Cay sitting up naked in Vivian's bed may seem rather precipitous, not to mention presumptuous; however, the move towards the sex scene had become a narrative inevitability.

Following Donna Deitch, who 'left the filming of the sex scene until the penultimate day of the short, thirty-one day shoot' (Finch 1986, p. 46), I have left the discussion of it until the penultimate section of this chapter (just to keep you reading). This is the scene in which it first appears that the differences between the two characters will be reintroduced: Vivian is dressed once again in the pink dressing-gown, echoing the earlier kitchen scene in which she hid self-consciously from Cay in the privacy of the darkness; Cay, on the other hand, comes into the domestic space of the bedroom in her work clothes. She is full of confidence and spontaneity, and Vivian has reverted to her inhibited state of denial and repression. This difference is intensified as the seduction becomes a battle of wills: once Cay has undressed and got into Vivian's bed, does Vivian want her to get dressed and leave or does she not? For some in the audience this scene is humorously familiar, for others it is painfully reminiscent of pressure or coercion (reinforcing the myth that, as the slogan goes, 'when a lady says no, she means maybe'?); however, for everyone it looks like the beginning of a classic butch/femme, active/passive scenario which contemporary lesbians have come to associate with romance and sexuality between women in the 1950s (see Nestle 1987 and 1992).

However, in a way that condenses and reproduces the narrative structure of the whole film, the sex scene also represents transformation, and plays with the shifting meaning of differences between women. It begins with the active dark-haired dyke taking the initiative and again 'teaching' Vivian the rules. She obeys less and less reluctantly. Cay continues to take the lead as the two are shot in close-up profile on the bed (echoing Cay and Frances earlier in the film). Throughout this long (almost a full five minutes) sex scene, a back-and-forth rhythm is repeated whereby Cay takes the initiative, but then Vivian follows, retrieving the lead with enthusiasm. This is punctuated by expressions of Vivian's anxiety, a sharp, nervous intake of breath, a pulling away, as she finally wins the battle with herself and 'lets her hair down'. Cay's first kiss is thus followed by Vivian's; Cay takes the lead as they begin to make love, cradling Vivian in her arms and then lying on top of her; Vivian then rolls her over and lies on top. The fade to the bedroom at twilight (they began at 11 a.m.) then shows Cay sitting back passively, presumably enjoying oral sex, orgasming as the camera moves down her body. Vivian seems to have lost all her inhibitions and has taken to lesbian sex like a duck to water. This is one of the few scenes unaccompanied by non-diegetic music, and despite criticisms that the sound of 'smacking lips' undermines the romantic illusion, it nevertheless conveys the physicality of the experience which is crucial in the transformation of Vivian's character.

In this scene, and in the one later that evening, back inside the hotel room, there is a visual emphasis on mirroring and similarity which further undermines the apparent differences between the two women. As they lie on the bed, a close-up shows breast on breast, nipple on nipple, and later their naked bodies form exactly the same shapes in the window against the lights of the city. Indeed, throughout the film there is a visual rhyming of shot and framing patterns which connects the two women; the close-up of their profiled faces as they begin to have sex, for example, echoes back to numerous previous scenes in which their intimacy is thus established, especially significant in their first 'face-to-face' meeting in the doorway of Cay's cottage. This mirroring of the female form in order to suggest 'the perfect match' is made possible by the physical 'fit' between these two white, slim, conventionally attractive actors.

These visual patterns also function to comment upon the place of lesbians in heterosexual culture. Both characters are repeatedly framed by doorways, windows, windscreens and mirrors. This frame-within-a-frame technique has a twofold significance here. Like its use within film noir in which 'femmes fatales' are constantly framed by doorways, spotlights or shutters, this double framing technique here might be read as symbolic of confinement and constraint.[16] Without the sinister or duplicitous connotations of 1940s film noir, the use of these devices throughout *Desert Hearts* has the cumulative effect of underscoring the limits upon lesbian relationships in the 1950s American West. The boundaries between inside space and outside space, such as doorways and windows, are continuously used to frame Cay and Vivian, and to mark their transitions from the relative safety of their 'private', domestic intimacy to the hetero-sexual world of the 'public' where different rules apply. Thus, contra-dicting the meaning of the 'Wild West' as the place where anything goes, we are reminded instead that, for lesbians, romances always take place within the 'frame' of heterosexual culture. Indeed, the development of the lesbian romance in the film takes place against the backdrop of the public institutions and rituals of heterosexuality: divorce, engagement, marriage, honeymoon. The public expression of Joe (Anthony Ponzini) and Silver's relationship (especially Silver's song for Joe at the party), and the amount of approval they receive for it, contrasts strongly with the lesbian romance which can only be fully articulated within the privacy of the anonymous hotel bedroom. When Cay and Vivian do venture outside to the restaurant after their day of sexual passion, it ends in a row because of the contradiction between how she feels for Cay and the public perception of their presence as two available women in a bar, made evident when complimentary drinks arrive from a group of men. Vivian's internalized homophobia resurfaces at the prospect of leading this bizarre double life and she insists on leaving. Again their differences emerge as, in the middle of the argument with Cay, she asks 'does it have to unravel this quickly?', to which the old hand replies 'it comes with the territory', reminding us precisely whose 'territory' they are inhabiting. Back in the safety of the hotel room, however, they are reunited. The shot of their naked bodies on the windowsill against the bright lights of the public space of the city condenses precisely this contradiction, especially when read in relation to the previous scene.

The other way to read this frame-within-a-frame technique is as a commentary on the conventions of film-making. This reading is made convincing when taken together with the other ways in which *Desert Hearts* draws ironic attention to the conventions of romance. It uses the iconography of romance films: train stations, sunsets and sunrises, close-up shots, rain-drenched kisses, lakeside confessions, 'I've never felt this way before' orgasms. The soundtrack of country music is nearly all songs of love and loss, unapologetic celebration of romantic sentimentality. How-ever, the use of these conventions, or rather clichés, takes on an ironic, and often humorous, meaning in the light of the 'perversion' of the usual narrative trajectory of 'boy meets girl'. The songs, many of which origin-ally told stories of heterosexuality, are redeployed here to accompany (and support) the development of the lesbian romance. Indeed, when I watched the film at an international lesbian and gay film festival, the audience was high on participation and frequently screamed with laughter and pleasure, as the conventions of Hollywood romance, which had excluded them for so long, were being used in a lesbian context. Thus, the film succeeds, I think, in both offering the audience the story of a romance whilst simultaneously commenting upon the romantic conventions it deploys as somehow 'other': in this case, unusually, highlighting the 'otherness' of dominant culture.

IMPOSSIBLE CATEGORIES?

As the narrative closure approaches, then, and we return to the railway station where the film opened, Vivian has overcome her homophobia sufficiently to invite Cay to ride with her (at least to the next station). To the tune of *I Wished on the Moon* sung by Ella Fitzgerald, the train begins to pull out and one final question is answered: will Cay leave this desert town where everything stays the same, and chance a new life in a strange city? Their roles have thus been completely reversed: Vivian now becomes the narrative agent, the initiator, the challenge-setter, and Cay must decide whether *she* can take the risk. Suddenly, Reno seems tame and predictable by comparison with the excitement of the unknown in the East. Thus, although dressed here in the same suit she arrived in (but with no hat and a less formal hairstyle), Vivian has nevertheless been transformed: she has discovered her body, her passion and even her temper. Similarly, Cay, has lost some of her dykey bravado, has even appeared as a bridesmaid in a suit not unlike Vivian's present one, and in this final scene appears fearful and timid. The confidence has shifted from Cay to Vivian as the transition begins from the West to the East coast (see Plate 9).

Plate 9 Will she? Won't she? A final moment of uncertainty for Cay and the professor. (Courtesy of the British Film Institute Stills Department.)

The 'happy ending' of the film is probably its most unusual characteristic when compared with its generic predecessors discussed earlier.[17] Lesbian audiences generally breathed a sigh of relief when both characters made it to the end of the film without being killed off or having nervous break-downs. However, they may have breathed a deeper one had there ever been any doubt in their minds that Cay would step on to that train with Vivian. In other words, all the problems which were put in the way of their romance, including that of Vivian's homophobia, seemed to find relatively easy solution: we never really felt on the edge of our seats, willing the relationship to succeed, fearing that without our collective desire for its fulfilment it would surely fail.[18] What I hope to have shown, then, is that if this is the first lesbian romance which offers its spectators an unapologetic celebration of lesbian love, then it is also, sadly, a film which does so at the expense of the emotional intensity we have come to expect from such genres. Thus, whilst challenging the traditional definition of lesbianism as 'unnatural', 'deviant', 'predatory' or 'depressing', *Desert Hearts* fails to introduce engaging new narrative formulae to replace these older unacceptable ones.

Given the conventions of the romance genre, then, we seem to be left with an impossible, and rather unfair, dilemma: for who would advocate the return to *The Children's Hour*-type narratives simply to ensure narra-tive tension and emotional engagement? One solution might be found in a strategy used in both *November Moon* (1984) and *My Beautiful Laundrette* (1985). These lesbian and gay romances both situate the narrative problems outside the relationship altogether: in *November Moon* (which perhaps overdoses on dramatic tension) the problem faced by the two women living in occupied France under Nazi rule is anti-semitism. One of the women is Jewish and the narrative revolves around the fear of her dis-covery. In *My Beautiful Laundrette* the narrative problems focus on the question of racism. This time, racism in Thatcher's Britain and the relation-ship between the disenfranchised white working class and the emergent Asian middle class is the focus for our anxiety. The lesbian and gay romances occur relatively unproblematically compared with the conflicts and violence of the wider context. Indeed, these romances are represented in moments of wonderful defiance: the restaurant scene in *November Moon* where the two women successfully avoid paying the bill by dancing together and flaunting their intimacy in public space; and the sex scene behind the two-way mirror in the launderette in which the two men keep everyone waiting for the grand opening while they have sex and drink champagne together. However, if the problems are located elsewhere in the narrative, there is a risk of representing lesbian (or gay) relationships as 'just like any others' and denying the specificity of forms of power and oppression. If the relationship is incidental to the narrative problems, does this depoliticize lesbian and gay identity?

So where does this analysis leave the 'popular lesbian romance film'? If we take *popular* to mean both 'use of recognizable Hollywood conventions' *and* 'appreciated by lesbian audiences', *lesbian* to denote 'some kind of female same-sex desire', and *romance* to mean 'the sexual and emotional union of two characters having successfully overcome certain obstacles which the audience believed they might not', then it would seem that the category of the *popular lesbian romance* film is a virtual contradiction in terms. Perhaps future films will prove me wrong.

ACKNOWLEDGEMENTS

Many thanks go to all those friends and colleagues who discussed *Desert Hearts* with me after its release in Britain in 1986: many of their ideas formed the basis of the argument developed in this chapter. I am particularly grateful to Louise Allen, Richard Dyer, Sarah Franklin and Lynne Pearce for reading and commenting on earlier drafts of this place, and most especially to Hilary Hinds for her detailed discussions of the finer points of lesbian romance. Finally, I am very indebted to Tamsin Wilton for her patience and her perseverance.

NOTES

1 For a more detailed analysis of the effects of Section 28, see J. Stacey (1991) 'Promoting normality: Section 28 and the regulation of sexuality', in S. Franklin, C. Lury and J. Stacey (eds), *Off-Centre: Feminism and Cultural Studies*, London: Harper Collins Academic/Routledge.

2 The novels on which these films are based represent lesbianism much more explicitly. See M. Pally (1986) 'When the gaze is gay: women in love', *Film Comment* 22, Part 2: 35–9.

3 For a discussion of 'queer cinema', see Bad Object-Choices (eds) (1991) *How Do I Look? Queer Film and Video*, Seattle: Bay Press; P. Cook and P. Dodd (eds) (1993) *Women and Film: A Sight and Sound Reader*, London: Scarlet Press; and B. Ruby Rich (1994, forthcoming) 'Reflections on queer screen', *GLQ: A Journal of Lesbian and Gay Studies*, 1, 1.

4 For an important critique of the celebration of 'transgression', see E. Wilson (1993) 'Is transgression transgressive?', in J. Bristow and A. R. Wilson (eds), *Activating Theory: Lesbian, Gay, Bisexual Politics*, London: Lawrence & Wishart.

5 For examples of 'queer culture' debates, see: *Differences: A Journal of Feminist Cultural Studies* 2, 3, Summer 1991; *New Formations: A Journal of Culture/Theory/Politics* 19, Spring 1993; and *GLQ: A Journal of Lesbian and Gay Studies* 1, 1, 1994.

6 For further details of Deitch's previous films, see J. Root (1986) 'Not the only game in town', Monthly Film Bulletin 53, 631: 228–9.

7 For a notable exception, see J. Roof (1991) *A Lure of Knowledge: Lesbian Sexuality and Theory*, New York: Columbia University Press; and M. Merck (1994).

8 For accounts of the fate of the lesbian at the hands of Hollywood, see V. Russo (1981) *The Celluloid Closet: Homosexuality in the Movies*, New York: Harper Row.

9 For a detailed discussion of the conventions of romance, see J. Radway (1984) *Reading the Romance: Women, Patriarchy and Popular Literature*, Chapel Hill and London: University of North Carolina.

10 For a brief discussion of romance as a cinematic genre, see J. Stacy (1990) 'Romance', in A. Kuhn and S. Radstone (eds), *The Women's Companion to International Film*, London: Virago.

11 For a discussion of desire in narrative cinema, see T. de Lauretis (1984) *Alice Doesn't: Feminism, Semiotics, Cinema*, Bloomington: Indiana; University Press.

12 Deitch, quoted in M. Finch (1986) 'Home on the range', *Gay Times* 95: 44–6.

13 For a critique of the use of these stereotypes, see L. Whitelaw (n.d.) 'Lesbians of the mainscreen', *Gossip* 5: 37–46.

14 I am grateful to Louise Allen for discussions on these points.

15 For further analysis of the relation between constructions of butch/femme identities and whiteness, see Louise Allen, this volume.

16 The use of such techniques in film noir is discussed in E. Ann Kaplan (ed.) (1978) *Women in Film Noir*, London: British Film Institute.

17 For a discussion of the 'happy ending' in lesbian film, see S. Hetze (1986) '*Happy-End Für Wen? Kino und Lesbische Frauen*', Frankfurt: tende Verlag.

18 An alternative reading suggested to me by Lynne Pearce might be that the somewhat open-ended *narrative* resolution is perhaps responsible for the audience's feeling of a lack of an *emotional* resolution as the train leaves Reno.

REFERENCES

Bad Object-Choices (eds) (1991) *How Do I Look?: Queer Film and Video*, Seattle: Bay Press.

Cook, P. and Dodd, P. (eds) (1993) *Women and Film: A Sight & Sound Reader*, London: Scarlet Press.

de Lauretis, T. (1984) *Alice Doesn't: Feminism, Semiotics, Cinema*, Bloomington: Indiana University Press.

—————— (1990) 'Guerilla in the midst: women's cinema in the '80s', *Screen* 31, 1: 6–25.

—————— (1991) 'Film and the visible', in Bad Object-Choices (eds) (1991) *How Do I Look?: Queer Film and Video*, Seattle: Bay Press.

Dyer, R. (1987) 'Screen scenes '86', *Lesbian and Gay Socialist* 9: 18–19.

—————— (1988) 'White', *Screen* 29, 4: 44–65.

Finch, M. (1986) 'Home on the range', *Gay Times* 95: 44–6.

Florence, P. (forthcoming) 'The sign of money: or, how to suppress popular lesbian film'.

Hetze, S. (1986) *Happy-End Für Wen?: Kino und lesbische Frauen*, Frankfurt: tende Verlag.

Jenkins, S. (1986) Review of *Desert Hearts*, *Monthly Film Bulletin*, 53, 631: 227–8.

Kaplan, E. Ann (ed.) (1978) *Women in Film Noir*, London: British Film Institute.

Koenig Quart, B. (1990) 'Donna Deitch', in A. Kuhn and S. Radstone (eds), *The Women's Companion to International Film*, London: Virago.

Lipman, A. (1986) 'Dykes, Deitch and dollars', *City Limits*, 24–31 July 1986, pp. 14–16.

Mackenzie, S. (1991) 'Wearing her heart on her sleeve', the *Guardian*, 20 March 1991.

Merck, M. (1993) *Perversions: Deviant Readings*, London: Virago.

———— (1994) 'Dessert Hearts' in Gever, M. *et al.* (eds) *Queer Looks: Perspectives on Lesbian and Gay Film and Video* in (eds) Parmar, Pratiba, New York: Routledge.

Nestle, J. (1987) *A Restricted Country*, Ithaca, New York: Firebrand Books.

———— (ed.) (1992) *The Persistent Desire: A Femme-Butch Reader*, Boston: Alyson Publications.

Pally, M. (1986) 'When the gaze is gay: women in love', *Film Comment* 22, Part 2: 35–9.

Radway, J. (1984) *Reading the Romance: Women, Patriarchy and Popular Literature*, Chapel Hill and London: University of North Carolina.

Rich, B. Ruby (1985) 'Desert heat', *The Village Voice*.

———— (1994, forthcoming) 'Reflections on a queer screen', *GLQ: A Journal of Lesbian and Gay Studies*, 1, 1.

Roof, J. (1991) *A Lure of Knowledge: Lesbian Sexuality and Theory*, New York: Colombia University Press.

Root, J. (1986) 'Not the only game in town', *Monthly Film Bulletin* 53, 631: 228–9.

Russo, V. (1981) *The Celluloid Closet: Homosexuality in the Movies*, New York: Harper Row.

Sheldon, C. (1977) 'Lesbians and film: some thoughts' in Dyer, Richard (ed.), *Gays and Film*, London: British Film Institute: 5–26.

Stacey, J. (1990) 'Romance', in A. Kuhn and S. Radstone (eds), *The Women's Companion to International Film*, London: Virago.

———— (1991) 'Promoting normality: Section 28 and the regulation of sexuality', in S. Franklin, C. Lury and J. Stacey (eds), *Off-Centre: Feminism and Cultural Studies*, London: Harper Collins Academic/Routledge.

Weiss, A. (1992) *Vampires and Violets: Lesbians in the Cinema*, London: Jonathan Cape.

Whitelaw, L. (n.d.) 'Lesbians of the mainscreen', *Gossip*, 5: 37–46.

Wilson, E. (1993) 'Is transgression transgressive? ', in J. Bristow and A. R. Wilson (eds), *Activating Theory: Lesbian, Gay, Bisexual Politics*, London: Lawrence & Wishart.

7

PORTRAIT OF A PRODUCTION

Penny Florence

The scene is the grounds of Knowle in Kent, the Sackville family seat. Vita Sackville-West and her childhood friend Violet Trefusis ('Lushka' and 'Metya') lie under a tree, Vita sprawled in her britches like the young boy heir she could never be. They look at the magnificent building in its deer-inhabited grounds, and Violet says, 'if you had been a man, I would most certainly have married you for it'. Thus in the four-part BBC2 TV serial *Portrait of a Marriage* (screened 19 September to 10 October 1990), the issue of inherited property linked to social position – aristocratic inheritance/class – is raised for a moment, only to be cast aside in favour

Plate 10 Vita and Violet at Knowle. (Courtesy of the BBC.)

of an almost hermetically sealed story of 'private individuals'. References to both women's literary careers are similarly marginalized and directly subordinated to the sexual tale; Violet, for example, seduces Vita with intense flattery, praising her as 'great poet'. Even if the audience already knows 'the background', this reference to her writing could as easily be lost to the audience of the serial as is Vita's contribution to the serious art of gardening, buried as it is by a little manly if unspecific digging.

In what follows I shall use *Portrait of a Marriage*, drawing on information about the production from the producers themselves, to address some of the questions involved in what is an important but intractable area of cultural critique: that of the interaction between production processes as a whole and what is seen as TV culture. The wider culture of the moving image is not my primary interest here (see Florence 1993a), although much of what I have to say is relevant to it, if in modified form. It is an awkward moment to be articulating these preliminary ideas about the socio-economics of cultural form because the structures of broadcasting in Britain are changing rapidly. What was true of the way in which costume drama was brought to the screen in the days of *The Forsyte Saga* (1967) had already changed by the time *Portrait* was produced, and that change is being accelerated through doctrinaire intervention by central government. Detailed commentary on some of the specifics of how the programme was produced are already historical, and my purpose is to contribute to the immediate future process. The way in which this essay is informed by information from the producers is thus more general than I had originally intended.[1] I hope also to counterpoint and complement the work that has been done on lesbian spectatorship (for example, Weiss 1992; Roof 1991; Stacey 1994), which has demonstrated how expert lesbians are as readers against the grain.

As I am approaching issues about TV production from a lesbian point of view, exclusion is clearly a central problem. While I would in no way minimize the need to understand how censorship and direct opposition work against lesbians and other perceived minorities (see Kuhn 1988), my aim is rather to explore the limitations of established processes when faced with cultural manifestations that may be inimical, or at best incomprehensible, to them. My emphasis is on finding ways through towards new possibilities rather than on the equally vital analysis of the barriers.

To some extent, this is an outline of a need within feminist TV and film criticism. The need is urgent and simply stated: it is that of finding a way of incorporating issues around production, including finance, into the critique of finished films, videos or broadcast programmes. This is not just special pleading for film-makers, although greater understanding of the conditions in which they often have to work could contribute to separating assumptions about form from exigencies of low production values.[2] Rather, as I hope to show, production issues have implications for the use of psychoanalytic frameworks in film criticism, and possibly have a contribution to make to crossing the boundary between psychoanalytic and sociological arguments and frameworks. The complexity of sites of production and reception now make it urgent that critical understandings are refined and extended. This applies to TV and film in general, but is particularly relevant to those who are marginalized; lesbian film production, and lesbian representation in general, are obscured by the relative critical silence over how films come to the screen, and how and where they are seen by their intended audiences, and by others.

THE IMPACT OF DEREGULATION

What, then, are the effects of the production processes of film and TV institutions on the way lesbians are represented? Do recent changes towards deregulation offer cause for greater optimism? On what levels do these processes affect us as artists (writers, directors, producers, crew) and as audiences? How can we find a way of describing these material and organizational factors that can mesh usefully with an already complex language of film criticism, particularly with notoriously blocking psychoanalytic paradigms? Psychoanalysis, for example, is at its most problematic when dealing with lesbianism, always producing it as 'other', pathological or inauthentic. It has also often been applied in ways that tend to foreclose on wider sociopolitical issues, such as the way issues around sexuality have arguably been narrowed down to a depoliticized conceptualization of individual 'adjustment'. Indeed, the challenging question of how to develop ways of analysing the intermeshing of psychic and social structures is especially important here, and it is another facet of the problem of critical frameworks which now require reformulation, since the languages of psychoanalysis and sociology have developed in ways that have made them very difficult to intercalate.[3] Women's and lesbian film and TV appear to me to offer an excellent way into these general theoretical problems. Since it is not usual to regard 'women's issues' as relevant to the generality – women are specific, men are the overall – this exemplifies how necessary it is for a culture to develop beyond habits, especially unconscious habits, which marginalize.

Portrait of a Marriage was produced as costume drama, and costume drama is prestige TV. It is a major earner in the international market for the BBC, which now has to consider profit in order to survive. The Corporation has been broken down into units working as profit centres, having to buy and sell services to each other and in competition with each other. Many of the changes consequent on British Government policy over deregulation are considered to be disastrous by those working in all aspects of broadcasting, none more so than in what is known as 'producer choice', where an apparent move towards a 'free' market (however mythical) is actually far more manipulative and less accountable than the old structure.[4] The reason why this is particularly important, here, is that it is a further shift in the direction of money-power; it is the producer who controls the money, right from the inception of a project, sometimes also initiating the idea. It moves the role of finance even closer to the centre in determining not only what gets made, but how. It is clear that developing programmes for maximum profit and according to commodified notions of marketing has a deleterious effect, especially for numerical minorities. Although minorities of all kinds are affected, the commercial significance of numbers specifically works against lesbians and gay men, not only because the percentage of the population that may be identified as gay in some sense is difficult to ascertain (is it 10 per cent? What kind of 'gayness' does this figure locate?) but also because the variety and extent of gay sexualities and cultures is still very largely invisible. The majority is indeed silent about aspects of itself which it regards as stigmatized. It is not simple to follow this understanding through into the more detailed and specific pathways and dynamics that structures of finance and production both set up and, importantly, preclude.

Women who choose to try and produce programmes with more humane or democratic production processes are further disadvantaged in this situation, and many of the gains won by them and the unions are currently being deliberately destroyed.[5] These factors directly affect the kinds of work that are possible, and the capacity of those on the margins to reach mass audiences is greatly reduced. What appears to be a numbers game, furthermore, is not simply that. The inequitable distribution of money and power, what I would call money-power, is not a neutral 'fact of life'. It is a historical and political situation, the legacy of patriarchal colonialism.

QUESTIONS OF GENRE

The reason for privatization is always the control of money. In *Portrait of a Marriage* the decision to exclude both Vita's and Violet's social and public lives was taken by those involved in the production at this level because of cost, but was seen as one of aesthetics; indeed a scene about the protagonists' literary connections, possibly referencing Virginia Woolf, was considered but rejected on these grounds. But this is a secondary reason. Costume drama lays claim to a certain historical 'authenticity', by which is generally meant 'realism'. Period details are attended to with minute care and a great deal of the creative and budgetary resources are spent on researching and representing them accurately. But historical authenticity, if there is such a thing, surely lies in an awareness of history's own factitiousness. If, as it seems, it would have been too expensive to fill in what is perceived as 'the background', the obvious questions about how and why that sense of what constitutes background and foreground is arrived at need to be asked, not just taken for granted. Vita's husband's career in the Foreign Office is simply and clearly suggested through scenes with him at his desk seeking *le mot juste* for his opinions on affairs of state. But it would have been awkward to use this kind of shorthand for a woman's career or public activity, because the usual silence over it (historical and representational) makes it appear too exceptional. Violet's need to get married in order to afford her the freedom to assume a social existence is treated as tangential, reduced to another example of her amorality as she pityingly uses Captain Trefusis as a means to 'do what she wants'. The fact that all women, including the rich, were/are subject to this kind of social control through heterosex, and its impact on women's and lesbian identity, is subordinated to characterization. In order to make these issues clear without the kind of straightforward exposition excluded from costume drama, dramatic incidents or formal structures would have to be developed because audiences cannot understand them according to the norms of the TV schedules into which they would be inserted. How husbands make their money is a recognizably 'important' piece of information; how women deal with the near necessity to be wives in order to function publicly is not seen as such (and this is not only economics, for many self-supporting lesbians have been forced out of public life, or even social recognition). Changing this would change 'costume drama'. The sheer weight of the penetration of masculinist economics into the form makes lesbian costume drama *for the mass media* (though not in itself) an impossibility because the history of which it is supposed to be some kind of realist interpretation itself excludes lesbians; it is a narrative within whose terms Vita's and Violet's values are inarticulable. In other words, the question of whether forms are or are not radical, or capable of carrying new meanings, is a relative one whose framing needs to take account of audience, and indeed the whole production, distribution and exhibition cycle – the socioeconomic context as it impacts on 'industrial' cultural form.

For instance, Judith Mayne has written about 'primitive' narration in early cinema, and how this relates to women's reconceptualization of narrative – not 'dismantling or bracketing' it, but reshaping it (Mayne 1990, p. 183). How might it be possible to reinscribe these issues into Mayne's analysis of the reconceptualization of narrative which women's avant-garde practice precipitates? The psychoanalytic conceptualizations of voyeurism, fetishism and exhibitionism require to be examined against the socioeconomics of cultural commodification. One way into this might be by looking at exclusions and exceptions. Here, Sally Potter's *Orlando* (1992), which clearly relates to *Portrait*, if only through its connection with Vita Sackville-West, is a revealing contrast.

Orlando was not produced within the commercial system, and critics found it difficult to categorize. In the film Potter breaks the taboo against direct address to camera (based as it is on the self-enclosure of the cinematic imaginary), significantly, with Orlando's first words, 'That is, I'.[6] The audience is being told in voiceover (another interruptive device, though not tabooed) 'who Orlando is', beginning with the ironic assertion that there could be no doubt about 'his' sex, and continuing with a catalogue of the social and economic advantages of his birth – which will be returned to later when, as a mother, Orlando visits 'her' former home as a member of the public. Orlando's direct remarks to camera are significantly placed; a further example is at the moment s/he has been contemplating her woman's body – or, importantly, its reflection – for the first time, and she comments that there is no difference in herself at all, just a different sex.[7] Potter has referred to her work as 'avant-garde show-business' (Florence 1993b, pp. 277–8), somewhat with tongue in cheek, but nevertheless the idea wittily and usefully exposes both the economic and formal separations which her work begins to transgress. Mainstream, or 'malestream', positioning of women now is more conscious than it was in the early days of cinema, which is not to say that in earlier times it was innocent, but rather to pay attention to the different meanings that inhere in unconscious structures, especially when an analogic function of the imaginary is at stake. 'Primitive' film, of course, is not singular, and 'malestream' film is also not necessarily singular, although its obsessional narrowing down to a limited set of narratives and concerns is arguably a defining feature.[8]

PRODUCTION (OF) VALUES

The kinds of feminist historical analysis that have already been done on the cinema need to be complemented with more detailed examination of the conditions of production, both economic and organizational, and how they enter into the dynamics of TV production and programming. This approach may produce insights into, and ways out of, some of the theoretical double-binds which appear to block us, such as those concerning women as narrative disturbance rather than agent (Rose 1986, p. 211),[9] because the ways in which they are symptoms of theoretical irresolvability may become clearer; that is to say, the points where our current frameworks betray their own limits may be made to read as indicators of ways forward. The really interesting point arising from this would be how to establish detailed connections between social and formal determinations with the psychoanalytic understandings developed over the past couple of decades in media criticism. The analogy between the cinematic and psychoanalytic imaginaries which underlies influential strands of film theory (and influences to an extent thinking about TV) has been questioned for some time, for example by Jacqueline Rose. Through a discussion of the problems of analogy and disavowal in the theories of Metz and Comolli, she raises again the overlooked question of sexual difference in the cinematic apparatus (ibid.). Sexual difference, she points out, functions as the vanishing-point of their theories. What female desire is or might be, how it might be articulated in terms of the cinematic apparatus, is an inevitable question which straddles the analogy central to her essay, that between the psycho-analytic and cinematic imaginary. Barely stated here, though, is the impact of disavowal on the issue of homosexuality and homoeroticism in/on the view of Woman/women. The investigation should be taken up and extended into the wider fields of production and audience under discussion, not as mere 'context', but as structural. The difficulty of putting this into practice is perhaps symptomatic of the split between psychoanalysis and sociology; or, if not of this separation directly, of the philosophical modes and paradigms that produce it.

The way that form appears to be inflected, or even determined in some cases, by the structural effects of money-power leads to the exclusion or distortion of lesbians' and women's meanings, even, or perhaps sometimes especially, where we appear on screen. Right now it seems almost inevitable without intervention. The problem with just accepting this and reading against the grain is that resources remain within the same mainstream circuit, ensuring the recirculation of the same meanings. Schedules, furthermore, are carefully calculated, and what are perceived to be minority issues or subjects kept within specific timeslots.

One straight portrait is another lesbian's erasure; to change women's acculturation to men's image of us and their use of it for their own self-representation is an urgent project. Luce Irigaray calls for 50 per cent of broadcasting and media coverage to be adapted to women (Irigaray 1991, p. 209), who pay the same taxes as men. Two fairly obvious features of deregulation make this even less likely in the future unless there is radical change: one is the notion of the 'free market' and notorious formulations such as 'producer choice',[10] and the other is the imposition of a process which sidelines discussion of issues other than financial survival or 'success' through destabilization (as the US has done politically in South America). A glance at *Stage, Screen and Radio*, the BECTU (Broadcasting Entertainment Cinematograph and Theatre Union) journal, shows how it has become dominated by these issues, and how the union's resources have been necessarily coopted to monitoring and resisting the worst effects.[11] Developing and refining the admittedly flawed Equal Opportunities model to further organizational change towards facilitating women's participation is once again off the agenda.[12]

A BRITISH MARRIAGE?

It was a cliché of my jingoistic childhood that 'X' in Britain was the envy of the world: the health service, education, you name it. Perhaps one instance in which this might be said to contain an element of truth is – or was – the BBC. In a sense, that form of serious and responsible public broadcasting presents for lesbians a microcosmic example of the difficulty of liberalism and of the evolutionary model of social change. It may well be preferable, on balance, that there exists a body prepared to make programmes that not only include lesbian subject matter, but that foreground it and treat it seriously in a prestige form. But in the end, lesbians and others with a stake in innovation need to be clear about the precise ways in which large corporations either reproduce or break away from received thought and its structures. To seek from them direct insight into lesbian thought and our structures would be to miss the point.[13] *Portrait* was a bold and serious piece of programming; only liberals would have been unaware that it would have to fail its subject (material and protagonist) if it was to succeed as an 'investment'.[14] Whether such programming acts to suppress us, and if so how, requires detailed thought.

Heterosexual marriage is of interest to lesbians and gay men because of its normative and public aspects: if there is a principal structuring form for the definition and control of sexuality in law, marriage is that form. Marriage, furthermore, is an economic institution, so it provides an example of a social structure within which sexuality, economics and the law intersect. When heterosexuals confront the possibility of a plurality of sexualities, the threat to their sense(s) of self is not only personal, it is also social and economic. This affects lesbians as a group far more than gay men, because women are still seen as the secondary and dependent half of the 'partnership', a sexual and social dependence reinforced by actual and perceived economics.[15] (I seek only to be clear about necessary differentiation, not to deny gay men's specific oppressions.) Lesbians who realize their sexuality after heterosexual marriage, for example, or who come out after it, stand to lose their social position in terms both of status and money, and are very likely to face a drastic cut in their standard of living. Those who have always been aware that they are lesbian have already faced the definitional limitations marriage places on their social sense of self and their potential for public activity. Marriage as social fact, metaphor and representation affords a means through which to explore the interface of sociological and psychoanalytic understandings of sexuality.

These issues are part of a major difference between homosexuality and heterosexuality that tends not to be explored in film criticism and theories of representation, which emphasize desire and looking. Heterosexuality and homosexuality do not have the same status in law. What this implies is that their social coding, the meanings to which they give rise within the overall representational system, are at variance. A psychoanalytic framework tends to occlude these levels of meaning, or to render them secondary. At its simplest, heterosexuality is on the 'right' side and the inside of the law, homosexuality on the 'wrong' side or the outside; recent developments such as in the Spanner case (in which more general legal charges were brought against gay men in place of specific anti-homosexual legislation)[16] have shown how vulnerable attempts at liberalization of this positioning are. I should like to see a shift in the way cultural criticism approaches the law, in order to facilitate understandings of psychoanalytic and juridical workings of 'law' as concept and means of control, while not losing sight of the valuable theoretical work along Foucauldian lines which takes account of regulatory effects of discursive power.

In different ways a possibly analogous asymmetry in relation to the law (juridical and psychoanalytic) occurs in relation to male and female homosexuality, and is reflected in contemporary uncertainty over terminology. 'Lesbians' is the most frequently used term among women for women, certainly in the United Kingdom. 'Gay women' is rare, and 'female homosexual' out of date and with overtones of medical or obsolete sexological discourse. The fact that many women, lesbian or straight, have felt uneasy about the elision of gender in the recent elaborations of 'queer' is also relevant here, although it is usually articulated in terms of sexuality itself rather than its status either before the law or within the polity. This is right and proper, because as much clarity as possible about the fundamental terms of the debate is essential. But lesbians have not been subjected to legal controls in the same way as gay men, at least partly because we are already controlled as women.

MATERIAL ISSUES

The economic dimension to the framework within which I want to think about the issues around the representation of lesbians is clearer in relation to film and TV than most other cultural forms, because their production and consumption (though I do not much like these terms any more) require substantial material and organizational resources. While all art and culture relate in some way to economics, mass film and TV do so in a particularly direct way. I have explored elsewhere some preliminary ideas about what I called the 'systematics' of film and TV, by which I mean the interaction of the inbuilt tendencies of the economic and organizational structures of film and TV with aesthetics, subject matter and what is produced by whom. Perhaps 'signification' is a better term than aesthetics, because it can cover the same kinds of textual analysis while also being applicable to understanding representational strategies. It is also useful in ensuring that such strategies are not confused with political action when the focus is on how signifying strategies are used politically. Where the mass media are openly incorporated into the political process, as for example in the case of the South American Mayor with his own TV station, or the US presidential and British prime-ministerial circuses, the politics of representation are acknowledged. But both capital and political representation are always in close proximity to the TV business. What is perhaps surprising is not that there is a relationship between representation and these broader socio-political structures, but that it is so little attended to outside specific examples or as a whole.

The representational strategies of *Portrait of a Marriage* are complex, both in terms of its production and its intended audience. On one level they are clearly masculinist and heterosexist, but how are the meanings of the piece changed through the addition of the straight female spectator and scriptwriter, and the actresses, whose discomfort with the love scenes was sympathetically publicized?[17] Lesbians were nowhere in the principal production roles or intended audience, and the idea that there should be any form of lesbian input was considered to be an irrelevance.[18] There is, of course, no guarantee of 'authenticity' through the inclusion of lesbians, and no single lesbian experience or sexuality to which appeal could be made to prove the point. The argument need not be made in terms of essentialism, however; the point is more usefully made as one of repre-sentational strategy, not because it is more true in some sense, but because it poses the issues in such a way as to ground them in social and psychic experiences which are both shared and sufficiently developed to have certain structural representations. Mandy Merck's essay 'Portrait of a marriage?', for example, indicates how public was Vita Sackville-West's interest in the then current debates over Marie Stopes's ideas concerning marriage and sexual pleasure (Merck 1993, pp. 104–10, 115). Annette Kuhn has explored the power-relations of the cinematic process in relation to the same period and ideas (Kuhn 1988). Both of these point towards ways in which the apparent neutrality of the treatment of marriage in the recent serial may be understood as historically specific and as participating in productive and regulatory discourses about sexuality and the law.

This is the kind of framework within which some of the recurrent definitional problems around women's and lesbian film could be reshaped. These are problems which give rise to a group of very simple questions, the answers to which are both complex in themselves and overlapping. Some of them have been much discussed, often with great subtlety, and they will remain unresolved until the process of development produces either answers or reformulations that more usefully move matters forward. I have in mind consistent psychoanalytic and sociological terms within which to explore and define the basic questions which recur but remain unclear, such as: What is a lesbian?; What is identity?; What is lesbian identity and how does it intersect with race and class?; Does it matter whether a programme-maker is a lesbian (woman, white person, straight)?; in terms of function (script, camera, direction) and in terms of form (aesthetics, signifying strategies) how do sex/gender and sexuality interact?; What is the relationship between what is already articulated and what it is possible to say/see?; What is the relationship between saying and seeing? To these questions I would add others such as: What is the relationship between identity and money?; How do sex/gender and multi-cultural social organization interact?; What is the relationship between mass cultural representation and the imaginary?

Unless some provisional simplifications are attempted and agreed cultural analysis will continue to re-cover the same ground; at present, the frameworks and terminology are sometimes either too restricted, and therefore exclusive, or too imprecise, so that the already slippery process of communication is rendered still more uncertain through reapplication of the similar as the same. (In its positive guise, of course, this is part of the generative power of sign systems; I make no call for spurious scientism or fixity.) I am talking about simple working hypotheses such as these that follow. But there is one further point, and that is that they derive from practice and application of theory before 'pure' theoretical considerations. Clearly, a certain pragmatism in the combination of both is necessary. A precise and agreed understanding of what lesbian identity is, and how it intersects with psychic construction, is necessarily a crucial question in terms of signification and representational strategies, not only because of the need for non-exclusive definitions of Subjecthood, but also because of the way the definition of the Subject defines the imaginary. It would be retrograde if recent influential and important notions of performativity (Butler 1990; Fuss 1991, pp. 1–12) were to appear to disallow such basic procedural definition.

TOWARDS NEW FRAMEWORKS

At the risk of seeming oversimplified, then, I would say that in working towards new frameworks lesbian identity and psychic construction remain useful abstractions; they carry meanings. But they are not monolithic, and factors such as race and class, and the economics associated with them, are not secondary. Psychic construction is not the same as identity, furthermore, and is not separable from the body; whereas identity is a socioeconomic phenomenon. Lesbian psychic construction is not the same as heterosexual female or gay or straight male psychic construction; for social reasons, masculine or feminine do not mean the same when applied to heterosexual or homosexual individuals. Both psychic construction and identity are produced and are not immutable givens, even if they have corporeal origins; but identity may be more amenable to change in the short term than psychic construction, since identity and psychic construction are marked by representation in different ways; and representation is marked by economics. No single aspect of psychic construction is necessarily privileged; socioeconomic conditions, however, may distort this.

Portrait of a Marriage is clearly far from advancing understandings of these issues. But it could be productive of useful meanings about lesbian identity (and in this I am not attempting to read against the grain). Vita is

Plate 11 Vita and Harold at Sissinghurst. (Courtesy of the BBC.)

clearly portrayed as male-identified in her relationship with Violet; and there is the irony of the portrayal as having been scripted by a straight woman, using men as a model,[19] directed by a man and played by a straight woman. But I shall assume for now that any woman, whether lesbian or straight, may identify as a male without in any sense becoming inauthentic.

126

This may not be an easy idea to assimilate. I have in the past resisted the idea of lesbian identification with the male as absurdly masculinist, which in some respects it may still be. But I think it may be true in some significant senses. It explains the relationship of some lesbians to the phallus, where a dildo appears to take on the attributes of the body, in common with fetishism and certain forms of S/M practice. Della Grace's photographs are examples,[20] as are Parveen Adams's arguments about the phallus (Adams 1989, 247–65).

This psychic experience is comprehensible through the idea of prostheticism in which bodily accessories or tools are experienced as bodily extensions (Grosz, forthcoming). The power of the social marking of clothes would then derive at least in part from their being similarly experienced (see Plate 11). Cross-dressing (Garber 1992) as a site of intercalation of the social and the psychic would then be far from marginal or superficial (except in the sense of 'surface', which it clearly is) in refiguring identity, as is indicated by the persistent strength of western taboos against 'serious' cross-dressing. (The paradoxes of power-dressing for women in business or public life testify to this, as does the persecution of male transvestites who venture to go public; the association of certain forms of dress with economic activity and power is an effective form of socioeconomic control, particularly when associated with sex/gender.) In *Portrait*, Vita was usually in some form of masculine attire such as jodhpurs and army uniform for the sex scenes; otherwise she appeared in appropriate female clothes of her class.

As I said at the beginning, I am only able in this space to raise some of the points which I believe could inform development of the kind of lesbian cultural criticism that would be instrumental in changing representational strategies for the better for all those who are under-represented. Programmes such as *Portrait of a Marriage* are relevant to this project, particularly if a way can be found to connect the distortions they evince with the exclusionary dynamic they attempt to transcend.

ACKNOWLEDGEMENTS

Colin Tucker and Anna Kalnars were both very generous with their time and knowledge. I am grateful to them for their cooperation and readiness to engage with these ideas. However, I am entirely responsible for the way the ideas have been used here, and for the opinions expressed in this essay, unless clearly indicated otherwise.

NOTES

1 A further limiting factor is confidentiality; detailed production information is commercially valuable, a further instance of the limiting intersection between knowledge and contemporary 'markets'.

2 Lesbian work is often criticized for its low production values and perceived

technical inferiority, and lesbian audiences can appear not to know why this is. Financial deprivation and lack of access to training and sustained experience inevitably limit the work produced and the forms; drama, for example, is extremely expensive.

3 Malcolm Bowie, for example, has pointed out that: 'a collaborative research programme between psychoanalysis and sociology has been called for since the early thirties . . . the need for a fully interactive theory of social and psychical structure is an urgent one' (M. Bowie (1987) *Freud, Proust and Lacan*, Cambridge and Melbourne: Cambridge University Press, p. 176).

4 'Producer choice' may be compared with the internal market of the reorganized National Health Service. The BBC is being divided into resource directorates and business units which have to break even. One of the most pernicious features of the system is that each unit is allocated a proportion of over-heads, which it has to recover by charging all other departments for what it provides. This prices them out of what is supposed to be a 'free' market. It is, effectively, rigged. Privatization will be the outcome, together with job losses for programme-makers and more jobs for accountants; this is already happening. (My thanks are due to BECTU – Broadcasting, Entertainment Cinematograph Technicians' Union – sources.)

5 The losses affect everyone, but women are always the worst hit, particularly in an 'industry' which has such disruptive working conditions; recession and privatization work as means of controlling us. While I prefer to argue for women's rights in our terms and not those of family commitments, those who have such commitments will be severely affected.

6 Direct address to camera is, of course, permitted in transgressive forms such as comedy and visionary film, where there is no 'realist' illusion, and in documentary. Some comedy relies for comic effect on this taboo-breaking. Potter pays tribute to Michael Powell in the credits to *Orlando*, and parallels could be drawn between her work and that of Powell and Pressburger, for example in the ways in which her relation as director to the camera is mediated through the narrative and/or the narrator.

7 The irony of this remark is played out in relation to property in the film. With considerable subtlety, *Orlando* pivots partly on the difference in her/his legal and economic position as woman or as man.

8 Classical Hollywood requires to be differentiated from present-day commercial cinema, not only because of drastic changes in the studio system but also because of TV.

Never one of the pack, Powell (see note 7 above), of course, found to his cost how the mainstream can act as its own censor. His brilliantly reflexive treatment of the extremes of cinematic voyeurism in *Peeping Tom* (1959) effectively ended his career until his rediscovery by a later generation.

9 I do not see, however, that confirmation of women's negative position is a problem beyond the theoretical, unless the dominant economy is maintained. This is neither Rose's aim nor mine.

10 See note 4 above.

11 See, for example, the issues from November 1992 to June 1993.

12 My opinion is that the model is based on a false notion of equity.

13 Elizabeth Wilson has pointed out how the programme might be symptomatic of straight society using homosexuality as a 'lens' through which to peer at its own 'problematic practices' (E. Wilson, 'Borderlines', *New Statesman & Society*, November 1990, p. 31).

14 I do not know if the programme has been successful as a money-maker, but it was not repeated as is customary.

15 It is, of course, not true that women are as economically dependent as most economic analyses assume, as feminists have been pointing out for at least two decades. Many women are breadwinners, and virtually all women perform work that is not recognized as 'productive'.

16 A group of gay men engaged in consensual S/M were charged with assault. This was deliberate policing of sexual practice, using the indirect means of laws intended for entirely different situations to control gay men once homosexuality itself had ceased to be illegal. It is comparable with the notorious Section 28, which forbids material 'promoting' homosexuality in schools and other specific situations.

17 In an article in the *Sheffield Star*, 19 September 1990.

18 *Radio Times*, 15–21 September 1990. It remains Colin Tucker's position that the story is the universal one of a woman torn between two lovers. If one happens to be a woman, that makes no difference. Lesbian views of the programme were sought, however, at the stage of editing – late in the overall process.

19 The scriptwriter was Penelope Mortimer, and she is quoted in the *Radio Times* (15–21 September 1990) as having modelled her characterization of Vita on a man.

20 See Della Grace's 1992 series *Xenomorphosis*. For other lesbian photography, including Grace's *The Ceremony*, see T. Boffin and J. Fraser (eds) (1991) *Stolen Glances: Lesbians Take Photographs*, London: Pandora.

REFERENCES

Adams, P. (1989) 'Of female bondage', in T. Brennan (ed.) *Between Feminism and Psychoanalysis*, London and New York: Routledge.

Boffin, T. and Fraser, J. (eds) (1991) *Stolen Glances. Lesbians Take Photographs*, London: Pandora.

Bowie, M. (1987) *Freud, Proust and Lacan*, Cambridge and Melbourne: Cambridge University Press.

Butler, J. (1990) *Gender Trouble*, London and New York: Routledge.

Florence, P. (1993a) 'Lesbian cinema, women's cinema', in Gabriele Griffin (ed.), *Outwrite*, London: Pluto.

———— (1993b) 'A conversation with Sally Potter', *Screen* 34, 3: 275–84.

Fuss, D. (ed.) (1991) *Inside Out*, London and New York: Routledge.

Garber, M. (1992) *Vested Interests. Cross-dressing and Cultural Anxiety*, London and New York: Routledge.

Grosz, E. (forthcoming) 'Psychoanalysis and the imaginary body', in P. Florence and D. Reynolds (eds), *Media, Subject, Gender*, Manchester: Manchester University Press.

Irigaray, L. (1991) 'The Limits of the Transference' in Whitford, M. (ed.) *The Irigaray Reader*, Oxford: Blackwell.

Kuhn, A. (1988) *Cinema, Censorship and Sexuality*, London and New York: Routledge.

Mayne, J. (1990) *The Woman at the Keyhole: Feminism and Women's Cinema*, Bloomington and Indianapolis: Indiana University Press.

Merck, M. (1993) *Perversions, Deviant Readings*, London: Virago.

Rose, J. (1986) *Sexuality in the Field of Vision*, London: Verso.

Roof, J. (1991) *A Lure of Knowledge: Lesbian Sexuality and Theory*, New York: Columbia University Press.

Stacey, J. (1987) 'Desperately seeking difference', *Screen* 28, 1: 48–61.

Stacey, J. (1994) *Star Gazing: Hollywood Cinema and Female Spectatorship*, London: Routledge.

Weiss, A. (1992) *Vampires and Violets: Lesbians in the Cinema*, London: Jonathan Cape.

Whitford, M. (ed.) (1991) *The Irigaray Reader*, Oxford and Cambridge, Mass.: Blackwell.

Wilson, E. (1990) 'Borderlines', *New Statesman & Society*, November 1990.

8

THE SPACE BETWEEN

Daughters and lovers in *Anne Trister*

Lizzie Thynne

In Hollyood cinema, classic and modern, lesbianism has either been marginalized or has remained the repressed underside of heterosexual romance. A popular Freudian conception of female sexual development continues to underpin dominant representations of lesbianism. In her journey to maturity, the girl must transfer her affections from her first love, her mother, to her father – a process which, Freud acknowledged, was fraught with difficulties. Lea Pool's feature *Anne Trister* (1986), one of a number of films with lesbian themes funded by the Film Board of Canada in recent years, questions this phallocentric model of female sexuality and reframes, rather than disavows, the protagonist's primary bond with the mother.

Like the majority of lesbian romances (*Desert Hearts*, 1985; *Lianna*, 1982; *Personal Best*, 1982; *Another Way*, 1982) the story of *Anne Trister* focusses on a straight woman falling in love with another woman – a discovery which takes place in isolation from any recognizable lesbian or feminist subculture. Yet the film goes beyond the conventional girl-meets-girl scenario in a number of ways. Pool attempts to symbolize the relation between the two women through a particular use of space, *mise-en-scène* and metaphor, at the same time exploring the connections between this romance and the original love for mother. In my discussion of *Anne Trister* I draw extensively on the work of Luce Irigaray, the French feminist theorist who reworks and critiques Freudian psychoanalysis, both tracing the obstacles to female subjectivity in the current patriarchal order and envisaging the alternatives. She highlights the need for a 'female homosexual economy' based on the articulation rather than repudiation of the initial link with the mother, and her construction of a female symbolic helps to illuminate the process of symbolization in *Anne Trister*.[1]

Many lesbians have resisted the notion that desire between women has anything to do with mother-love, apparently because the association has commonly been used to dismiss lesbianism as an immature and/or pathological sexuality.[2] I am not proposing that there is any direct equivalence between the two, but that reconceptualizing the primary relationship of our

131

early life and the way that it subsequently figures in adulthood is an important part of validating the choice of a woman lover. I believe that psychoanalysis is a valuable tool in exploring the unconscious roots of our desires but, as Irigaray and others have argued, its terms need to be different to allow for less constricting notions of difference and sexuality.

A NON-PHALLIC LANGUAGE

In both Freudian and Lacanian accounts of subjectivity, separation from the mother is tied to her relegation to the status of object/lack because lacking the penis/phallus. The infant's acquisition of a distinct identity is made conditional on its recognition of the phallus as primary signifier, that which marks out the difference between the sexes. As Frank Krutnik summarizes:

> The male subject's acceptance of his destiny as a man requires a patent denigration and denial of the possibilities of satisfaction and identity which lie beyond the phallus. The mother literally embodies the pre-Oedipal regime and through the Oedipus complex, the female organs, womb, breast and vagina become recast as signifiers of phallic lack rather than productive feminine presence. . . . The denigration of the mother functions as a strategy whereby the importance of her earlier nurturing role, and the child's very reliance on her as a fundamental mirror for his own identity, can be disavowed.
>
> (Krutnik 1991, p. 83)

What then happens to the little girl in this phallic regime? Since entry into language and culture is predicated on the recognition of the phallus as primary signifier of sexual difference and the presence of the father as the representative of a wider social network, she too submits to this law (see Lacan 1977). In doing so, Irigaray argues, she relinquishes the possibility of her own emergence as a specifically female subject; her connection with a subject like herself – her mother – finds no representation in a language based on the male metaphor of the phallus. For women, to give up their first love of the mother is to 'sever them from the roots of their identity and subjectivity' (Irigaray 1991, p. 105). She does not deny the need for the mother–child dyad to be broken in order for the girl to participate in a cultural and linguistic order beyond her – what she does question is why the phallus/penis should have this special place in securing/marking the subject's place in the social.

In the Freudian and Lacanian systems woman represents lack, she represents the danger of castration for the male, his 'having' has meaning only in relation to her 'not having'. Irigaray's project is to create a different set of meanings, where differences necessarily still exist but without this hierarchy of male and female, where woman can exist for herself and not only in relation to a masculine norm. What is needed is a feminine symbolic where the language that stands in for the original loss of her mother as primary object is not masculine symbols and imagery but a language which allows for female identification. She tries to break the neo-Freudian link between language and the phallus, creating instead a language which embodies the connection with the mother's body recalled in the title of her work 'Corps à corps avec la mère' ('Body against body in relation to the mother'). She asserts: 'We need to discover a language that's not a substitute for the *corps à corps* as the paternal language seeks to be, but which accompanies that bodily experience, clothing it in words that do not erase but speak the body' (Irigaray 1992, p. 18). In the male psychic economy, woman is categorized only as mother; in order to exist the woman must oust/substitute her own mother. This situation can have negative consequences for our relationships with other women; since there is room for only one 'mother', together we often become our own worst enemies, embroiled in self-destruction and envy. Irigaray proposes an alternative: distinguished from each other and yet similar (as in her image of femininity as two lips) we can be contiguous with our mothers, *with* them instead of being in rivalry for their place. This association, rather than substitution, can provide the basis for solidarity with and love for other women.[3] Because Irigaray's writing refuses the sexual status quo it provides an invaluable tool for the analysis of women's cinema which is also trying to imagine a new sexual order.

NARCISSISM, SYMBOLIZATION AND LESBIAN SEXUALITY

Both *Anne Trister* (1986) and Pool's recent short *Rispondetemi* (1992) juxtapose childhood and adult experiences of sexuality. In the former, Anne, a young Jewish art student, goes on a journey from Montreal to Switzerland to recover from the death of her father, who is buried in the Israeli desert. She leaves behind her long-term lover, Pierre, and her mother. In Montreal, she meets Alix, an older woman who is professor of child psychology, and Simon, an old friend of her father who finds her a disused warehouse to use as a studio. The loss of her father repeats for Anne her earlier loss of her mother who was always too busy to look after her. Alix seems to provide the nurturance and support that Anne needs and she soon falls in love with her. Visual echoes of gestures and actions across the film highlight the connection between this relationship and that of mother and daughter. In the opening shot, Anne lies, back to camera, sobbing over her father's death while her mother sits looking on in the background, physically and emotionally distant, unable to comfort her. In the penultimate sequence, this shot is mirrored in a scene between Anne and Alix. Anne is again weeping over another loss – this time the demolition of her studio and with it the vast *trompe l'oeil* mural she had painted. Alix at first sits beyond her and then climbs onto the bed to comfort her.

The scene culminates in a kiss as they start to embrace. The analogy between the two moments is clear but this is no simple regression even though in loving Alix Anne is reconnected with the lost object of her childhood love.

Other lesbian romances have also presented same-sex love in terms of a maternal relation. In *Personal Best*, Chris, a budding young athlete, is brought on by older fellow athlete, Tory, who gives her the affection and gentle encouragement denied by her authoritarian father and homophobic coach. Linda Williams comments, 'the film's notions of authentic human intimacy tend to reduce this relationship to a kind of pre-verbal, pre-oedipal narcissism', and notes that when Chris is sick all night, Tory cradles her in her arms in 'a pose recalling that of a madonna and child' (Williams 1986, p. 150). Chris's eventual rejection of Tory in favour of a 'sensitive' male lover relegates the lesbian affair to an immature girlhood phase, a step on the road to adult heterosexuality. The attachment to a mother-figure is transferred to a man, who has what Tory lacks – a penis– as the film makes pointedly visible. The sex scenes – tickling each other's slim girlish bodies – also help frame Chris and Tory's involvement as a prelude to mature heterosex.

By contrast, Pool's protagonist, Anne, does not divert her love from a female to a male lover – maturity is not equated with becoming straight. Instead as part of her process of self-discovery she gives up her boyfriend,

Plate 12 Anne forces a kiss on Alix when she visits her studio. (Courtesy of Contemporary Films and the British Film Institute Stills Department.)

Pierre, in favour of her attraction to Alix. Their interaction contains echoes of a mother–daughter relationship but is not defined by narcissism or overidentification in the way that bonds between women have often been represented. (See for example, the destructive obsession with her house-mate of the principal woman character in *Single White Female*, 1992). Instead Alix and Anne's relationship is mediated through shared images and objects – a symbolic dimension of non-phallic signifiers, in particular the desert. The desert – as a landscape without clear confines – evokes Irigaray's image of the 'threshold', a relation between two subjects where there is no rigid boundary or hierarchy but rather a border which may be crossed and recrossed. During their first evening at Alix's house, the two women share reminiscences of the desert, and the image of the desert recurs in various forms throughout the film, including in the handful of sand which Anne sends Alix. Other symbolic objects are Anne's mural and the model of the mural they build between them. The exchange of symbols establishes boundaries so that they do not merely mirror or merge with each other. They are connected like mother and daughter – as the analogies between Anne and the child Sarah, and between Alix and Anne's mother – suggest, but not as in a pre-Oedipal union. Apart from achieving a symbolic dimension, the adult nature of their relationship is emphasized by their changing roles – Anne is sometimes the nurturer, as, for example, when Alix rows with Thomas; the younger woman takes the initiatives and

Plate 13 Alix reestablishes a connection symbolically by taking Sarah's hand. (Courtesy of Contemporary Films and the British Film Institute Stills Department.)

at the end it is Alix who is left alone when Anne leaves, echoing Anne's earlier abandonment.

Both Anne's and Alix's work involves them in a struggle to establish boundaries, to make space literally or figuratively – Anne through her painting and Alix through her therapy sessions with the young girl, Sarah, whom she encourages to communicate. Scenes of Anne at work in her studio and Alix at the clinic with Sarah are intercut. Sarah's and Anne's sexual advances towards Alix are compared – both initially want to possess her. Anne forces a kiss on her when she visits her in her studio, just as Anne's mother clung to her daughter on her departure from Switzerland. Accompanied by the sound of children's voices and then a heartbeat (recalling the mother's heartbeat in the womb), Sarah strokes her own and Alix's lips and tries to reach inside Alix's shirt to touch her breast. Sarah withdraws into a corner but Alix reestablishes the connection in a symbolic way by taking her hand. The scene is disturbing because of the girl's suggestively erotic caresses – they evoke an earlier infantile state (the child's first expression of its sexuality by sucking at the breast), but also reveal an unnerving sexual awareness (has she been abused?). The infantile position is no longer appropriate – the girl is about eight – nor is a direct sexual encounter with the older woman. Alix helps her symbolize her emotions towards her as a mother figure through an intimate but not erotic gesture, and through her play. When Anne kisses her Alix reacts in the same way as she does to Sarah – and the juxtaposition of the scenes points to the same unsettling boundary between the intimate and the erotic, which is so policed by the incest taboo.[4] The difference though, as Alix comes to realize, is that Anne's desires for her, which may have their origins in infancy, need not be censored as taboo and can be happily revived in a mutual lesbian affair.

Irigaray's thoughts on the different ways in which the little girl deals with the absence of her mother are a useful reference-point here. According to Freud, the boy masters the absence of his mother through substituting an object for her in the 'fort-da' game, a notion which Freud theorized on observing a baby boy throwing a cotton reel from his cot and then retrieving it (Freud 1955). The reel stands in for the mother's body and as such becomes one of the boy's first experiences of language, accompanied by the verbal description 'fort' (gone) and 'da' (there). The girl's gestures, Irigaray argues, aren't the same because her mother's sex is the same as hers and she can't have the objective status of a cotton reel. To see her mother as an object is to become an object herself. She says there are three possible reactions on the part of the young girl to the absence of her mother:

1 She is overcome by distress if deprived of the mother, she's lost, she can't survive, she neither speaks nor eats and is anorexic in every way.

2 She plays with a doll, transferring the maternal affects to a quasi-subject which allows her to create a symbolic space.

3 She dances, thereby creating for herself a vital subjective space.

(Irigaray 1989, p. 32)

In her therapy sessions Sarah uses her toy bears ('quasi-subjects') to represent herself and her relationship to her mother. Initially she bandages one and unbandages it. Then she paints its outline. In the same scene, cross-cut with Anne's attempt to spoil her mural with white paint after Alix won't kiss her, she daubs the bear red. Later she wreaks her anger and hatred, her sense of abandonment, on the body of Alix (taping her mouth, tying her to a chair and calling her a 'bad mommy'). When she becomes violent, Alix tells her to pretend, not to play for real. The game and the bear become a way of articulating limits between the woman and the girl so that there is a 'space for sublimation'. 'In analysis between two female subjects, this space is necessary', Irigaray argues, 'to combat the limit of the transference [which] would appear to be this distanceless proximity between mother and daughter, distanceless because no symbolic process can account for it' (Irigaray 1991, p. 107). Faced by the loss of identity threatened by bereavement, Anne too creates 'a vital subjective space' for herself. No longer content with the standard format of canvas, she paints red outlines on the window-panes of her art school, just as Sarah later draws round her bear in red; in Montreal she paints windows on to the walls of her studio, giving them the impression of three-dimensionality. The space of the studio thus embodies attachment to the past, the walls defining a closed space, combined with the desire to go beyond it – through the optical illusion of a space outside. The hall she is given to paint is initially a shell, deserted like the derelict building which she wanders through near the beginning of the film. The graffiti in the first building shows two adults and a child, reinforcing the idea of the place as representing her past infantile life and sense of loss.

When Alix, initially unable to respond to Anne's advances, moves in with her lover Thomas, Anne is again left in an empty space, repeating the trauma of separation. This time it is Alix's apartment, denuded of furniture. When her long-term lover, Pierre, arrives from Switzerland, she leaves him in bed in the empty flat to go to her studio where her beautiful *trompe l'oeil* painting is finished. This space seems to her more like home; Alix has helped her to produce it through their work together on the model design – a process which Anne describes as 'two little girls making a doll's house'. It is a space claimed in the teeth of resistance from Thomas, Alix's boyfriend who, when Anne is given the warehouse, cajoles her to trade it for his own much smaller workshop. The emphasis is on the possession and creation of space and structures by the women for themselves, where their own subjectivity can be established outside what is prescribed for them within patriarchy.

Plate 14 Anne is again left alone in an empty space repeating the trauma of separation (Courtesy of Contemporary Films and the British Film Institute Stills Department.)

HOME AND THE DESERT

Both the male lovers in the film want the women to represent home for them, to be their space, although neither is shown as particularly 'sexist' in an obvious sense. Thomas pressurizes Alix into living with him, away from her own place. When Anne claims Alix's attention, he threatens Anne at her studio causing her to have an accident. (She forgets to put the brake on her scaffold and falls when it slips. Concussed, she lies unconscious in hospital and comes round with Alix at her side.) Anne's long-term lover, Pierre, sends Anne the story of a small boy, clearly representing himself, who leaves his mother, gets lost in the vast expanses of the world, wreaks havoc and then returns to her womb – it is a fantasy of an impossible return to her body as a secure place for his identity. Since, for men, women unconsciously constitute the fantasized body of the mother, Irigaray argues, they do not exist as subjects for themselves (Irigaray 1985a). Pool gives her women characters symbolic shared spaces where mutual recognition is possible. When Alix comes to see Anne's mural at her studio their conversation is given in voiceover as they look admiringly at each other. This mutual gaze recalls that of mother and child in the pleasurable bonding of infancy before speech begins,[5] but this moment of mutuality is not presented as a simple romantic resolution, each fully comprehending the other. Instead, it is succeeded by Alix's confusion and surprise at Anne's attempt to kiss her. Similarly, the studio is not a permanent refuge for Anne – she cannot return to the home it represents – but its symbolic value is perpetuated in the other shared image, the desert, which is also a spatial metaphor and signifies her connection with the other woman. There is no fixed 'home' for Anne's identity – her studio is demolished while she is in hospital recovering from the accident. Pool's rather clichéd use of a fluttering dove bruising its wings as it tries to escape the studio via the false windows indicates that while it creates an illusion of freedom her obsession with the space has also made it a prison. The project has become exhausting and out of proportion. The *trompe l'oeil* structure she has painted is only a place of transition between the blank desert where her father's funeral is held in the opening sequence and the flowering one to which she returns at the end.

If her environmental painting reconnects her with her girlhood home, the desert suggests the freedom to become autonomous. It is an imaginary space which she shares with Alix. Other recent features looking at the relationship of two women have put them into open spaces – suggesting a new place for female desire beyond the confines of domestic interiors. The landscape previously colonized by men trying to conquer nature and native peoples, often designated as feminine, becomes the arena of women: Thelma and Louise speed across the desert on the run from patriarchal law; Kotz (kd lang) lures Roswitha out of her warm but constricting haven to glide through the spectacular snowscapes of Alaska. Similarly for Anne, Canada is a thrilling expanse after the confines of Switzerland.

The blizzard which falls the first night Anne spends with Alix is the frozen counterpart of the desert sandstorms. Alix tells Anne her 'desert stories' – of the time when she went to the Arabian desert to forget the past, spent days hearing only Arabic and stuffed her suitcase full of the beautiful rocks she found. As Anne's father is buried in the desert, for her it evokes death but Alix's experience suggests its beauty. Its openness and formlessness are also full of possibilities. When Anne returns there at the end of the film she sends Alix a handful of sand and a super-8 film of herself. Sand as a symbol suggests change and fluidity – as such, it is an appropriate image for female sexuality characterized as open-ended and flowing as opposed to the end-orientated solidity of male sexuality. Alix lets the sand slip through her fingers – it is not an object that can be fixed and held.[6] She projects the super-8 movie; it shows the desert in bloom and then Anne places herself smiling in front of the camera, moving backwards and forwards to make sure she is in frame, with her father's tomb behind her. She is both subject

– in shooting the film – and object of Alix's loving look as she watches it. The super-8 picture is only part of an otherwise dark screen, suggesting that Anne has found her own limits in relation to the void, through her relationship with the older woman. (Earlier in the film Sarah refuses Alix's look by splattering the screen through which she is observed at the clinic – she refuses the position of object and only progresses when Alix interacts with her directly.) The super-8 film, the final image of self-representation for the look of another woman, completes the film's project of charting a course for the female subject, in the words of the closing song 'celle qui n'a jamais parlé' ('she who has never spoken').

Five languages are either spoken or referred to in the film – French, English, Yiddish, Italian and Arabic – but the key moments between the women characters are wordless, suggesting the Irigarayan notion that women are in exile from language as it does not figure their bodies and their sexuality. The multiplicity of languages also reinforces the idea that Anne lacks a home. Her exile as a woman has affinities with the historic Jewish experience of statelessness, an experience suffered by director Pool's father, a Polish Jew. In an interview, Pool remembers how, when she took the boat with her family to Evian as a child, her father had no passport and so was left standing on the dock – an image she has never forgotten. Later she took the same journey as her protagonist from Switzerland to Canada, realizing after her father's death that she didn't really belong there: 'A cause de mon père justement, je ne me suis jamais sentie suisse' ('because of my father I never really felt Swiss') (Raillard 1986). As a Jew, Anne's father in the film also belonged nowhere; Simon, his friend, tells Anne that he spoke ten languages, to which she replies 'but none of them well'. Likewise, women have no passport to their own identity in a masculine system of meaning. Since a child, according to Freud, begins to speak when it senses something is lost – its first object, the mother – language becomes a substitute for the mother's body. In the 'fort-da' game, 'there is an imaginary equivalence between playing with the body of the mother and manipulating the corpus of language' (Whitford 1991, p. 44). When the girl starts using language she is objectifying her mother and herself, therefore women need their own system of exchange, their own 'house of language'. Thomas's language, Italian, acts as a barrier between Anne and Alix; when Alix comes to visit Anne, a noisy Italian song on her cassette-player stops her hearing Alix's voice.

In her short film, *Rispondetemi* (1992), Pool uses the differences between languages to signify the difference of female desire. A lesbian couple are involved in a car crash in which one is killed and the other is rushed to hospital barely alive. As the medics battle to save her, childhood experiences of abuse and memories/fantasies of her lover flash through her mind. Seduced by her father, she is distant from her mother when he beats his wife. Finally, still a child, she seems reconciled with her mother. Damaged by her father's sexual exploitation of her, her expression of affection for her mother has sexual overtones to which her mother responds only with a reassuring hug. The reconciliation with her mother is a prelude to her last memory – lying on her bed with her lover, who repeats the Italian words *rispondetemi* ('answer me'). At this point she crosses the threshold from near death to life and we know she will survive. As in *Anne Trister*, the links are suggestively drawn between a language which is other than the dominant one, love between women and between mother and daughter. In both films, the girl's Oedipal trajectory is reconceptualized: the relationship to another woman as mother is not repressed but given expression to provide the ground for a separate sense of female subjecthood and a reevaluation of femininity that makes lesbian love possible.

ACKNOWLEDGEMENTS

Special thanks to Linda Anderson for her inspiration in writing this article.

NOTES

1 Most relevant here are L. Irigaray (1992) 'Body against body in relation to the mother' in *Sexes and Genealogies*, New York: Columbia University Press; (1985a) *Speculum of the Other Woman*, Ithaca: Cornell University Press; and (1985b) *This Sex Which Is Not One*, Ithaca: Cornell University Press.

2 This point is discussed further in J. Ryan (1983) 'Psychoanalysis and women loving women', in S. Cartledge and J. Ryan (eds) *Sex and Love: New Thoughts on Old Contradictions*, London: Women's Press.

3 I have drawn, here, on Margaret Whitford's overview of Irigaray's writing in M. Whitford (1991) *Luce Irigaray: Philosophy in the Feminine*, London and New York: Routledge, esp. pp. 169–91. The following extract inspired the title for my article: 'Women are nomadic, their "living house" should move with them, they need to escape the properties in which they have been legally confined by the paternal genealogy. But love, instead of being a space between, an angel, a vehicle, has been delegated to women, and men, fearing their dereliction, confine them in the house, in the law, in their genealogy, cutting them off from their own space-time' (pp. 164–5).

4 As Tamsin Wilton has pointed out to me, the scene in *Desert Hearts* where young Cay tucks up Frances in bed in a sexually suggestive way is likewise shocking because of its incestuous connotations.

5 E. Ann Kaplan notes that 'this mutual gazing is not of the subject–object kind that reduces one of the parties to the place of submission' (*Women and Film: Both Sides of the Camera*, London and New York: Methuen, 1983, p. 205).

6 As a counter to Lacanian phallomorphism, Irigaray proposes a different set of metaphors for sexuality which more closely evoke the female body – at least two lips, mucous – images which suggest multiplicity, fluidity, lack of distinction between inside and outside. Other women's films have used the aqueous to represent women's bodily/erotic experience, for example, Ulrike Zimmermann's *Touristinnen* (1986), which features a sexual game between a female harbour worker and a mermaid shot partly underwater, and Maya Deren's *At Land*

(1944), where the protagonist finds herself beached from the sea on to the alien territory of land.

REFERENCES

Freud, S. (1955) 'Beyond the pleasure principle', in J. Strachey (ed. and trans.), *The Standard Edition of the Complete Psychological Works of Sigmund Freud* vol. XVIII, London: Hogarth Press and the Institute of Psychoanalysis.

Irigaray, L. (1985a) *Speculum of the Other Woman*, trans. G. Gill, Ithaca: Cornell University Press.

—— (1985b) *This Sex Which Is Not One*, trans. C. Porter and C. Burke, Ithaca: Cornell University Press.

—— (1989) 'The gesture in psychoanalysis', trans. E. Guild, in T. Brennan (ed.), *Between Feminism and Psychoanalysis*, London and New York: Routledge.

—— (1991) 'The limits of the transference', in M. Whitford (ed.), *The Irigaray Reader*, Oxford: Blackwell.

—— (1992) *Sexes and Genealogies*, trans. G. Gill, New York: Columbia University Press.

Kaplan, E. Ann (1983) *Women and Film: Both Sides of the Camera*, London and New York: Methuen.

Krutnik, F. (1991) *In a Lonely Street: Film Noir, Genre and Masculinity*, London and New York: Routledge.

Raillard, F. (1986) 'Une femme se penche sur son passé', *Le Matin* 23 July 1986, p. 16.

Ryan, J. (1983) 'Psychoanalysis and women loving women' in S. Cartledge and J. Ryan (eds), *Sex and Love: New Thoughts on Old Contradictions*, London: Women's Press.

Whitford, M. (1991) *Luce Irigaray: Philosophy in the Feminine*, London and New York: Routledge.

Williams, L. (1986) 'Personal Best: women in love', in C. Brunsden (ed.), *Films for Women*, London: British Film Institute.

9

ON NOT BEING LADY MACBETH

Some (troubled) thoughts on lesbian spectatorship

Tamsin Wilton

How do I look at the film? How do I appear in its fantasy? Am I looking on? Do I see myself in it? Is this my fantasy?

(de Lauretis 1991, p. 236)

If 'spectatorship' is simply a textual position, then there may only be a masculine or a feminine option; however, if spectatorship refers to members of a cinema audience, surely the possible positionings multiply.

(Stacey 1994, p. 29)

Come, you spirits/That tend on mortal thoughts, unsex me here
(Lady Macbeth, *Macbeth* I.V.)

TEXTS AND READERS, SIGHTS AND SEE-ERS

Film theory, including much from feminist and queer perspectives, has come to be dominated by a psychoanalytic paradigm that itself is dominated by a highly restrictive binarism whereby masculine/feminine are not only understood as the definitional polarities of gender but also coopted unproblematically as the exemplary paradigm for understanding sexual desire, pleasure and identity. Film theory is not unique in this, rather it is merely obedient to the hegemonic paradigm which has structured mainstream thinking about both gender and the erotic since Freud (and indeed, on and off since Plato). It also reflects, as Cindy Patton points out (this volume), what has tended to happen in film itself, whereby a pop-Freudian paradigm has profoundly influenced film-making. This obedience to the paradigm has presented difficulties for those who would claim a place for women as spectators rather than as spectacle of film, for, within the psychoanalytic paradigm, agency (and this includes ownership of the gaze), is masculine. Feminist film theory has tied itself up in increasingly baroque knots trying to establish a coherent and radical theory of

143

female cinema spectatorship and of female identification as part of that spectatorship within the terms of this binarism (Stacey 1994). For lesbian film theory, there is the added problem that psychoanalytic binarism has no place for lesbian desire.

Issues of identification and spectatorship remain moot within and between competing theories of film and audience, and are of course especially problematic for a lesbian viewer, for only a tiny proportion of films construct a lesbian viewing position or enable lesbians to enjoy uncomplicated identification with either onscreen character or voyeuristic camera. Indeed, if Laura Mulvey is to be believed, it is impossible for any woman to get pleasure from a mainstream narrative film without temporarily unsexing herself in order to carry out what is understood to be an intrinsically male set of behaviours, à la Lady Macbeth (Mulvey 1981). Yet lesbians still go to the movies and still get pleasure from watching films. Because it has no place within film theory, and because it is largely excluded from authorial intent or textual construct, this is a pleasure which many lesbian film critics have described as being somehow 'against the grain' (Florence 1993), a reading disobedient to intended address. Some critics have even gone so far as to suggest that queer consumers (and producers) of culture are so accustomed to self-consciously inhabiting contradictory viewing/reading positions as to make us preeminently skilled deconstructionists, subtle cynics about the various performative gender/sex roles which the less sophisticated still assume to be somehow natural or real (Dyer 1991; Traub 1991). As Dyer puts it:

> In this perspective both authorship and being lesbian/gay become a kind of performance, something we all do but only with the terms, the discourses, available to us, and whose relationship to the imputed self doing the performing cannot be taken as read. This may be a characteristically gay (I hesitate to claim lesbian/gay) perception, since for us performance is an everyday issue.
>
> (Dyer 1991, p. 188)

The notion of camp is of use here, and Dyer's hesitation to do violence to the question of gender marks a significant difference between lesbians and gay men with regard to camp. Queer theorists have mounted a resounding (and I think successful) challenge to Susan Sontag's interpretation of camp as apolitical and assimilationist/assimilated (see the essays collected in Meyer 1994), and insist rather on its political and its specifically queer status. Camp is understood within this queer paradigm to be rooted in gay men's lack of access to the machinery of representation (which is cultural reproduction). For Cynthia Morrill,

> Camp discourse is the epiphenomenon of the queer subject's proscription in the dominant order; it is an effect of homophobia. . . . Camp

results from the uncanny experience of looking into a nonreflective mirror and falling outside of the essentialized ontology of hetero-sexuality, a queer experience indeed.

(Morrill 1994, p. 119)

Furthermore, it is claimed that, because gay men have been obliged by the homophobic elision of sexuality and gender identity to pay critical atten-tion to gender, camp has emerged as a radical paradigm within which gender becomes artificial and open to deconstruction: 'To some extent, Camp originates in a gay male perception that gender is, if not quite arbitrary, certainly not biologically determined or natural, but rather that gender is socially constructed, artificial, and performed (and thus open to being consciously deformed)' (Kleinhans 1994, p. 188). This may be the case, but camp is a concept which is itself clearly gender-specific and hence problematic for lesbians. Gay men may lack access to the machinery of representation *qua* gay, they certainly do not *qua* men. It is the execrated sexuality 'gay' which finds no reflection in the mirror of cultural produc-tion, *not* the privileged gender 'man'.[1] Camp is less a product of lack of access to the machinery of representation and more a product of *compro-mised* access to that machinery. It is the lesbian who, vampire-like, must look in vain for her reflection in the glass, invisible by reason of the desire that her gender makes impossible. It is the lesbian who, more than any other sexed and gendered subject, cannot be successfully incorporated into the body of psychoanalytic film theory, and it is the question of lesbian spectatorship, and specifically of lesbian identification within that spectating, that I am concerned with here.

DOING THE LOOKING

The question of identification looms large in film theory and is assumed by many to be the key to understanding the processes whereby films (and indeed all texts) are made meaningful. It is a question which, according to Jackie Stacey, is contested between, on the one hand, film studies which generally understand spectatorship as a product of textual address and meaning as being production-led and, on the other, cultural studies which generally understand spectatorship as a process of negotiation between product and consumer and meaning as consumption-led (Stacey 1994). It seems clear to me that there is little evidence to suggest that film is in any significant way different from other cultural products. To say that film is polysemic and that its many possible meanings are contingent and, more-over, located at the meniscus between film as product (located within the social and economic relations of production) and viewer as consumer (similarly located within specific social and economic relations of con-sumption) is only to claim that film is no more and no less intrinsically meaning-full than painting, poetry, novels or any other cultural product. 'The meanings', as Penny Florence argues, 'are not locked up in the can with the celluloid' (Florence 1993).

I take for granted here that the sense of a film is made by the spectator – whom we may understand for our purposes as both receptive and engaged, and as bringing to the process of spectating a temporally and culturally specific set of signs, meanings, codes and languages. It is also I think important to focus on the sensory/social experience of sitting in the darkened cinema, temporarily disembodied and removed from the mundane context of tasks and obligations, with someone else's meanings playing across your retina.[2] I agree with Stacey that the materiality of 'the audience' and the *sociology* of that audience offer us dykes a way out of the impasse that psychoanalytic film theory has got us into.

Good, old-fashioned symbolic interactionism surely comes into its own in attempting to make sense of the (altogether rather peculiar) social experience of cinema spectatorship. If nothing else, to sit in the dark with a number of strangers releases one for a while from the unremitting pressure of presenting the self – and retaining control of that presentation as 'correctly' gendered, sexed and desiring – under the surveillance of the public arena. This unique social experience, unexplored by theorists of the cinema, certainly shapes the different pleasures which women, men, queers and non-queers extract from film spectatorship, variously oppressed/privileged as they may be by the relentless policing of dress, gesture and behaviour.[3] It also undoubtedly resonates differently for black and non-black spectators, whose quotidian experiences of surveillance are marked by their relationship to the machinery of racism.

If this (social) experience has potential pleasures to offer the lesbian spectator (and I argue below that it has), then it is also a potential source of anxiety when events on screen abruptly return us to our social location. For example, this sudden recoil happens (for me) when watching a lesbian sex scene in the company of a largely heterosexual audience. Suddenly to become aware of the heavy breathing of the straight men surrounding me, as happened when I was watching Monika Treut's *Virgin Machine*, (1988) is to be suddenly thrown back into the relations of surveillance which structure my social life. This recoil may, on rare occasions, be a source of pleasure itself, as it is at the end of *Desperate Remedies* (1993) when the two women board the ship together at the conclusion of a skilfully engineered 'will she, won't she?' suspense gradient, at which point I looked with triumph around the (largely heterosexual) audience, my own deviant choices validated.

Film theory, unlike media studies, has no place for this sensuous and social experience of the spectator. Sociological variables such as social class are taken for granted as significant in studies of television audiences, whether within the academy or in the context of viewing figures continually gathered by television companies themselves; this is (bizarrely) not the case with film.[4] What I want to explore, here, is how the social position of the spectator, when brought to the private experience of watching films impacts on the business of reading/spectating and, in particular, how the sensuous and social experience of being a lesbian influences lesbian spectatorship, and how important 'identification' is in that process. If I had a whole book to do this in (and a lot of money), I might have recruited a statistically significant number of lesbians;[5] since this chapter is all I have, I have donated my own eyes and brain to the cause, and what follows is a discussion of my own lesbian responses to two films using what might loosely be termed auto-ethnographic methodology. I have chosen two films: *The Living End* (1992) and *Strictly Ballroom* (1992).

The reasons why I have chosen these particular films are partly pragmatic, partly wilful and in part because I think they offer particularly useful material for this exercise. The two films intrigue me because, despite the fact that one purports to address (or at least include in its address) a queer audience while the other does not, both appear quite consciously to pre-empt the possibility of lesbian identification (see pp. 148–9 below), despite which I enjoyed watching both of them. A text-determinist position would suggest that my pleasure in watching two films that demonstrate hostility to and foreclose the possibility of a lesbian spectator position must be not only perverse but masochistic. A position that goes beyond textual determinism to consider the politics of location (Stacey 1994) enables me to map my social and political position (self-as-lesbian) on to the textually determined (and hence usually non-existent) lesbian viewing/reading position, and carve out a theoretical space for the spectating dyke. It is a mapping which demands that I distinguish between the two, which I do by designating the social, active meaning-maker as 'spectator', and the textually determined meaning absorber as 'audience'.

PERVERSE PLEASURES? LOOKING IN AT A GAY MEN'S FILM FROM OUTSIDE

The Living End, a film made by Gregg Araki in 1992, is a fairly conventional narrative of the road-movie genre, following the collision between the lives of two young, white HIV+ gay men, Jon and Luke. It is an independent film, and had a limited showing in Britain on the arts cinema circuit; it is also available on video and distributed largely through the gay press. Hailed by *The Village Voice* as being at the cutting edge of New Queer Cinema, the film was treated to a scathing and contemptuous review by *Gay Times*'s film critic, Mark Simpson. Characterizing the film as 'a spoilt West Hollywood queen's bohemian daydream', 'a straightforwardly romantic film badly disguising gushing sentimentality as nihilism' and 'headed . . . straight for Pretentious Crap City', Simpson accuses Araki of using the two protagonists' HIV status as 'just another accessory to their lip-curled designer disaffection . . . just cheap props in an impotent attempt to be transgressive' (Simpson 1992, p. 78). I have to say that, having seen and enjoyed the film, I was rather stunned by the sheer vitriol of the review, which led me to muse on the vexed question of (sexualized and gendered) identification. Did I only enjoy the film because I *wasn't* a gay man? Watching a gay men's film from the outside, was I obliged to rewrite my gender and my sexuality in so convoluted a fashion that I missed the inadequacies of the film by expending too much energy and concentration on repression of/compensation for my own inadequacies as watcher-without-a-dick?

That I enjoyed *The Living End* is especially intriguing because the film quite clearly doesn't want me to – or at least the 'me' that watches with lesbian eyes. There is a scene at the beginning of the film which nastily 'gets rid' of lesbians in no uncertain manner. Jon, the alienated drifter, thief and stereotypical antihero, thumbs a lift with two women in an open-top car who turn out to be lesbians. They also turn out to be off the wall, neurotically obsessed with men and with penises in particular, and dangerous to gay men. They use Jon's presence in the back seat to goad one another and eventually threaten him at gun-point. Jon takes advantage of a pee break in the desert to steal their car and their gun, leaving them stranded.

The episode is a nasty one which makes unrestrained use of all the anti-lesbian stereotypes in the book, and which makes a triumphant joke of Jon leaving the two women alone, vulnerable and without transport in the desert. Switching temporarily into psychoanalytic mode, the theft of gun and car – both paradigmatic phallic symbols – is also quite clearly a moment of phallic recuperation. Given the currency of anxiety about the penetrating penis and the lesbian dildo in the AIDS-aware queer milieu, this theft of the phallus from the lesbian by the gay man takes on a somewhat overburdened significance. It is a significance that is accessible to me as a queer/lesbian/feminist spectator, though I suspect that it would remain opaque to non-queers and non-feminists. As such, it is a meaning that I am able to make by reason of my precise, gendered, sociopolitical location between feminist and queer milieux, in postmodernity, at the height of the epidemic. Nuff said.

Watching from the dark of my local arts cinema, in an audience largely made up of gay men, I experienced a familiar gut sensation of vulnerability and rage at Jon's treatment of the women. The expectation of the film was that I should find this sequence funny. I didn't. Another clear expectation of the film was that I should find Jon sexy (even the rancorous Simpson had noticed his body beautiful). I didn't.

Since the central object of desire failed to move me, and since the film had shown itself to be at the least unfriendly to lesbians, one might presume that, as far as my viewing pleasure was concerned, *The Living End* was just that. What I recognize in retrospect is that in fact I put a remarkable degree of effort into my eventual enjoyment of the film, and that in order to get pleasure from it I resorted to a number of what I will call 'engagement strategies'. First, of course, I wanted to know what happened. This desire came from my own anxieties about illness, dying and HIV,[6] and from identifying *as queer* with the protagonists as they vanquished various representatives of homophobia. When Jon beat one such homophobe to death with a ghettoblaster I must confess to triumphant sympathetic bloodlust.

Second, there is the figure of Luke's heterosexual female friend Darcy, who is There For Him to a quite farcical degree. Darcy is the one who we see offering support to Luke over his HIV status, and she spends a significant chunk of her life anxiously waiting by the phone for him to ring after he has taken off into the wide blue yonder with Jon. She also has an entertainingly abysmal heterosexual sex life. I could identify with Darcy all right by dredging deep into my own heterosexual past. It wasn't much fun identifying with her – in the social, political and emotional narrative which I brought with me to my spectating she stands for everything about heterosexual womanhood that I thought I had escaped when I became a lesbian – but it kept me in my place, 'there' for the film, metaphorically waiting on the phone to see what the gay man's film had to say to me.

Then there was Jon. Take away the muscles and the blonde hair, and Jon was a lot like a boyfriend I had in the 1960s; selfish, destructive, often gob-smackingly childish but with an in-your-face intolerance of cant which sometimes provided a useful antidote to immersion in the culture of *Dixon of Dock Green* and *The Lucy Show*. This meant that I could just about manage to identify with Luke. A bit. Sometimes. What I could most certainly identify with was Luke's powerlessness and helplessness in his relationship with Jon. Jon has hurled them both into the hostile and inhospitable vacuum of the road, they are on the run. Luke is very sick, he is increasingly troubled by a dry cough – immediately intelligible to an AIDS-aware queer audience as *pneumocystis carinii pneumonia*, an AIDS-related opportunistic infection that is likely to kill him fairly swiftly if he doesn't get suitable care and medical help. The diegetic tension set up through the film coalesces around the question of whether Jon will risk capture and take Luke back home where he will receive care (we know he will get that care because Darcy is frantically hanging in there for him) or whether he will force him to face an unadorned and naked death on the road.[7] It is an existential crisis.

The spectators' investment in this diegetic anxiety is informed by their social, political and emotional relation to death, illness, care, medicine and the wider business of incorporation into mainstream society, factors which in turn are shaped by the spectator's social position and status. A white, non-gay male spectator may, for example, perceive medical care as comforting evidence of man's supremacy over a chaotic natural world while an African American may think of Tuskegee,[8] or a queer viewer of various (mostly sadistic) attempts to 'cure' homosexuality, etc., etc. As a feminist queer with a primary critique of hegemonic constructs of sexuality and of gender, I was rooting for Luke to maintain his 'escape' from the hetero-patriarchal machine. I knew only too well what would result from capitulation: Jon would be arrested and imprisoned for murder, and prison is not a good place for gay men, let alone gay men with HIV; Luke would be absorbed into the oppressive institution that is Western Scientific Medicine; and Darcy would be lumbered with being his primary carer. Not good for gay men, not good for women. As a lesbian feminist with a primary critique of masculinity, I was also furious with the self-indulgence and existential game-playing of Jon, and with his (familiar, male) failure to pay attention to or to care for his sick and vulnerable partner. At the climactic scene, when Jon fucks Luke with a gun in his mouth, I expected that diegetic resolution would be attained by the killing off of Jon, (coded as overmasculine, incapable of intimacy, dependent on violence to fight homophobia) and the blood-soaked survival – albeit time-limited – of

Plate 15 The existential wasteland at the end of living? *The Living End*'s Luke and Jon in a typical interchange. (Courtesy of the British Film Institute Stills Department.)

150

Luke (coded as sympathetic to femininity, capable of and desiring intimacy, with a more intellectual/theoretical approach to the problem of homophobia). This would have fitted in with a current trend in certain feminist-influenced approaches to gay masculinity (see, for example, Edwards 1994), and would have been a consummation devoutly to be wished for as far as my lesbian feminist position was concerned. The diegetic tension, then, was heightened and reflected in a private tension within myself as spectator. What is important is that this privacy does *not* mean that my personal tension may best be understood within a psychological paradigm. Rather, it resulted from a specifically *social* and *political* location, and was indicative of a wider tension between my allegiance as a lesbian to feminism and to queer. Other, differently located spectators, would have made other, quite different meanings out of this tension, and may not even have experienced it as a tension at all.

YES, BUT WAS IT FUN?

So far, then, I had managed to attain the three elements thought by James Linton (cited in Dyer 1992) to be essential to my entertainment: identification with characters, absorption in narrative and reassurance – Jon does agree in the end to take Luke home. Yet these were not things which, on the whole, the film had made unproblematically available to me as a lesbian viewer. I had had to work very hard indeed to come up with enough engagement strategies to keep me paying attention. Once I became aware of this degree of effort, watching this film began to feel less like an act or process of 'reception' and more like the kind of adversarial engagement involved in, for example, playing chess. This process of engagement suggests to me that it would be helpful to think in terms of what might be called a 'cinematic contract', whereby the spectator agrees to draw upon the personal emotional/political/social narratives which she brings with her into the cinema in order to devise engagement strategies which she puts at the service of the film.

These narratives in turn are expressive of and rooted in her social and political location. Thus, although the climactic diegetic dilemma of *The Living End* might appear to be on the level of the existential (where is meaning, in human contact or in lonely death?), it is in fact on the level of the social and political. Whether you are rooting for Luke to die in a hospital bed or in the desert, in the arms of Darcy or of Jon, largely depends on your own sociopolitical status *vis-à-vis* the normal and the deviant, the mainstream and the oppositional/marginalized. Social factors such as ethnicity, socioeconomic class, dis/ability and gender will shift and nuance the meaning-making of different spectators of this film, as much as being queer or not, being black or not, being HIV positive or negative. As a lesbian spectator, I fulfilled my side of the contract by drawing on remembered as well as current social and political locations, on remembered heterosexuality as well as present lesbianness; as a queer and an ally of gay men against homophobia and in this epidemic, I was prepared to ride out the anti-lesbian opening sequence and 'be there' to make meanings in cooperation with the film. (A less queer, more separatist lesbian feminist spectator would refuse to pay this degree of attention to men's (misogynist) speech, and indeed would probably not have gone to see the film in the first place.) This suggests to me that a production/consumption model of film spectating/reading is inadequate. The 'cultural product' which is the meaning of the film must be understood to be produced by this act of cooperation, and hence to be located in the intersections of *two* cultures, that of the auteur and the production system and that of the spectator.

Such are the strategies I employed to milk pleasure from a film supposedly addressed to a queer audience, to honour my part of the cinematic contract and cooperate in the cultural production of meaning for *The Living End*. What of a film which has no such queer address? How can a dyke enjoy a heterosexual romance like *Strictly Ballroom*?

WHEN IS A PARTNER NOT A PARTNER?
WHEN SHE'S A WOMAN!

Unlike *The Living End*, *Strictly Ballroom* (1992) was hailed by *Gay Times* (this time by video reviewer Peter Burton), as: 'Beautifully constructed, emotionally involving and a riot of sheer camp. . . . a thoroughly satisfying movie – a glorious mix of tears and laughter' (Burton 1993). In case you missed it this Australian-made film, a 'surprise international hit' of 1992, tells the story of how the handsome Scott brings a dash of authentic passion to the ersatz posturings of the ballroom dancing competition circuit, by scavenging on the Spanish heritage of his ugly-duckling partner, Fran. Camping it up to the hilt in a riotous blizzard of Frocks and 1950s pastiche, the film struck me as being a softened up, less cynical and decidedly less queer version of *Hairspray* (1988). It is, of course, not authentic (i.e., queer) camp. Rather it is vestigial or assimilated camp, evidence of what Margaret Thompson Drewal (1994) calls the 'camp trace'. In postmodernity, subcultural codes and vernaculars are constantly incorporated into the body of mainstream culture, witness Madonna's assimilation of S/M. 'The media world's cannibalization of subcultures' as Chuck Kleinhans puts it, 'is a structural feature of the culture industry' (1994, p. 187), and *Strictly Ballroom* is a good example of this cannibalism.[9]

The main theme is a familiar one: white kid from alienated, artificial, colonialist culture goes out and steals some authenticity from another, less civilized, immigrant/oppressed culture and brings back the booty. His peers are at first scandalized, but what he brings back calls to something buried in them beneath the thin veneer of that civilization, and narrative closure is attained when their alienation (seen as the inevitable price of civilization) is breached and their lives enriched by this enforced contact with authenticity. This may only be accomplished by breaking through (not breaking down) the social barriers between (in this case) white Australian and Spanish Australian culture, a task which takes the form of transforming Fran: reforming her immigrant poverty, ugliness and nonconformity into a predictable docility to the prevailing white Australian standards of female beauty.

From a lesbian point of view – especially a lesbian feminist point of view – the film sucks. Fran is introduced as a beginner with *no partner*, when in fact she is partnered by a (fat) woman.[10] During one of the diegetic moments of crisis, we see her, transformation temporarily suspended, back in beginners with 'no partner', whirling miserably around the floor with the fat woman again. The message is almost farcically anti-lesbian: to have a female partner *means* to be unattractive to men (both women are presented as ugly when they are dancing together) and *means* 'really' to have no partner at all. In addition what Scott needs to learn from the authentic Spanish dancing lessons Fran's parents give him is not merely passion but passionate heterosexual masculinity. What would Freud have to say about the scenes where Fran's father teaches him the steps of the male dancer, where her mother stands in for Fran and teaches Scott how to dance properly with a woman, or where mother's dancing dress is handed on to Fran to enable her to dance with Scott!

Ironically, the hidden text of this gay cult film is profoundly anti-gay. Heterosexuality is clearly in crisis on the ballroom dancing circuit, with male/female partnerships disintegrating faster than you can say 'passa doble'. The suggestion made by the film is that this crisis in heterosexuality is due to the artifice and alienation of the postmodern world, where authentic manliness and womanliness are no longer passed on through the generations. What saves Scott and Fran is that they are privileged to have access to real, genuine, 100 per cent authentic traditional heterosexuality, as represented by Fran's immigrant Spanish family where the men and the woman know their places and are content. We are being seduced back to basics.[11]

In order to reach this place of safety for heterosexuality and as heterosexuals, both Fran and Scott must be rescued from the alternative. Scott is quite clearly at risk of homosexuality, simply because he is a dancer. In addition, his father is a hen-pecked failure – nurturing a dangerous secret from his inadequate dancing past – and hence not in a position to initiate his son into the mysteries of virility. Fran is quite overtly saved from lesbianism – a salvation symbolically represented by the ritualistic removal of her glasses by Scott. Mary Ann Doane has suggested that the clichéd transformation of the female ugly duckling by ritualistic removal of the glasses represents a cinematic defence against female usurpation of the gaze, and the agency that comes with it:

Plate 16 Scott's heterosexual masculinity is uncompromised by his camp get-up in *Strictly Ballroom*. (Courtesy of the British Film Institute Stills Department.)

Glasses worn by a woman in the cinema do not generally signify a deficiency in seeing but an active looking, or simply the fact of seeing as opposed to being seen. The intellectual woman looks and analyses, and in usurping the gaze she poses a threat to the entire system of representation. It is as if the woman had forcefully moved to the other side of the specular.

(Doane 1992, p. 236)

In Fran's case, the usurped gaze threatens to be doubly dangerous, because the implied object of her bespectacled gaze is her female dancing partner. Strange things are done to the cinematic gaze when it associates with Fran. That female partner, whom we see quite clearly, is rendered invisible, nonexistent, by the script. Although we *see* a woman, we *hear* that Fran has *no* partner. Interestingly, hearing takes precedence over seeing *while Fran is wearing her glasses*. Once Scott removes her glasses, she becomes more dependent on his guidance, and much more active in looking. Stripped of the means to see clearly, she gazes long and increasingly lovingly into his face. A disobedient lesbian reading which springs to mind is that she only fancies Scott once she can't see clearly.

As an apology for white colonialism and an active 'promoter' of heterosexuality, it is clear that the universally positive gay response to *Strictly Ballroom* must have to do with something other than its narrative content. The attractions of Paul Mercurio, who plays Scott, loomed large in the promotion of the film, with his suitably confrontational face gazing directly at you from the publicity poster. Certainly the film offers him as object of desire as much as or perhaps more than Tara Morice (Fran),[12] and it is hardly surprising that, given the hegemonic status of the *male* sexually desiring gaze, any object of desire of whatever gender should be assumed to be an object of desire for men. The film was promoted with full page adverts in *Gay Times*, in which context Mercurio became a sexual product alongside porn star Jeff Stryker and the Foto Fantasy Guys.

But I am not a gay man, and found myself unable to take either Fran or Scott seriously as objects of desire, despite having Scott's moderate amount of chest hair looming at me from the screen and being privileged witness to the despectacling of Fran. Yet I thoroughly enjoyed the film, as did many of my lesbian friends, weeping and laughing in all the right places and telling other dykes that they simply had to see it. Why?

ON LYING BACK AND ENJOYING IT: A (LESBIAN) SPECTATING POSITION

In contrast to *The Living End*, there was no hard work involved in my engagement with *Strictly Ballroom*. The film is a clever pastiche, giving off very clear messages that you are not *supposed* to take it seriously, any more than you are supposed to regard candyfloss as food or Mills & Boon as literature. The terms of engagement set by the film are that you should 'simply' abandon yourself to the pleasurable superficialities of the sensuous experience it offers. German and Germanist scholars, not least Heidi Schlüpmann, have resurrected *Zerstreuung*, a word current in Weimar Germany meaning 'abandoning oneself to pure appearances, to the "dazzle", renouncing concern with meaning' (Schlüpmann, cited in Dyer 1992, p. 9), and it is a useful word to sum up the process by which I got great pleasure from *Strictly Ballroom*. For the 'dazzle' of the film is delightful and very well done; the self-consciously clichéd romantic narrative preempts cynicism, and the colour and sparkle of the world it depicts seduce the eye.

But that leaves open the question as to why *Zerstreuung* should be in and of itself pleasurable. I am forced to conclude that the pleasure I took from *Strictly Ballroom* lay simply in my queer-chameleon ability to adopt an alien reading position for the night. This ability to spectate/consume from multiple positions is becoming a given in lesbian cultural criticism. There is a tendency to assume that such a change of position is necessary for pleasurable lesbian consumption of all cultural products, and indeed, for lesbian cultural production: '[we can all] read from more than one position (what other explanation is there for lesbian enjoyment of mainstream novels?) and write multifaceted texts' (Lewis 1992, p. 20). But my (guilty) pleasure in *Strictly Ballroom* lay in being able to *set aside entirely* my lesbian reading position and have a rest from it. As 'who I am', namely a queer feminist with a critique of racism, I could not possibly have sat through the film without considerable discomfort. But far from 'not sit[ting] easily and shift[ing] restlessly in [my] borrowed transvestite clothes', as Mulvey insists all women must at the cinema (Mulvey 1981, p. 33), I revelled in my successful temporary escape from my social and political position.

There is an influential sociology of escapism (Cohen and Taylor 1974) which characterizes cinema (among other sites) as a 'free area' wherein the fantasies which maintain sanity may flourish, safely contained. It is this perspective which much Freudian/Lacanian-inspired film theory seems to me to lack. The question is not, which sex position does a woman (or a man, or a lesbian) have to occupy in order to get pleasure from film, but what pleasures are to be gained from that positioning itself? Mulvey admits that the fantasy of control offered by identification with a male protagonist may present women with something denied to them in their 'real' lives: 'She may find herself secretly, unconsciously almost, enjoying the freedom of action and control over the diegetic world that identification with a hero provides' (Mulvey 1981, p. 29). I think that a less complex set of pleasures is at issue, one which does not depend for its success on identification with onscreen characters but on the degree to which the film facilitates the viewer relinquishing her 'self', escaping for a while from identity.

This isn't a new idea. Peter Wells, the New Zealand writer and film-maker who wrote and codirected *Desperate Remedies* (1993), told Rose Collis that the film was 'trying to reconnect with that extreme world which, on one level, doesn't have anything to do with reality, but does answer the need to pop into another life' (Collis 1994);[13] and 'escapism' has long been recognized as a desirable feature of 'entertainment' (Dyer 1992). Of course, some political commentators believe the power of escapist fantasy to be a dangerous drug, the sugar on the pill of capitalism/patriarchy/homophobia. This may well be true, although some sociologists have suggested that political radicalism itself is merely a different kind of strategy for escaping an intolerable existence (Cohen and Taylor 1974). What remains to be asked is, what is to be gained by sitting in a darkened room and 'popping into another life'?

This is where I want to pull back once more from the screen, glittering seductively with frocks and jocks from the Pan-Pacific ballroom dancing finals, and pan around to me, sitting in the dark, face turned obediently up to the screen, lesbian feminist self switched off for the duration. What is going on?

POPPING OUT OF THE LESBIAN SELF?

Watching a film is clearly hard work for the lesbian spectator. To read much lesbian film theory is to understand lesbian spectatorship as a constant struggle to insist on and locate 'lesbian' as a reading/viewing position. This is in itself a mightly battle, in the teeth of Freudian/Lacanian film theory which sets up a rigidly (one might say, anxiously) gendered polarity whereby the unstable, multiple inflections of genders, sexualities and desires are mercilessly beaten into the square hole[14] of heterosexuality (see Dyer 1992, pp. 4–5, or Stacey 1994, for sensible deflations of psychoanalytic film theory). The lesbian spectator is forced to defend herself against a plethora of fantastic phallocentric assumptions that psychoanalysis has bred, and that have become influential even within feminism. Thus, for example, Teresa de Lauretis is obliged to rescue lesbian desire from Julia Kristeva's declaration that:

> Lesbian loves comprise the delightful arena of a neutralized, filtered libido, devoid of the erotic cutting edge of masculine sexuality. Light touches, caresses, barely distinct images fading one into the other, growing dim or veiled without bright flashes into the mellowness of a dissolution, a liquefaction, a merger.
>
> (cited in de Lauretis 1991, p. 253)

As a lesbian reader I chuckle and ask myself *who* she has been having lesbian sex with,[15] and what recreational drugs were involved at the time. I also recognize, as does de Lauretis, that ignorance and silence about lesbian sexuality is so utter that non-lesbians reading Kristeva will have no doubt that she is speaking the truth, and will be grateful for having their own phallocentrism reassured and their anxiety about lesbians assuaged. Public speech about lesbians (and film is in this category) is thus an automatic source of anxiety for lesbians, who fear having to defend themselves against misrepresentation.

In addition, the elision of sexuality and gender makes it almost impossible for any film theory informed by psychoanalysis to make sense of lesbians. Jackie Stacey is right when she calls for an untangling of the two:

> This insistence upon a gendered dualism of sexual desire maps homosexuality on to an assumed antithesis of masculinity and femininity. Such an assumption precludes a description of homosexual positioning. . . . In arguing for a more complex model of cinema spectatorship, I am suggesting that we need to separate gender identity from sexuality, too often conflated in the name of sexual difference.
>
> (Stacey 1992, p. 249)

Unless the separation that Stacey advocates occurs, the unfortunate lesbian viewer is doomed in film theory to ricochet back and forth between 'castrated male' and 'fetishized phallic female', existing only as an antidote to male anxiety, a salve for the cruelest cut of all. Having spent so much time and energy fighting the windmills of penis envy, castration anxiety, etc. (themselves a form of cultural misrepresentation), insisting that 'a lass (is) not a lack' (Doane 1992, p. 230), there is little left to expend on the business of watching.

What we are watching also presents us with a struggle. Saturated as it is in patriarchal, heterosexist signs, codes and ideologies, privileging as it does the sexual and erotic as sites of scopophilic pleasure, film by and large obliges its lesbian spectators to engage with an undiluted reflection of mainstream cultural hostility to lesbian existence. Either there are no lesbians, or, if there are, they must bear the burden of representing the whole class 'lesbian'. As Sander Gilman notes in the context of race: 'the representation of individuals implies the creation of some greater class or classes to which the individual is seen to belong' (Gilman 1992, p. 171). Any onscreen lesbian must meet the demands of every other lesbian looking at her that she represent *their* lesbianness. Clearly this can only end in tears.

There is, further, the social as opposed to the theoretical business of being a lesbian. For all the (interesting, valid and useful) challenges posed by social construction theory to the 'reality' of a lesbian identity, the materialities of lesbian oppression continue. Even social construction theory does not propose that 'lesbian' is any less real than any other social category, and as such, 'women' who identify as 'lesbian' inhabit a particular set of interstices among social notions of gender, desire, deviance, criminality, sin, naturalness, etc. It is a complex positioning, but what it boils down to is oppression. As a lesbian sitting in a cinema I bring personal and social narratives of oppression – both material and ideological – along with me. When called upon, as I am by *The Living End*, I make use of that set of narratives to construct engagement strategies with which to make meaning of the film; such is the nature of the cinematic contract. But the delight of spectating *Strictly Ballroom* lies precisely in the film's persuasive invitation to set all that aside, to step out of the tight and beleaguered social space which, as a lesbian, I inhabit as a matter of course. Is this perhaps the simple solution to the appeal of escapist fantasy cinema for gay men? Can the success of such films as *The Wizard of Oz* or *Strictly Ballroom* in the gay milieu be due not to the production side of the cinematic contract, but to the consumption side?

If we understand the cultural product which is the 'meaning' of films to occur, as I have suggested, at the meniscus between production (determined by and expressive of specific social and economic relations of power) and consumption (equally determined by and expressive of such relations), then the relative significance of the social factors impacting upon production and consumption will determine the success or otherwise of the reception of a particular film by a particular social group. When the weight of homophobia (or racism, or sexism/misogyny) is present as a determining factor on the consumption side of the contract, the business of simple escapism takes on added significance. To be able to sit in the dark, temporarily released from one's own performative obligations, and be allowed to take unproblematic pleasure in the joys, sorrows and fantasies of the wider culture, is like going on queer holiday; an experience that partakes of the painful and poignant illusion of stepping out of the (cold, dark) margins and being included within society for a change.

CONCLUSION: GROPING IN THE DARK

It is no longer appropriate to rely on the individualistic, heterosexist myth system of psychoanalytic film theory to explain lesbian spectating. 'Lesbian' is not amenable to enclosure within a polar model of gendered sexuality or sexualized gender. Rather, it partakes of a far greater range of social and political issues which may include, but are not limited to, the questions of male anxiety and control foregrounded (albeit at times unwittingly) in the psychoanalytic paradigm. In order to begin to understand the processes by which lesbian spectators make sense of film, we must pay attention to the sociology of lesbianism as it impacts on the business of film-making, but more importantly, as it impacts on the business of lesbian spectating. This investigation should take account of, among other factors: the temporary relief from gendered/sexualized performative obligations which watching in a darkened cinema affords; the importance of the fantasy genre as an 'escape mechanism' whereby homophobia/misogyny may be survived; the willingness or otherwise of lesbian spectators to enter into the cinematic contract and cooperate in the business of producing meaning; the implications of different forms of address (whether hostile or friendly to lesbians/women/queers) for that willingness to honour the cinematic contract; and the use of 'engagement strategies' to milk pleasure from a lesbian-hostile film.

I am not proposing 'auto-ethnography' as the exemplary methodology for this sociology of lesbian spectatorship(!). It has been useful here, but leaves unexamined by default the intersections of race, age, class and dis/ability in lesbian spectating. I find it useful to foreground the 'lesbian' in lesbian spectating, precisely because it is the 'lesbian' whose visual pleasure is unallowable within psychoanalytic film theory, and because as a queer feminist I find 'lesbian' to be the paradigmatic site for disentangling the threads of gender and sexuality, but other vectors of oppression clearly need to be incorporated into 'lesbian' if we are to develop an adequately inclusive theory of lesbian cinematic spectatorship.

NOTES

1 Although, of course, the execrated sexuality does 'contaminate' the privileged gender.
2 Stacey argues for the importance of the cinema as a physical environment to the experience of watching films, in *Star Gazing: Hollywood Cinema and Female Spectatorship*, London: Routledge.
3 'Policing' quite literally in the case of gay men, women sex workers, consensual sadomasochists, etc. – lest the metaphorical use of the word lull us into forgetting that state surveillance of our erotic behaviours has a more than academic impact on our lives.
4 I am grateful to Jackie Stacey for drawing my attention to this anomaly.
5 Although, according to some authorities, 'a statistically significant number of lesbians' is oxymoronic. A national funding body which shall remain nameless refused to consider funding my research into lesbian safer sex practices because: 'You couldn't possibly find a large enough number of lesbians for it to be statistically significant.' Well . . . hello to my three lesbian readers!
6 I have worked in the field of HIV/AIDS since 1986 and have lost friends to the epidemic, so my anxieties are more specific than most people's. I am not suggesting that anxiety about HIV will be an important factor shaping everyone's response to the film, although since it is addressed to a gay male audience, that will probably be the case for most viewers.
7 Or at least, it coalesces around this question for me. The idea of spectatorship as an active process implies of course that this diegetic tension is established by my spectating of the film, not necessarily by/in the film itself and, as such, will not necessarily be experienced as significant by other spectators, other readings.
8 Tuskegee is a Southern US town where black Americans suffering from syphilis were fraudulently recruited to a research programme, left untreated and their syphilis allowed to run its course, in order that medical researchers

might familiarize themselves with the natural progression of the disease. Many died.

9 In contrast, Stewart Main and Peter Wells's queer-produced film *Desperate Remedies* (1993) is authentic camp, making hay not only with the codification systems of heterosex, but with heterosexuality itself, something that *Strictly Ballroom* conspicuously refuses to do.

10 Bigness is familiar as a property of the heterosexist caricature of the 'manly' lesbian, in implied contrast to a 'real' woman, whose principal obligation is to be thin.

11 'Back to Basics' was the slogan for an ill-fated 1994 Conservative Government campaign to return Britain to 'traditional' (hetero)sexual morality.

12 An indication of the film's popularity among a British gay audience was the inclusion of Morice as one of the celebrities interviewed in Australia by Julian Clary in his 1993 Christmas season television show, 'Brace Yourself, Sydney'. In this, Clary asked Morice if she came to Bondi Beach to cruise, to which she replied that she usually did that 'up at the other end' of the beach. There is an assumption here (which Morice does not challenge) that gay men and heterosexual women share a similar sexual interest in men – an assumption which presumably says much about the gay male response to *Strictly Ballroom*.

13 Although, interestingly, *Desperate Remedies* does not encourage the kind of absorption in the narrative which 'popping into another life' requires. Employing hyperextravagant costume, distracting camera techniques (jump cuts in all their dislocating glory), self-consciously theatrical sets and OTT acting styles, the film constantly pushes the spectator away from suspension of disbelief or identification with onscreen character.

14 Yes, I know it's 'square peg into round hole', but I can't make myself see heterosexuality as anything other than square – on any number of levels.

15 Actually, it's probably the two lesbian heroines from *Desperate Remedies*!

REFERENCES

Burton, P. (1993) Review of *Strictly Ballroom*, in *Gay Times*, July 1993.

Cohen, S. and Taylor, L. (1974) *Escape Attempts: The Theory and Practice of Resistance to Everyday Life*, Harmondsworth, Penguin; new edition, London: Routledge, 1994.

Collis, R. (1994) 'Peter Wells: throwing naturalism aside', in *Gay Times*, January 1994.

de Lauretis, T. (1991) 'Film and the visible', in Bad Object-Choices (eds), *How Do I Look? Queer Film and Video*, Seattle: Bay Press.

Doane, M. A. (1992) 'Film and the masquerade: theorising the female spectator', in M. Merck *et al.* (eds), *The Sexual Subject: A Screen Reader in Sexuality*, London: Routledge.

Drewal, M. Thompson (1994) 'The camp trace in corporate America: Liberace and the Rockettes and Radio City Music Hall', in M. Meyer (ed.), *The Politics and Poetics of Camp*, London: Routledge.

Dyer, R. (1991) 'Believing in fairies: the author and the homosexual', in D. Fuss (ed.), *Inside/Out: Lesbian Theories, Gay Theories*, London: Routledge.

———— (1992) *Only Entertainment*, London: Routledge.

Edwards, T. (1994) *Erotics and Politics: Gay Male Sexuality, Masculinity and Feminism*, London: Routledge.

Florence, P. (1993) 'Lesbian cinema, women's cinema', in G. Griffin (ed.), *Outwrite: Lesbianism and Popular Culture*, London: Pluto Press.

Gilman, S. L. (1992) 'Black bodies, white bodies: towards an iconography of female sexuality in late nineteenth century art, medicine and literature', in J. Donald and A. Rattansi (eds), *' Race', Culture and Difference*, London: Sage.

Kleinhans, C. (1994) 'Taking out the trash: camp and the politics of parody', in M. Meyer (ed.), *The Politics and Poetics of Camp*, London: Routledge.

Lewis, R. (1992) 'The death of the author and the resurrection of the dyke', in S. Munt (ed.), *New Lesbian Criticism: Literary and Cultural Readings*, Hemel Hempstead: Harvester Wheatsheaf.

Meyer, M. (ed.) (1994) *The Politics and Poetics of Camp*, London: Routledge.

Morrill, C. (1994) 'Revamping the gay sensibility: queer camp and dyke noir', in M. Meyer (ed.), (1994) *The Politics and Poetics of Camp*, London: Routledge.

Mulvey, L. (1981) 'Afterthoughts on "visual pleasure and narrative cinema" inspired by King Vidor's *Duel in the Sun* (1946)', in L. Mulvey (1989) *Visual and Other Pleasures*, London: Macmillan.

Simpson, M. (1992) 'London Film Festival: being in the vanguard', in *Gay Times*, November 1992.

Stacey, J. (1992) 'Desperately seeking difference', in M. Merck *et al.* (eds), *The Sexual Subject: A Screen Reader in Sexuality*, London: Routledge.

——— (1994) *Star Gazing: Hollywood Cinema and Female Spectatorship*, London: Routledge.

Traub, V. (1991) 'The ambiguities of "lesbian" viewing pleasure: the (dis)articulations of *Black Widow*', in J. Epstein and K. Straub (eds), *Body Guards: The Cultural Politics of Gender Ambiguity*, London: Routledge.

10

GIRL'S CAMP?

The politics of parody

Paula Graham

In the context of the New Queer Cinema, and as some groups of lesbians try to claim a lesbian art and culture that is more open about lesbian sexuality, the question of lesbian camp is on the agenda. Parody, performance and subversion have largely replaced positive-images feminist politics with 'riskier' images of 'queer' sexuality. The question of what constitutes a risky image is not one on which all lesbians will necessarily agree, however. Meanings of the term risk are particularly complex for lesbians. Queer cinema sees itself as risking homophobic responses by being more open about homosexual or gay sexuality. Feminism sees the risk in representing female sexuality in terms of promoting violence against women generally. Lesbians committed to anti-pornography politics would argue that it is the feminist *challenge* to the (hetero)sexualization of women which is most risky for lesbians, in terms of provoking anti-lesbian responses.

A greater openness to the 'undecidability' of representational effects can be seen as positive – arising as it does from a greater sense of security in self-defined cultural spaces. Over the last three decades in the West, marginal groups have been successful to varying degrees in achieving greater visibility and greater confidence in asserting cultural difference. Lesbian willingness to risk sexually explicit imagery is a function of increased security in lesbian-made cultural space. Lesbian cultural space can be seen as 'an oasis where we are, for a time, beyond patriarchy. . . . We have freedom which straight women access at their peril' (Axton 1993). Lesbian space is where gender is, arguably, meaningless, or its meanings inverted. There has been some shift of focus away from critical confrontation with patriarchal representational regimes, characteristic of 1970s and 1980s lesbian politics, and towards performative subversion of gendered roles.

This means, put as simply as possible, that instead of tearing up porno mags in Soho in confrontation with dominant constructs of 'woman' as sexual object, lesbians play about with and redo the heteropatriarchal language of sex in their own sweet way. This shows that: 'woman' can be lots of things; 'woman' can speak for herself; and if 'woman' can behave like 'man' *or* like woman *or* like both at once, then gender cannot be fixed and natural like it says in the Bible. The hope is that, in this way, the man/woman split will be broken up into many different ways to act like a human being – and gender-oppression will ultimately cease to exist.

Despite the shift in critical emphasis from dominant meanings to marginal readings of popular culture, queer activism still feels moved to mount 'in-yer-face' campaigns against mainsteam images of homosexuality which it reads as homophobic (the term homophobic is, in itself, problematic for many lesbians). Queer reaction to *Basic Instinct* was illuminating in that it barely sought to interpret the images of *women* which it offered, but campaigned under the liberal/gay rubric that the image of gay (woman/ man) as violent sociopath was *homophobic*. Exasperated, one lesbian commentator wryly enquired as to what could be wrong with a film in which women have sex with each other and kill men!

It seems important to consider more closely the frames of reference in and through which female parody and performance operate. In shifting a primary alliance from a now demonized feminism to queer politics, some lesbianisms risk losing a language in and through which to articulate a fuller range of lesbian identities. Feminist lesbianisms may reject a language associated with masculine practices and agendas which may, or may not, be appropriate to lesbian identities and interests. Lesbianisms coming out of different cultural traditions may also feel little involvement with white/English language and traditions on which camp performance draws.

The subject of camp and female parody has long been a bone of contention between feminists, lesbians and gay men. There has also been similar conflict around the deployment of codes of race in white gay culture. Critical work in both areas is tending towards more open reading practices, but these conflicts continue to problematize the incorporative claims of queer discourse. It seems useful to contextualize *who* is risking *what* . . .

ACADEMIC CAMPS

Arguments about lesbians and camp need to be seen not only in the context of a shift from lesbian feminist critical perspectives to queer perspectives, but also in the context of wider (or just controlling) critical discourses of subjectivity and subversive practices inherited from Marxist cultural debates and through poststructuralist theory. New left and poststructuralist critical languages oppose the deployment of a referential play of signification to the realist aesthetics of positive-images practices (or social realism). The idea of a female essence, located in the female body, is not only seen as an ideological 'own goal' for feminism, but also goes against the controlling discourses of left-liberal academia.

Feminist film criticism has operated mainly within a psychoanalytic framework, with its positive–negative characterization of gender that makes it difficult, if not impossible, to construct a subject position which is both positive and feminine. At the current state of play, much hetero-sexual feminist film criticism seems worn out by the struggle to construct a figure of a 'strong' woman on hostile discursive terrain, and has become concerned with deconstructing the purportedly controlling stability of the male subject of psychoanalysis. Academic lesbian film theory also works mainly along psychoanalytic lines; but the effort to mould a grown-up, healthy, female, lesbian out of the stuff of psychoanalysis often seems a losing battle. In the teeth of these academic disciplines, radical feminism implied an intuitive female integrity as ontological source of confrontation with male language – and was marginalized. New feminist perspectives are tending, instead, towards a Foucauldian discursive subject of micropolitics. For Butler:

> The feminist 'we' is always and only a phantasmic construction . . . which constitutes itself only through the exclusion of some part of the constituency that it simultaneously seeks to represent . . . the question of agency is reformulated as a question of how signification and resignification work. . . . The loss of gender norms would have the effect of proliferating gender configurations, destabilizing substantive identity, and depriving the naturalizing narratives of compulsory heterosexuality of their central protagonists: 'man' and 'woman.' As the effects of a subtle and politically enforced performativity, gender is an 'act,' as it were, that is open to splittings, self-parody, self-criticism, and those hyperbolic exhibitions of 'the natural' that, in their very exaggeration, reveal its fundamentally phantasmatic status.
>
> (Butler 1990)

To anyone acquainted with theorizations of gay male camp, this is not unfamiliar territory:

> As a practical tendency in things or persons, camp emphasises style as a means of self-projection. . . . Style is a form of consciousness; it is never 'natural', always acquired . . . it signifies performance rather than existence. . . . Camp is often exaggerated . . . the emphasis shifts from what a thing or a person *is* to what it *looks* like; from *what* is being done to *how* it is being done.
>
> (Babuscio 1984)

Concepts of 'camp' and 'gay sensibility' are not a million miles from concepts like Barthes' 'textual jouissance' or Butler's 'performative iden-tities'. Camp has been theorized as a gay reading strategy deployed to construct identifications and pleasures denied by dominant, heterosexual culture. Camp expresses the disruptive distance of an estranged homosexual subjectivity. It is argued that it was through oppositional readings and performative transformations of popular culture that homosexual subcultures initially defined themselves. Camp reading and performativity, though ill-defined, has undoubtedly been central in forming male gay culture, art and criticism. However, as the language of camp becomes increasingly incorporated into left academic discursive formations, a disciplinary, controlling effect can develop. Exclusion, estrangement and opposition take many forms. To what extent has this specific effect – of camp, parody and play – actually informed or structured other oppositional discursive practices?

ON THE SELF – THE INS AND OUTS

Opponents of realism take the basic view (expressed in a variety of ways) that: (a) we have no access to 'the real' because of the preconceptions we require to organize perceptions (without which we could not make any sense of sensory experience); and, consequently, (b) any effort to reproduce 'reality' will only succeed in reproducing preconceptions. The idea that there is *an* objective 'real world' which 'any sensible person' must interpret the same way is a hegemonic one (a middle-class, white male perspective masquerading as common sense). But opposition to realist practices has often also covertly assumed a white, male subject position and interpreted *all* forms of contestation which it encounters from this position.

Mercer's comments on the use of realism in black British independent film-making within both documentary and narrative genres seem useful here:

> This insistent emphasis on the real must be understood as the prevailing mode in which independent black film has performed a critical function in providing a counter-discourse against those versions of reality produced by dominant voices and discourses in British film and media . . . [but] how can the 'colonised' express an authentic self in an alien languge imposed by the imperial power of the 'coloniser'?
>
> (Mercer 1988)

Mercer argues that the deployment of semiotic concepts of signification in new black film-making may tend only to produce another form of mimicry – of European modes of 'high' artistic practice and semiotic analysis. He goes on to trace out a potential for subversive mobilization of the multiplicity of every-day-life aesthetic practices of black peoples in Britain to 'decentre, destabilise and carnivalise the linguistic domination of "English" – the nation-language of the master-discourse' (ibid).

Waugh sums up a feminist perspective on a mimetic tendency in contemporary feminist writing which is an expression of a related problem of subjectivity:

During the 1960s, as Vonnegut waves a fond goodbye to character in fiction, women writers are beginning, *for the first time in history*, to construct an identity out of the recognition that women need to discover, and must fight for, a sense of unified selfhood, a rational, coherent, effective identity. As male writers lament its demise, women writers have not yet experienced that subjectivity which will give them a sense of personal autonomy, continuous identity, a history and agency in the world.

(Waugh 1989)

Despite an increasing understanding of the totalizing tendencies of realist representation which problematize positive-images demands, lesbians still frequently express a preference for 'realistic' images of lesbian life and relationships. Despite essentialization tendencies in 1970s and 1980s lesbian feminism, however, lesbian writing and film-making of the same period does not prioritize realism. It is often playful, ironic, experimental and expressive of estrangement. 'Transgressive' practices such as cross-dressing are also part of lesbian tradition. But can such practices be interpreted as exactly analogous to gay male transgressive/subversive or camp practices?

Lesbians, traditionally constructed by heteropatriarchal culture as repressed and/or asexual, are often attracted by the rampant phallic-feminine excesses of gay male culture. Searching for a framework within which to construct a powerful sexual subject which does not essentialize and is deconstructive of male subjective authority, camp seems to offer such a paradigm. However, the uncritical use of semiotic concepts or camp practices by lesbians may simply reproduce the boundaries of exclusionary discursive practices, offering an equivocal inclusion on its own linguistic terms only.

Foucauldian feminism – which tends to locate the lesbian in the category of (homo)sexuality rather than gender – marginalizes or elides frameworks in and through which to theorize the specific gender–power relations which continue to structure lesbian identity and experience. These are not the same gender–power relations which structure male gay identity and experience. In expressing a displaced subjectivity, camp is above all positional. I will here be considering popular film, white lesbian reading practices, and their relationship to camp traditions.

SUBCULTURAL CAMPS

Camp is based in sex – even when it is 'the Brown Derby restaurant on Sunset Boulevard in LA' (Sontag 1982). But, mostly, camp is unmistakably sex – and unmistakably deviant sex.

> camp taste draws on a mostly unacknowledged truth of taste: the most refined form of sexual attractiveness (as well as the most refined form

of sexual pleasure) consists in going against the grain of one's sex. . . .
Allied to . . . a relish for the exaggeration of sexual characteristics.

(Sontag 1982)

Traditionally, gay male camp takes the fetishized Hollywood female star as
its focus – not just any female star, but the 'strong', highly sexualized
feminine images, the sirens, vamps and femmes fatales; in other words,
what psychoanalytic language would designate as the fetishized phallic
feminine. Camp pleasure – that most refined and ecstatic sexual pleasure –
lies in a fetishistic tease of presence/absence of phallic control: power and
the threat of its loss. Camp expresses the relation of gay men *to* male
authority, *mediated by* a relationship to representations of 'the feminine'.

Existential gender categories are necessarily asymmetric – spectator and
spectacle. Constructed as that which does not have the phallus, as 'absence'
or non-being, how might women, lesbians or even black/Asian gay men
(frequently situated in 'the feminine' by white gay culture) make sense of
this thrilling flirtation with the *surrender* of (phallic) power so dear to
white gay male hearts?

White masculinity signifies as rational being. Femininity (as one of its
constitutive others) signifies as irrational non-being. Therefore, when a
white man enters the feminine he becomes sinister, false, non-being (the
cat-stroking/art-loving/mother-loving villain); or sexually excessive, hysterical, non-being (screaming queen). Because 'the feminine' is by definition negative, a man entering the feminine can only be irrational, evil or
ludicrous. It is assumed that a white woman entering the white masculine
will be similarly inverted – will take on the codes of homosexuality.
Indeed, a woman attempting to negate or invert male power by subjecting
men to a feminine regime signifies as lesbian through one of the two basic
lesbian stereotypes: either oversexed, perverse and mad, or neurotic,
repressed and authoritarian. But a young girl may aspire to a male subjective position as long as she upholds the *principle* of male dominance
(she may emulate male power but may not appropriate it to female ends).

In the English tradition, plucky heroines (warrior maids, principal boys,
cross-dressing heroines of romantic novels, Amazons and Virgin Queens)
are stripped of feminine sexuality and acquire a boyish subjectivity. The
English-speaking Amazon is not, however, traditionally a lesbian stereotype. Contemptuous of male 'inadequacy', she works to restore the male
order in times of crisis. Traditionally, the Amazon is pitted against the
lesbian invert-queen (or more recently the lesbian, repressive boss-woman
– a popular stereotype in the women's prison and convent genres, amongst
others).

The masculinized 'tart-with-a-heart' is reminiscent of the appeal of
Pretty Polly Perkins (who went to war in her brother's clothes), hoydens,
roaring girls and the principal boy. A pretty boy/girl in breeches, and a

Plate 17 Oh no, she's not! . . . Oh, yes she is!! Jean Peters' swashbuckling tomboy hits off the not-so-innocently androgynous charm of the principal boy. (Courtesy of the British Film Institute Stills Department.)

bad-girl figure which appeals most strongly to lesbians, ranging from Dietrich's assorted tarts, to Crawford in *Johnny Guitar* (1953), Bancroft in *Seven Women* (1966), and Peters in *Anne of the Indies* (1951). Her masculine clothing emphasizes her girlish sexual attractiveness. This Amazon is not at all chaste. Her cross-dressing symbolizes freewheeling,

169

masculine attitudes to sexuality, money and aggression. She has 'positive male' attributes, such as honour, courage and decisive action, and she is sexually active on her own terms. It is this kind of freewheeling, self-defining sexual power which seems to attract lesbian identification, even though the tart-with-a-heart is always restored to a heterosexual order, and usually ends up dead for good measure.

Lesbians tend to go for the boy–girl/Amazon character – even when she is dedicated to the vengeful destruction of an explicitly lesbian character. This might be more understandable when the tart or Amazon is represented as attractive and/or freewheeling whilst the 'lesbian' is represented as repressive and repellent. But why should the heterosexualized or asexual Amazon be preferred so often by lesbians over sexually aggressive, dominant and feminine-attractive lesbian witch queens?

Camp reading parodies popular genre forms by foregrounding the suppressed implications of deviance from which the genre draws its pleasurable intensities. The camp sensibility, alive to the 'difference . . . between the thing as meaning something, anything, and the thing as pure artifice' (Sontag 1982) lends itself easily to genre spoofs, and camp crossed over to the mainstream some time ago. Medhurst (1991) makes an important distinction in separating texts which *become* camp through gay reading, from mainstream texts self-consciously capitalizing on the self-reflexivity and parodic wit of camp. Finch (1986) questions camp's effectiveness in challenging culturally constituted gender roles; particularly now that camp is so popular in the mainstream and no longer a specifically gay discursive practice – or even necessarily gay addressed.

Camp, expressing the disruptive distance of estranged subjectivity and revealing culture as a construction of dominance, cannot be seen as quite the same phenomenon as a self-affirming, 'knowing', bourgeois sophistication and/or adolescent cynicism – however pleasurable (and even affirming) the resultant sexual spectacle may be for gay people. In the mainstream, 'camp' may articulate either reformative liberal attitudes to sexuality and gender (a containment project) or a conservative sense of threat to the heteropatriarchal hegemony and attempts at neutralization. Mainstream camp generally offers preferred readings which are neither lesbian nor gay nor feminist. 'Camp' has become the permissible form in which sexual deviance may be displayed as spectacle for heterosexual consumption (and its threat neutralized).

POPULAR CAMPS

The opposition of Amazon versus an excessive lesbian, or tomboy tart versus repressed lesbian, occurs in a number of films which have been popular with gay and lesbian, as well as mainstream, audiences. *Red Sonja* (1985) has a gay/lesbian camp following, and has camp codings in its mode

of representing 'perverse' sexuality as pleasurable spectacle for a principally heterosexual male audience. Generically, it is classifiable more or
less as sword-and-sorcery: it has generic connections to the *Conan* cycle
(1982–4) and is based on the works of the same writer. *Conan* films are
hybrid sword-and-sorcery, gladiator-muscle-epic, and ape-man flicks
which circulate through the video market to male adolescent rather than
cult audiences.

Red Sonja has many elements from the literary traditions of the female
warrior and evil queen in a contemporary context, and is a variation on a
standard formulaic sword-and-sorcery plot. Schwarzenegger, as Kalidor,
occupies a controlling position in the narrative, both in terms of genre
codings and the scopic structure. The lesbian implications of the female
warrior's appropriation of 'male' rule are brought to the fore, but contained
both by the narrative closure and by the overseeing male gaze of Kalidor.
His controlling, phallic gaze is signified by the setting up of the relay
through which the male spectator controls the image of the woman. There
is an establishing shot as Sonja rides off across the plains to begin her quest
filmed in longshot with the camera positioned behind Kalidor's shoulder
from a vantage-point in the mountains. This constitutes a point of insertion
for the male spectator which positions both women as spectacle, disarming
the threat of exclusive female bonding. The male spectator is able to have
his cake and eat it between sadistic-voyeuristic looking and masochistic-
fetishistic looking at the eroticized spectacle of feminine excess.

In the opening scenes the voiceover narration explains that the evil
despotic queen Gedren wanted Sonja for herself, and Gedren attempts to
abduct her. But Sonja's 'disgust was clear' – enacted by slashing Gedren's
face with her own orb/mace (symbol of authority). Gedren's face, which
was covered by a veil, is thus exposed and scarred, combining clichéd
metaphors: veil = duplicitous femininity, scar = homosexuality. Sonja is
granted strength by a divine visitation in order to fight for justice, and she
goes off to a warrior school borrowed from the kung-fu genre.

In the meantime, an order of warrior priestesses, of whom Sonja's sister
is a member, is massacred by Gedren, and Gedren steals the talisman used
by 'God' to create the world. The talisman can only be touched by women,
and becomes dangerous in the light (reason), causing earthquakes and
storms (traditional powers of witchcraft). It must be kept buried in the
dark (the feminine). In the hands of the lesbian Gedren, it will destroy the
world in thirteen days if Sonja cannot get to the talisman and destroy it.

Sonja is warned that 'hatred of men in a lovely young woman could be
your downfall'. Sonja, however, does not hate all men, but has taken a vow
that 'no man may have me unless he has beaten me in a fair fight'. In other
words, she is dedicated to the restoration of the 'natural' order of heterosexuality disturbed by Gedren's deviance. As she sets out in her quest to
find and destroy the talisman, Sonja arrogantly refuses Kalidor's help (he

is guardian of the talisman unbeknownst to her). However, subsequent events show that she does need Kalidor, who repeatedly saves her life.

On the way, Kalidor and Sonja acquire a boychild, a prince dethroned by Gedren, and his servant. Sonja adopts a motherly role in relation to the boy. The relation of the prince to his servant/mentor is 'unbalanced'. Although the civilization in which the servant's deference made sense has been destroyed (by Gedren), he continues to obey the child, although to do so often puts the child in danger. Sonja restores the 'natural' order by spanking the boy. Finally, Sonja kills Gedren, destroys the talisman of female power and goes off with Kalidor and the boy.

During the scene in which Kalidor sets out to conquer Sonja (sexually) in a 'fair fight', the boy leaps on to Kalidor's shoulders attempting to defend Sonja who is, of course, metaphorically making love. The fight scene is constructed in the boy's point of view, and the boy shadows the lunges, feints and parries with his own small sword until losing interest, remarking: 'Why does she fight so hard, she doesn't want to win!' Sonja and Kalidor finally sink down exhausted on the ground, evenly matched. Besides the obvious reference to the Freudian 'primal scene', there are resonances of 1960s male buddy films in which the buddies (or sometimes father–son) fight to exhaustion before embracing in mutual recognition – the homoerotic subtext of which has frequently been remarked on.

This scene makes the function of the Amazon in patriarchal culture fairly clear. Gedren's feminine regime has destroyed the 'natural' order of authority, from father to son via mother. Sonja represents feminine self-control as the mainstay of the family. She is supposedly equal to Kalidor, the guardian/father, but in the feminine sphere. She concerns herself with the talisman which Kalidor explains is ultimately his responsibility, but which is entrusted to the priestesses because it cannot be touched by men. That is to say, the sexes have 'equal' power in their appointed spheres, although ultimately the 'divine right' belongs to males. Sonja has to learn to rely on him, and not to try to exist alone. The boy must accept the 'proper' order of accession to power in the correct Oedipal configuration. He must learn that a 'real' man respects his mother/wife as having an important task in the moral sphere.

The contrast between Gedren and Sonja is underlined in a sequence in which Gedren observes Sonja watching the child go to sleep. Sonja has an expression of maternal softness. Gedren's hand is clenched and she has an expression of hard lust for possession: 'Spare her, I want that beauty here with me' (hatred of men – lesbianism – will be *her* downfall as Sonja is, of course, the vengeful fury who, having been spared, pursues and kills the lesbian Gedren). Gedren will not listen to the advice of her male advisers, insisting on using the talisman although she is told that it will become beyond control. Gedren's minions are inadequate males. Sonja gradually respects Kalidor's authority. As earthquakes shake the castle and storms rend the sky, Gedren curls up on her tyrant's throne laughing in uncontrolled hysteria. It remains to the chaste maiden to exert feminine self-control. All in all, Sonja represents an extremely traditional, protestant ideal of 'companionate' heterosexual femininity.

Gedren is mad, bad femme fatale, and a thoroughly histrionic excess of signification. The *mise-en-scène* associates her with the female genitals. Her castle is deep pinky red with round openings and subterranean tunnels. In contrast to the 'shinie cleare' priestesses and their temple, Gedren and her castle are obscured by dim lighting and smokey atmospheres. She wears black and gold, hiding her scarred face with a gold mask. Besides her veils, scars, masks, witchcraft and supernatural vision, she has a pet black spider (significant of voracious female sexuality and lesbianism). The *mise-en-scène* also inflects Gedren with the codes of 'orientalism', which emphasizes her lesbianism by further 'overheating' her feminine sexuality.

It is interesting to note that lesbians who say they enjoyed *Red Sonja* usually say that it was the image of Birgitta Nielson's Sonja which attracted them – which gave them pleasure. It is particularly telling, in such a narrative, that lesbian spectators will identify with the heterosexual figure dedicated to the overthrow of lesbian rule. The implication of *Red Sonja's* narrative and *mise-en-scène* is mentally 'edited out' by many lesbians because of its 'knowing' camp excess. The triteness of the imagery and plot begs a camp reading – a further source of amusement for audiences.

This would not explain, however, why lesbian identification should focus on Nielsen rather than Bergman. Extratextual subcultural gossip that Nielsen is lesbian or bisexual may go some way to explaining this paradox. However, similar structures can be seen in many other films without the element of subcultural identification attaching to the actresses playing the boy/girl. Clearly, the scopic relay and narrative structures also facilitate identification with the boy/girl protagonist, but gay men often read against both narrative structure and scopic relay and identify with the witch. Could this be explained in terms of a 'mindset' which these two subcultural audiences bring to reading the text?

FEMINIST CAMPS

A sexually excessive female figure which often *is* popular with lesbians is the female vampire. Could this be connected with the difference between the predominantly voyeuristic scopic structure of the vampire film as opposed to the predominantly fetishistic scopic structure of the gladiatorial spectacle? However, although the lesbian vampire is not always subjected to the male gaze through an intradiagetic male look, the image is still presented as fetishized spectacle for the male. Studlar (1990) suggests that heterosexual male spectatorial pleasure in phallic-feminine images does not depend on a fetishistic covering for the missing phallus (as suggested by Mulvey's analysis), but on a disavowal of the father's phallic power and its redistribution on to the authoritative, pre-Oedipal mother. In the absence of a male protagonist, lesbians would also be brought into a direct erotic rapport with the image along the lines suggested by Mulvey (1975) for the male spectator, and by Studlar (1990) for the lesbian spectator of the campy Dietrich–Sternberg cycle. Lesbian pleasure in the lesbian vampire film would then consist in a playful, subversive female-to-female looking, disseminating lesbian identification between desire for and identification with the authoritative woman.

In films such as *Red Sonja*, the gay male spectator is likely to identify with the phallic-feminine wicked queen (possibly along the lines suggested by Studlar). However, the lesbian spectator, if offered a choice between 'transvestite' (Amazon) and 'phallic-feminine' (witch queen) identifications, will tend to prefer what Mulvey (1981) describes as 'transvestite', 'tomboy pleasures'. The heterosexual male spectator may, however, respond masochistically to the phallic feminine – and this raises important issues for feminism.

Modleski (1991) points out that when the (heterosexual male) masochist fashions the woman as the symbolic father (who beats out his narcissistic love for the male parent), the substitution renders male *authority itself* ridiculous. For many critics, this is the very subversive or satirical edge of camp. There are double-edged effects for women, however, in these mainstream camp classics. It makes little difference whether pleasures are pre-Oedipal or fetishistic. Such images either straightforwardly represent female power as sick, ugly and ineffectual, or clearly draw satiric power from the cultural inappropriateness of a woman acting powerfully. Whilst parodying specific *forms* of male authority, they simultaneously confirm the illegitimacy of female authority itself. This may very well explain how counteridentification against 'lesbian' characters is produced in lesbian spectators of mainstream 'camp'.

Forms of parody in which 'feminine excess' (i.e., feminine power) signifies an illegitimate form of power are usually an index of tensions within the heteropatriarchal order. They may express either conservative fears of moral breakdown, liberal satirical attacks on conservative moral authority, or other forms of contestation – either within the male order or in responses by the male order to the challenge of feminism itself. Efforts to contain fears of female power (often symbolized by lesbianism) are readable in many camp classics. In *Red Sonja*, a conservative text, the lesbian Gedren's rampant female sexuality threatens 'civilization' itself. In the liberal *Daughters of Darkness* (1971), feminine authority ('mother' and the Countess) functions as parody of an anachronistic aristocratic class-power signifying moral decay and corruption (as a twist on the traditional middle-class values of the genre).

The liberal *Johnny Guitar* (1953) also focusses on a struggle between two women. The film's camp following tends to be attached to the image of Joan Crawford, playing Vienna, a cross-dressing tart-with-a-heart. Pleasures in the confrontations between the two central female characters also draw on the lesbian-erotic implications of the 'cat-fight', which in turn draws on homoerotic subtextual elements in westerns. There is an interesting similarity in the ways in which codings of lesbianism circulate through this text and through *Red Sonja*. Against her gun-slinging and cross-dressing proclivities, Vienna is narratively heterosexual and reliant on a male helper. Her equally gun-slinging adversary, Emma, is, on the other hand, a classic lesbian stereotype of the time, which is still recognizable in the popular stereotype of lesbian feminism. She is conservative, authoritarian, repressed, hysterical, anti-sex, will not accept male help or advice, and subjects the men around her to (an 'unbalanced') feminine agenda.

In a liberal text, delineation of the forces of 'good' and 'evil' may approximate more closely to a lesbian or gay spectator's 'own' values and therefore be less easily visible as such. In *Johnny Guitar* the stereotypical lesbian opposes the (good) liberal, masculine rationalism of 'progress', 'civilization' and 'tolerance', and is interested only in her own conservative-landed (evil) power base and (evil) repressed feminine desires. Female power (lesbianism) is again linked to the forces of evil, and the Amazon tart linked to the forces for 'good' – which, in a liberal universe, are forces of 'irrational conservatism' versus forces of 'progress' and 'civilization'. Vienna's cross-dressing is symbolic of and also narratively offset by her heterosexual alliance with rational tolerance. Emma's 'man-hating' spinster (lesbian) figure is, again, deployed (by men) to ridicule a particular form of *male* power – in this case, a liberal critique of conservative morality. Lesbians counteridentify against this figure of ridicule, preferring 'transvestite' identification with the (narratively and culturally) privileged position of the boy/girl.

In *Seven Women* (1966), a similar pattern can be observed. Convents, and in this case a predominantly female mission post, are a favourite setting (along with female prison movies) in which women-without-men and particularly feminine authority are represented as repressed/repressive, hysterical and unbalanced (often as allegorical condemnation of conservative repressive society). In *Seven Women*, a repressive, authoritarian lesbian character presides over a remote mission in Asia. The only male character is weak and dominated by female rule. In the opening scenes, we are shown the lesbian character's predatory lust for a young girl, along with outbreaks of hysteria amongst the women who are anxiously waiting for a doctor to arrive. As in *Red Sonja*, the codes of 'orientalism' are deployed to express a sexual 'overheating' of the relationships between women, suggesting lesbian undertones. The depiction of the Asian men as sexually barbaric counterpoints the absence of (white) male 'civilizing' authority over the women.

The narrative sets up the expectation that the doctor will be a strong, white male character who will provide a reassuring masculine presence – a 'true' authority and a rational order. But when the doctor does arrive, *she* is a variation on the tart-with-a-heart, a masculine authoritative (as opposed to feminine repressive) figure with riding-boots, jodphurs, and a bowling stride. This heterosexually and masculine-identified character coolly returns the cinematic gaze as an expression of her phallic presence, juxtaposing the 'illegitimate' authority of the 'bossy' lesbian, which crumbles.

In the final scenes, she sacrifices herself heroically to save the other women – and chooses death in preference to submission to sexual domination. Her return to the feminine is signified by the wearing of Asian clothing, which further emphasizes the slippage between 'the feminine' and 'the barbarous'. Although the narrative suggests that it is not only rape that she cannot bear, but specifically rape by a man of colour, lesbians, particularly white lesbians, may still prioritize a reading of pleasurable defiance of male control and 'civilizing rationalism'. (It is worth noting, as regards narrative closures, that it tends to be a lesbian majority view of

Plate 18 Spot the lesbian? No – *not* the cute one in trousers! Anne Bancroft's sexy defiance of Margaret Leighton's repressed, bossy lesbian gets smoke in our eyes. (Courtesy of the British Film Institute Stills Department.)

Thelma and Louise that the protagonists are positively better off dead than returned to the 'feminine'.)

In *Johnny Guitar* and *Seven Women* it is more immediately obvious why lesbian spectatorship should align itself with a 'transvestite' position. Some feminist critics would argue that these films merely 'con' lesbians into alignment with white, male values and projected self-hatred. Indeed, such tropes do continue to inform stereotypes of femininism (female power or female aspiration to power) as conservative, repressive and anti-sex. Narrative and scopic structure do seem to align lesbians with masculine subject positions. All the films, with the possible exception of *Anne of the Indies*, offer preferred anti-feminist and anti-lesbian readings. *Red Sonja* and *Seven Women*, in particular, have pronounced racist subjects. Why, then, should any lesbians, or gay men, find pleasures in these films?

LESBIAN CAMPS

Gay men usually seem to identify with the feminine excess *and parody of authority* embodied in the mad-bad-pervert-witch or repressed but sexually seething boss-woman. Lesbians, on the other hand, seem to prefer the cross-dressing Amazon or tart – even though she is heterosexualized and defeats a female order to restore a patriarchal one. This difference is probably due principally to a characteristic feeling on the part of gay men that their sexuality is repressed by masculine authority; as against a characteristic feeling on the part of lesbians that they are excluded from authoritative action by passive sexualization (as spectacle) for men.

The Amazon's chastity is childlike, awaiting sexual 'awakening', recalling a relative freedom prior to oppressive sexualization for women at adolescence. Lesbian identification with the masculinized woman may not be located primarily in specifically sexual desires, or the transgressive (sexualized) pleasures of parodic subversion of gender categories, but in the pleasurable illusion of physical presence and active control conveyed by the masculinization of the female body. In practice, lesbians seem not to identify so much with feminine sexual excess as with a masculinized agency which is sexually active, but not reducible to sexualization.

Which brings us back to the question as to whether such 'masculine' identifications by lesbian spectators are equivalent to straightforward alignment with a masculine/patriarchal point of view. Apart from the obvious disruptive effect when a woman occupies a male position, how do lesbians 'subvert' these male identifications?

'Camp' films are usually also in genres associated with male audiences: westerns, sci-fi, swashbucklers, sword-and-sorcery, horror. Camp readings play on the homoerotic undercurrents of the male bonding (homosociality) foregrounded in these genres. There is a another aspect of camp which is raised in these popular male genres – that of sexual exaggeration. The

Conan films, for example, are muscle fests. It has been noted that if masculinity is sufficiently exaggerated, the result tips over into 'the feminine'. The adolescent heterosexual male spectator of Schwarzenegger's oiled pecs is in perpetual danger of having his homoerotic subtextual pleasures burst in upon his consciousness (cf. Neale 1983).

Typically, mainstream 'camp' picks up and spoofs on such underlying forbidden pleasures. In the genre spoofs under consideration, the male gladiatorial spectacle is feminized in order to exploit its homoerotic potential without challenging a heterosexual male audience. Amazonian protagonists, such as Sonja or Vienna, must be de- or heterosexualized in order to suppress lesbian implications which result from this substitution.

The masculinized female protagonist such as Vienna, or the principal-boyish character of Anne from *Anne of the Indies*, can also be a point of heterosexual male identification *and* desire – a social impossibility resolved by her narrative heterosexualization and/or self-sacrificing death, returning her to the feminine. Masculine coding of the female body probably has a fetishistic effect for the male spectator; he identifies with her 'masculinity' *and* desires her. This desire is clearly not unambiguously heterosexual, a problem which need not be acknowledged because it is mediated by a female body. Occupying a sexually ambiguous subject position in the (male) scopic relay, however, the lesbian can re-appropriate the disavowed homoerotic pleasures offered to the heterosexual male spectator.

If both positions in this relay are quasi-male, this might imply that lesbian sexuality and homosexuality are structurally the same. However, whilst gay male sexuality positions the phallus as object of male desire, lesbian sexuality positions woman as (phallic) subject. Gay male camp disrupts an illusion of coherence. Lesbians, as women, posited as incoherence in the first place, strive to enter the illusion of coherent identity and physical presence.

Exaggerated heterosexual femininity is more likely to be a point of identification for gay men than for lesbians. A gay man positioning himself in the feminine does disrupt male authority. Women, indelibly marked as the site of the feminine, necessarily have a different relation to this category. Lesbians more characteristically experience western standards of femininity as unattainable, exclusive and oppressive, and counteridentify. Femininity is, after all, a relatively privileged category from which lesbians are excluded, but which is also, for women, a mark of subordination to masculine authority, and not a form of resistance to it. Even an 'excessive' femininity which, like excessive masculinity, tips itself over into the opposite sex, reveals itself as spurious, and which can therefore be seen as subversive, still seems to have considerably less appeal to lesbian audiences than to gay male audiences.

In spite of the problems surrounding camp, particularly mainstream

Plate 19 Disavowing the lack? Well, I think this just about covers it! (Courtesy of the British Film Institute Stills Department.)

'camp', for lesbian spectators, camp films and reading against the grain are very popular with many lesbians – although often lesbians do not enjoy the same 'canon' of camp that traditionally appeals to gay men. On the whole, lesbians do enjoy the spectacle of sexual excess. But a spree of female strong-arm action and a satisfying spurt of gunfire is usually far more likely to rivet lesbian attention.

A survey carried out by Channel 4's *Out* programme showed that lesbians' most popular star was Sigourney Weaver in *Alien* (1979; see Ros Jennings, this volume). More recently, apart from the rest of the *Alien* trilogy, a lot of lesbians also go for Linda Hamilton in *Terminator II: Judgement Day* (1991) and some also for Jodie Foster in *The Silence of the Lambs* (1990), or even Sharon Stone in *Basic Instinct* (1992). Lesbians seem less likely to register the negative representation of male homosexuality in *The Silence of the Lambs* and more likely to read Foster's character as positively lesbian. If lesbians read these films (or films such as *Daughters of Darkness*, 1971) as lesbian-negative, it is more likely to be articulated on the feminist grounds that they depict and/or promote sexual violence against women rather than homophobia or 'queerbashing' – the distinction being a moot one, anyway, for lesbian experience of male violence.

Weaver, Hamilton and Foster are 'masculinized' as protagonists, but these texts do not do their subversive work through transgression (in the camp sense of pleasurably overstepping the line for the sake of forbidden pleasure) or parody. These contemporary lesbian icons do not fit into camp traditions. Male culture *is* revealed as a structure of dominance, but one which works, on women, through exclusion before repression. White gay men are excluded by the fact of their resistance to repressive male authority and appropriations of (feminine) 'artifice' and 'incoherence' have been a mark of that resistance. All lesbians are excluded already from male authority as women. Appropriation of a subjective 'presence' has, traditionally, been a mark of their resistance. Lesbian appropriation of positive subject positions and realization of same-sex desires suppressed in the texts are, indeed, disruptive and gender-destabilizing – but not *camp*.

The histories of lesbian discourses, particularly in the past three decades, diverge quite radically from the historical development of the discourses of homosexuality, gayness or queer (although constantly contesting and incorporating one another). The most obvious reason for this is that the position of women differs quite radically from that of men. As queer lesbianism sprints to distance itself from feminism (restigmatized as conservative, killjoy and frumpy), the question as to whether there is a lesbian camp seems to be more a strategic question about where lesbianisms might now find a strong political ally rather than a question about lesbian cultural and discursive practices. Otherwise, why not just ask the question, what *are* the discursive practices of lesbianisms?; and among what multiple and historically specific power-relations do lesbians struggle to constitute ourselves as such?

Oppositional readings of popular culture do play a substantial part in the construction and reconstruction of oppositional cultures. But oppositional culture, or even lesbianism, are not homogeneous categories. Borderlines between what constitutes construction of forbidden pleasures, what is open to subversive readings and what is unacceptably sexist, racist or homophobic, are subject to constant renegotiation between and within oppressed cultural groups. Oppositional reading strategies develop in response to specific, if overlapping, forms of oppression. To apply terms such as camp or queer to lesbian reading practices is more likely to obscure both the diversity and the specificity of the practices themselves, as well as the power-relations which structure them, than to facilitate a productive diversity of cultural reading and aesthetic practices.

REFERENCES

Axton, E. (1993) 'Radical cheek', *Shebang* 2.

Babuscio, J. (1984) 'Camp and the gay sensibility', in R. Dyer (ed.), *Gays in Film*, New York: Zoetrope.

Butler, J. (1990) *Gender Trouble: Feminism and the Subversion of Identity*, New York: Routledge.

Finch, M. (1986) 'Sex and address in *Dynasty*', *Screen* 27, 6.

Medhurst, A. (1991) 'Batman, deviance and camp', in R. E. Pearson and W. Uricchio (eds), *The Many Lives of Batman*, New York: Routledge.

Mercer, K. (1988) 'Diaspora, culture and the dialogic imagination: the aesthetics of black independent film in Britain' in Andrade-Watkins, M. B. and Cham, C. (eds) *Blackframes: Critical Perspectives on Black Independent Cinema*, Cambridge, Mass: MIT.

Modleski, T. (1991) 'A father is being beaten', in T. Modleski, *Feminism Without Women: Culture and Criticism in a 'Postfeminist' Age*, New York: Routledge.

Mulvey, L. (1975) 'Visual pleasure and narrative cinema' and (1981) 'Afterthoughts on "Visual pleasure and narrative cinema" inspired by *Duel in the Sun*'. Both reprinted in Penley, C. (ed.) (1988) *Feminism and Film Theory*, London: BFI.

Neale, S. (1983) 'Masculinity as spectacle', *Screen*, 24, 6.

Sontag, S. (1982) 'Notes on camp', in S. Sontag, *Against Interpretation*, New York: Farrar.

Studlar, G. (1990) 'Masochism, masquerade, and the erotic metamorphoses of Marlene Dietrich', in J. Gaines and C. Herzog (eds), *Fabrications: Costume and the Female Body*, New York: Routledge.

Waugh, P. (1989) *Feminine Fictions: Revisiting the Postmodern*, London: Routledge.

Weiss, A. (1991) 'A queer feeling when I look at you: Hollywood stars and lesbian spectatorship in the 1930s', in C. A. Gledhill (ed.), *Stardom: Industry of Desire*, London: Routledge.

——— (1992) *Vampires and Violets: Lesbians in the Cinema*, London: Cape.

11

LOOKING AT *PUMPING IRON II: THE WOMEN*

Jocelyn Robson and Beverley Zalcock

THE AGENDA

Contemporary interest in gender theory and its currently privileged position in the field of cultural studies has two key sources: feminism and lesbian/gay politics. As such, we might be forgiven for supposing that debates around gender would be a liberating force in the struggle for meaning in postmodernity. Not so. Manifestations of gender interest in popular culture seem principally concerned with masculinity in crisis,[1] and in the academy the postmodernist theoretical preoccupation with gender is functioning to replace (if not efface) feminism, (see Fuss 1989; Graham 1991).

In this article we want to explore the radical elements of reading gender, most particularly as it relates to images of the deviant (or unruly) 'female'. The film *Pumping Iron II: The Women* (1984) will provide the focus of our analysis, since it requires of the audience a questioning of what it is to be a woman, which clearly links with a number of ongoing feminist concerns (political and theoretical), including the usefulness of an identity politics and the struggle for a voice, a space, a subjectivity. The film is also crucially about gender trespass and, as such, throws up a number of issues arising from gay subversive discourses, including camp and drag, which – like the impetus of women's liberation – have done much to destabilize our strict positioning under patriarchy. It is also worth noting that it is at the point of intersection of the two key discourses, feminism and gay identity politics, that we may locate the 'deviant female'. She is represented in the film *Pumping Iron II: The Women* via the body of Bev Francis and represented in contemporary culture by the lesbian.

Women's liberation, gay liberation and the struggles of black communities against oppression and repression occupy increasingly important oppositional positions – positions once held to be the sole prerogative of the working class. In terms of women's struggle for identity and power, the discourse of sexuality provides the backdrop.[2] Psychoanalysis, as feminists have noted, reveals sexuality as the subtext of power-relations within western culture. Sexuality and the issue of gender is, then, potentially a radical site for challenge and contestation. But as we have remarked, there is a tendency in contemporary theory to recuperate this drive by isolating gender from the context of feminism (where it clearly belongs), which has resulted in the debate becoming defused. Similarly, with regard to contemporary practice around sexuality, notably gay activism and the rise of so-called 'queer politics', we witness the attempted merging of notions of gay male and lesbian identities under a 'queer' umbrella, as though their interests were one. This failure to take account of the two groups' differences in terms of social power and positioning, as well as historical formation, results in at least the relegation of the lesbian to the margins of the struggle, at worst in her invisibility. Hence, in terms of the trends in cultural practice, we can observe that just as feminism is being excluded from contemporary theory, so lesbianism is being effaced by contemporary practice.

The exclusion of feminism from the theoretical locus of gender is not necessarily a *fait accompli*, since the 'repressed', as work on the monster in horror has indicated, tends to return (see Wood 1985). It returns in a number of forms and representations, as 'monster' or as 'masquerade'. Consider, for example, the persona of Divine, whose female impersonations, as Judith Butler has noted, 'implicitly suggest that gender is a kind of persistent impersonation that passes as the real' (Butler 1990, p. x). Divine's radical drag grows out of a subversive camp sensibility, and serves to uncover the 'monstrous feminine' at the heart of the gender debate, particularly in his/her role in the film *Female Trouble* (1978). We hope to show that the same impetus is provided by the representation of Bev Francis, the central character in *Pumping Iron II: The Women*, whose violation of the so-called gender boundaries is about challenging the roles and positions assigned to women in our society. But before going into a detailed examination of the role of Bev Francis, we want to indicate the theoretical context in which 'gender studies' has so effectively hijacked the feminist project.

FEMINISM AND POSTMODERNISM

Feminism

A popular rallying call of the women's liberation movement in its resistance to patriarchal domination was 'why be a wife?'.[3] This slogan not only foregrounded the repressive social structures, the apparatus of the state, which functioned to keep women in their place (for example, within the home in marriage) but also served to identify the concealed mechanisms which fixed women within heterosexuality. It was, on the whole, radical feminism that took this analysis forward with the development of the concept of 'heteropatriarchy', thereby ensuring the central place of the question of sexuality for women's liberation.[4] It is no coincidence that many of the most committed radical feminists were lesbian separatists – a logical consequence, one might argue, of the rejection of patriarchal law and heterosexual order. The development of a lesbian politics and the debates within the lesbian community throughout the 1980s have kept this issue alive and kicking (see Ardill and O'Sullivan 1989). Despite controversy, it has always represented a radical strand in the development of feminism; it is, after all, one thing to identify and challenge the repressive function of state institutions, and quite something else to expose their psychosexual foundations. However, the contribution of (1970s or 1980s) feminism is rarely acknowledged in contemporary work around gender.

Postmodernism

It is ironic, but no real coincidence, that just as 'woman' was busy getting born, 'man' was busy dying; that is to say 'man' (master of the 'master narratives') was swept away on the crest of the electronic tidal wave that was breaking over the earth's surface – there was no depth (see Jameson 1984). In just one decade (the 1980s), aspects of history such as material reality, the class struggle and the binary opposition were called into question and found wanting. In this climate, formations and formulations cut loose into ecstatic free fall (see Baudrillard 1983). Traditional and hitherto reliable concepts dissolved into multiplicities; the soviet bloc dispersed, the western bloc did not. In fact, as the fallout settles, it is becoming clear that while some constructs have deconstructed (in some cases, self-destructed) others have appeared stronger than ever. So that while, in theory at least, women, people of colour and the poor have all but disappeared, white male masters (minus their narratives) have thrived. This period has been called (by them) 'postfeminism'. Feminism, of course, was not dead, only deconstructing.

Meanwhile, postmodernity devised a new question to replace the old feminist one. Instead of 'why be a wife?', we are proffered 'why be a woman?'. Suddenly we have choices! In the pick-and-mix-and-match atmosphere of the cultural marketplace, 'gender play' becomes a fun range of up-to-the-minute lifestyle options. In popular culture, Madonna and Prince demonstrated how to 'play' with gender and race. Politics, of course, was not dead, only self-destructing.

Body

One increasingly important zone or commodity in postmodernity is the body *per se*. While we suggest that the impact of 'new theory' is generally reactionary, work around the body does open up a space, a place, a site around which meanings can be contested. The body as crucial signifier of identity crisis is not particularly new. In Cartesian thinking, it was one of the horns of the dilemma – mind versus body; more recently, for feminists and gays it occupies an important position in establishing new meanings and subverting old ones: for example, the importance of the reproductive body in feminism and the sexual body in gay life. In the 1980s, the body as a site of panic represents escalating crisis as well as providing the forum for the playing out of repression and resistance (see Jacobus *et al.* 1990). For lesbians, the crisis is perhaps even more acute. The question facing many young dykes is 'Am I gay or am I a woman? '. Either choice involves denial – the former of her 'femaleness', the latter of her 'gayness'.

In *Pumping Iron II: The Women* it is the body that is offered as central in the resistance stakes. This new articulation is in many ways a reworking of the classic debates which inform the oppositional pairing of nature/culture and of male/female. The body is simultaneously the locus of gender definition and the site of sexuality, which perhaps accounts for what might be called the category confusion between anatomy and appearance. Gender definition is in fact much more about imagery (style and shape) than it is about biology, to which it is often mistakenly reduced.

Gender trespass, or more particularly the challenging of those imposed roles which specify identity and mark out our relationship to social power, is hence linked to appearance, that is to say, image. For example, deviation may take the form of 'inappropriate' dress (gender inappropriate) and/or body adornments – hairstyles, make-up, jewellery. Cross-dressing from male to female is a feature of camp and (as noted above) Divine's extreme use of this tactic, amounts to breaking the rules in a quite radical way. As Judith Butler observes: 'His/her performance destabilises the very distinctions between the natural and the artificial, depth and surface, inner and outer through which discourse about genders almost always operates' (Butler 1990, p. x). Reaction to imposed gender positions has often, in the case of women, led to much more drastic measures than cross-dressing. For instance, the requirement to stay young and beautiful (one among many of the impossible demands made upon us) has led to serious body reconstruction, ranging from eating disorders to plastic surgery.

Like it or not, all of us in postmodernity, but women in particular, are situated within an imperative which starts with careful eating and exercise and leads to harsher programmes of dieting and working out, in a scenario where the compulsory and the compulsive become one in the merging of social and personal goals. A kind of body fascism prevails, in which fitness equals 'strong, beautiful, powerful' and fatness equals 'weak, ugly, power-less'. It's perfect for the state, since everybody polices themselves. Women (whose experience of shape dictatorship is not new) have throughout the centuries amassed valuable experience *vis-à-vis* means and modes of resistance.

Body-building for women, which is the subject of *Pumping Iron II: The Women*, raises many of the concerns and anxieties that accompany body-policing. This particular form of body-restructuring has implications for gender, since the effect of weight training/body-building at competition level is to develop muscles and a masculine shape. The implications of such gender deviance are much more serious than in the case of camp – taking on feminine attributes – since the issue is not simply about rejecting assigned gender roles, which in camp is tolerated, but about women seizing power – that is, becoming masculine.

THE FILM

As already indicated, *Pumping Iron II: The Women* is a film about women body-builders; it traces the activities of key competitors in their preparations for a body-building contest held in Las Vegas in 1984. Through a series of cameos, the audience (like a fly on the wall) witnesses the physical preparations in the gym, the discussions amongst the competitors themselves, the support offered by family and friends to individual contestants, the discussions and arguments amongst the judges, as well as highlights from the actual contest itself. The narrative, such as it is, draws us forward to this final contest and focusses on the question 'Who will win? ', with its associated question 'Who *should* win? ' Of pivotal importance in the film is the entry in the contest of Australian Bev Francis, who is known by contestants and judges alike to have taken the sport into new and controversial realms. Her arrival, her preparations and her final performance provide much of the dramatic tension in the film, and stimulate most of the debate. She is also the focus for much of what we wish to say about the film in this article.

The consequences of pumping iron for women (and these elements have always been of particular interest to lesbian women) are socially, politically and culturally very interesting. The practitioners of this sport are seen to take on masculine attributes: the body image changes dramatically as breasts disappear, biceps bulge, periods cease and hips streamline. The film *Pumping Iron II: The Women* has, as its whole focus, this struggle to change the body and to redefine (as it were) femininity itself. The body becomes (in a sense) the social body, in a postmodern phase, in danger of erupting from within, or bursting its chains and breaking its boundaries. As the women's bodies change and become strongly muscular, a crisis is instigated in ways that we shall describe.

It has been noted that the concept of a border is one of the things that is central to the construction of the monstrous in the horror film; those things that highlight the fragility of the law, which cross or threaten to cross the border have been described as 'abject' (see Creed 1986). The abject threatens life but it also helps to define life. The women body-builders are truly monstrous and, in this sense, the film illustrates the work of abjection; these women refuse to take up their proper gender roles as women and are as monstrous, therefore, as those who cross the border between the normal and the supernatural, the human and the inhuman, in such films as *Rosemary's Baby* (1968) or *Cat People* (1982). Furthermore, contemporary interest in the female body, evident in films such as *The Brood* (1979) and *Aliens* (1986) and often focussing on the female body's reproductive processes, is echoed in *Pumping Iron II: The Women*. As the women's bodies start to lose their reproductive features, they become (as it were) metaphors for the uncertainty of the future – the uncertainty of a species and a society unwilling (or unable) to reproduce itself in its contemporary forms. In this respect the monster is a mutant who represents the violation of both biology and the social programme.

Faced with a display of women's bodies that are oiled, ripped and cut (and changing (mutating) even while we watch) the film's audience, so accustomed to the task of assigning gender identifications, is thrown into crisis. Furthermore, the film's genre remains unclear: is this a sport documentary about real body-builders? (a real event) or is it a fictional story of passion and ambition? Which women are we to identify with (or desire)?

In ways we shall come to describe, the audience is eventually invited to judge, to decide which body is best, which image is the most desirable, which woman is beautiful. Through its relentless focus on the body, the film strives to challenge our codes of masculine/feminine and to confront us with a crisis. Through a close reading of some key moments in the film, we shall look, first, at these issues of judgement in the film, and second, at the crisis of the body itself.

Judgements

In a series of short, telling sequences near the beginning of the film (before the contest takes place) several points of view concerning the validity or otherwise of a range of body images are explored. The women competitors crowd together in a steaming jacuzzi and compare their reactions to the body of Bev Francis (who is absent). The audience is already aware of the fact that the competitor, Bev Francis, has gone beyond the muscularity of other female body-builders and that the contest is in many ways a test of the acceptability of her project. The discussion in the heated pool focusses primarily on body aesthetics (underpinned by the visuals of the near naked female forms) but it is informed by a politics of gender: The main criterion offered here is of beauty, of a shape developed in the gym, of toned muscle, and so on, but it conceals a more fraught issue relating to femininity. As the contestants laugh and splash in girlish high spirits, we are left in doubt: 'a woman is a woman' remarks one contestant, and the real question is left begging.

In the next sequence the judges debate the need to preserve femininity whilst holding fast to similar criteria, namely those relating to athleticism and aesthetics. The chief judge is unwilling to engage with anything too masculine: 'women are women and men are men', he says; 'and thank god for that difference', concludes another judge. With the exception of one token woman, the judges are all men and their pronouncements have a strong sense of the judgement of Paris (a motif which is underlined by the classical statues and Doric columns of the decor) and of traditional patriarchal power. The analysis of femininity, such as it is, rests on what men want to see – aesthetic femininity and muscle tone: this is ultimately not a discussion about female beauty but about gender power. Whatever their decision, it remains a judgement of women by men, who in turn defer to a god-given (i.e. 'natural') difference.

The next sequence shows Carla, the only black competitor, formation-swimming alone in the pool. She is spatially separated from her co-competitors (seen earlier in the jacuzzi) and is also, as we discover very soon, separated from them further by her forthright, thoughtful and radical views. In this sequence she is filmed with flowing camera movements, in a style which luxuriates in the almost abstract beauty of her body in rhythmic, graceful and powerful motion. Of all the sequences in the film, this one perhaps comes nearest to a definition of beauty: the body here, almost neither masculine nor feminine, simply *is*. The euphoria of the scene comes partly from the beauty of the decor but also from a sense of relief from fixity. This sequence, in contrast to those immediately before it, is all about flowing and pleasure: It does not perform for an audience nor defer to an intellectual judgement. It is simply beautiful. Carla becomes here not 'woman as beauty' but much more 'the body as beauty'.

Her centrality is reaffirmed in the next sequence in which she has a conversation with Bev in the massage room. Interestingly, it is finally Carla who wins the contest and who is (in a sense) the central voice of the film. During the massage session, a dialogue takes place which is informed visually by some important details. Crucially, Carla is black and Bev is white – a difference never referred to in the film, whose chief preoccupation is with gender difference not race. There is also a shot of the red varnished nails of the masseuse – foregrounded to accompany Carla's remarks about the importance of a multiplicity of notions of female beauty. She rejects fixed notions of femininity and discusses with cutting analysis the sexist implication behind the notion of an ideal body shape for a woman. Her voice is certainly the most radical in the film and the most just. She is concerned at the idea of a woman who has had a mastectomy not being considered a real woman and she highlights in the film the feminist aspect of the gender debate – an aspect often elided in contemporary theory as we have shown. She rejects the shallow centrefold mentality of the judges and is able to relate to Bev's love of muscularity without in any sense regarding her as a freak. Her conversation lacks the competitive edge evident amongst the women in the jacuzzi earlier, and is sisterly in tone and spirit. Her point of view is that which we, as audience, are finally invited by the film to share.

These four short sequences, then, are extremely important to the issues raised by the film as a whole. Bev's trespass of gender boundaries, which throws up a crisis and the question 'What is a woman?' has evoked a range of emotions from bemusement to anger, and no clear solution has emerged. Our faith in the judges, and in their decision to relegate Bev Francis to eighth place, is undermined by the film's representation of them as incompetent and confused. As an audience, we are left with a question. It is the question 'What is a woman?', put literally in an address to the camera by Bev's coach who ends with the words 'You tell me!'.

Body in crisis

Two further sequences are worth considering, this time as specific instances of heightened focus on the woman's body, primarily the body of Bev Francis.

The first extract selected here is a brief interlude where Bev delights friends and family with her parody of the typical European body-builder. A friend records this performance on video, as Bev's muscular body mimics the poses of the glamour girl. Her simpering smiles and coquettish gestures are belied by her strong body. The resulting incongruity is indeed entertaining, for friends and film audience alike, but there is, too, an underlying pain (registering partially on her father's face) and an underlying seriousness. Bev's body has changed dramatically since the beginning of the film. Her family joke about it when they arrive for the contest ('Where's your face?'), but there is also some sense of shock as her family (and the audience) try to come to terms with her new body. The parody in the hotel room indicates that Bev is aware of the real issues behind the contest. Is she to be herself or is she to be (falsely) 'feminine?'

The disturbance arises chiefly, however, through the audience's and family's recognition that the real Bev (herself) is in fact (falsely) 'masculine' and that during her parody what she most resembles is a drag artist, a man parodying a woman, which is indeed very reminiscent of the impersonations of Divine. Her friends and family (and we, as viewers) have an important role in that we/they are invited to confirm or not to confirm her image, her self, her social acceptability. Our decision is made harder by the film's use of documentary technique, through the camera's sympathetic record of Bev in natural as well as unnatural surroundings and by our knowledge that she is a real woman participating in a real contest. In this sense, we know she is not a character at all but a genuine open person who faces the impossibility (for her) of being other than she really is.

Bev's parody is therefore a key moment in the film because it throws into crisis the real and the unreal, the masculine and the feminine, the natural and the unnatural). For the lesbian spectator, there is a very special recognition at this stage; we identify with Bev's fragile positioning in terms of these polarities. Her inability to signal effectively any conceptual distinction between her performance and her parody makes her a spectacle which invokes our pity and our fear. In violating the boundaries, and in failing to take up her assigned gender role (either socially or within the terms of the contest), Bev becomes monstrous. She is centred by the film because she (more than any of the other female body-builders) has pushed and broken the boundaries of acceptable female form and because she is engaged in a struggle to attain a personal grail that puts strength and muscularity over and above femininity (however defined). As far as most of the judges are concerned, she is a freak, an object of disgust, and despite the film's discrediting of the judges' viewpoint, the crisis is not resolved in her favour (Carla wins the contest) and it becomes increasingly difficult for the audience to share Bev's point of view.

Alongside Bev's parody of the typical female body-builder, it is worth considering Bev's performance in the final contest, particularly her solo. In the line up, Bev is called forward with Rachel (a flirtatious and humourless drama queen); as a fellow competitor observes, they are total opposites. Rachel is in fact the typical subject of Bev's earlier parody – the sultry woman of the *Playboy* centre page – whose need to cheat (her bra is padded) cannot be separated from her need to attest publicly her woman-hood and her heterosexual femininity. By comparison, Bev's presentation of herself is open and good-humoured and, again, a dilemma presents itself to the viewer: which image should we accept?; should we accept (vote for) the genuine likeable Bev whose body (though 'real') is quite unlike anything we have seen before, or should we vote for Rachel, who is deceitful and has sly, mincing movements, along with a body that is *not* completely real? Bev's solo performance does nothing to help us (as viewers) resolve the issues. On a darkened stage, as *2001 Space Odyssey* music fills Caesar's Palace, Bev poses; powerful and controlled, like a warrior of a future time, she shoots imaginary arrows from an archer's bow, and for a moment or two, we are caught up with her on a venture into the unknown.[5] As the music changes to a disco beat, and as Bev begins to move forward and (most importantly) to smile, somehow the warrior image falls away and we see a heavily muscled figure that moves awkwardly, without grace, and is at moments grotesque, in ways that are distinctly reminiscent of her earlier parody.

Afterwards, she questions her coach anxiously; 'Did I look like a girl? ';

and a minute later, more seriously, 'Was my feminine quality enough there?'. These questions (like the parody) reveal Bev's understanding of some of the issues at least on a personal level: 'You're not allowed muscles if you're a girl', she says.

CONCLUSION

Representations of gender play (in cinema as in life) have, as we have noted, traditionally resided in camp – an aspect of gay male discourse, and as such, an established cultural form (Medhurst 1990). At its most radical, drag functions to offer a critique of notions of both masculinity and femininity (for example, Divine) by focussing upon the impersonation aspect of gender identity – calling into question the signifying moments of cultural performance and thereby pointing to its constructed nature so that it appears as a parody of naturalness.

Like Divine, Bev Francis's identity is constructed around a body that is outrageous. Her ripped and cut muscular body in a bikini is as incongruous as Divine's massive flabby one in hot pants. While Divine is able to play upon this incongruity, Bev has no such culturally assigned space, although both function to throw the paradigm of a stable gender identity into question. Divine's performance in *Female Trouble* represents the camp, comic moment of cultural performance, sustained and given meaning by a theatrical gay male subculture. As such, the impersonation is liberating. For Bev, the converse is true – it is a moment of repression involving (as it does) not laughter and jouissance but fear and loathing.

Bev's final performance from powerful 'superhero' to simpering strip-tease artiste does not merely parody the natural feminine but it represents finally a kind of self-mutilation; she is a parody of a parody having no stable point of identity and nowhere to go. The taboo for her is so much greater because she is a woman assuming the attributes of male power, signified via masculinity. Conversely, Divine represents no real threat since he is a man impersonating the feminine (i.e., the powerless). While Divine's 'feminine' invokes laughter, and is truly comic within the tradition of the burlesque, which is both crude and risqué, Bev's 'masculine' invokes the pity and fear of tragedy, and even sheer terror, as the monster, the castrating woman, the Medusa who turns men's gaze to stone (see Creed 1986).

It becomes increasingly difficult to elide feminism with an 'indifferent' or non-gender-specific 'gender studies' because in so doing it becomes impossible to account for the difference described above. Without an analysis which takes on board the 'monstrous feminine' as a threat to patriarchy, there can be no real understanding of the political aspects of gendering in its various cultural manifestations.

Finally, to gaze upon the forbidden female, contemporary gender theory would have to come to terms with her multiple manifestations. Like Medusa, she is mythical, monstrous and murderous. She has many names. Today she is called 'lesbian'.

NOTES

1 The Summer 1991 series on BBC2, *From Wimps to Warriors*, which explores our 'myths of manhood', is a good example of such preoccupations.
2 For an exploration of the impact of the nineteenth-century paradigm, see M. Foucault (1981) *The History of Sexuality: An Introduction*, by Harmondsworth: Penguin.
3 There was a campaign during the mid-1970s, presented visually via posters and postcards printed by the See Red Women's Poster Workshop, using the slogan 'YBA Wife'.
4 See, particularly, the Radical and Revolutionary Feminist publications of the 1970s, for example the magazine *Scarlet Woman*.
5 Richard Strauss's *Thus Spake Zarathustra* has associations with the notion of the superman in the work of the philosopher Nietzsche. The music at other times is equally significant, as in the song *Future Sex* over the opening titles.

REFERENCES

Ardill, S. and O'Sullivan, S. (1989). 'Sex in the summer of 1988' (this volume).
Baudrillard, J. (1983) 'The ecstasy of communication', in H. Foster (ed.), *The Anti-Aesthetic; Essays in Postmodern Culture*, Port Townsend, W.A.: The Bay Press.
Butler, J. (1990) *Gender Trouble: Feminism and the Subversion of Identity*, London: Routledge.
Creed, B. (1986) 'Horror and the monstrous feminine – an imaginary abjection', *Screen*, 27, 1: 19–21.
Foucault, M. (1981) *The History of Sexuality. An Introduction*, Harmondsworth: Penguin.
Fuss, D. (1989) *Essentially Speaking: Feminism, Nature and Difference*, London: Routledge.
Graham, P. (1991) *Radical romantics: essentialism in feminist discourse*, unpublished dissertation, Middlesex Polytechnic.
Jacobus, M., Keller, E. and Shuttleworth, S. (eds) (1990) *Body Politics: Women and the Discourses of Science*, London: Routledge.
Jameson, F. (1984) 'Postmodernism or the cultural logic of late capitalism', *New Left Review* 146: 11–12.
Medhurst, A. (1990) 'Pitching camp', *City Limits*, 10–17 May 1990.
Wood, R. (1985) 'An introduction to the American horror film', in B. Nichols (ed.), *Movies and Methods*, vol. 2, University of California Press.

12

DESIRE AND DESIGN – RIPLEY UNDRESSED

Ros Jennings

When I left the cinema after seeing *Alien* (1979) for the first time, I do not claim that my life was changed in any significant way. Nevertheless, despite the occasional twinges of fear and discomfort that I felt at certain sections of the film, I sensed that I had encountered something in that film that I had not come across before. More importantly, I had found something that I had constantly found to be missing up to that point. It was the start of my love affair with Ripley, and though I would not declare my interest as being in anyway unreserved, Ripley became the object of my admiration because she was the first female protagonist that I had ever encountered, who in my opinion, was wholly intelligible, attractive and heroic.

As far as my own lesbian sensibilities were concerned, it was too much to hope that she might be a lesbian character, but in a film culture so starved of positive lesbian representations, I grasped at her because although she was not coded as lesbian or bisexual, to my immense surprise/relief, neither was she specifically coded as heterosexual.

Back then in 1979, the vogue for high-profile sequels had not yet come into fashion, I thought that my encounter with Sigourney Weaver as Ripley would be a one-off – a moment to treasure. The fact that Weaver would play Ripley on another two occasions, in *Aliens* (1986) and *Alien 3* (1992), not only gave me great personal pleasure, but also provided a rare opportunity to observe the development of a strong female character who was to remain central to the project of each of the *Alien/s* films.

In the thirteen years that elapsed between *Alien* and *Alien 3*, we have moved from a time when cultural debates and discourses were dominated by radical feminism to an era when the orthodoxies of radical feminism have lost influence in favour of more plural positions. The move away from the idea of a unitary category or group called 'women' or equally a unitary category called 'lesbian', has not been unproblematic or entirely welcome in many areas. If this change in political and cultural concern has led us to a situation where the sentiment 'nothing is true: everything is permitted' (Burroughs 1983) holds sway, then there are dangers involved for the

193

future of political organization and critical arguments against oppressions that still face us, both individually and collectively.

Politically, it would seem that we are in a period when we are trying to find a way to organize and unite around issues that allow us to recognize and embrace our differences, whether they are based on race, gender, class, sexuality or multiples of these positions. Culturally and artistically, however, it is my belief that the move away from controlling orthodoxies has enabled a more diverse engagement with issues of difference and in particular, sexual difference. In many ways, the special significance of Weaver and her role as Ripley has been in providing a distinctive site of change and engagement with film and sexual difference. As Mary Ann Doane explains, film as a cultural practice is able, by virtue of its very nature, to create 'space for considering differences and shifts in the representation of gender which may amount to new patterns of definition with real effects on how we can visualise ourselves' (Doane 1982, p. 6). The impact of film as part of our individual and collective cultural capital is not to be underestimated. Shifts in the representation of gender can have unique resonance for the lesbian viewer, especially when an active female protagonist such as Ripley emerges, and especially when no attempt to validate her existence is made by placing her in a relationship with a man.

When Caroline Sheldon claims that 'on the whole, lesbians (and indeed feminists) are attracted by films containing independent and sensitive women' (Sheldon 1980, p. 23), Ripley would seem to fulfil the necessary criteria, and indeed in order to shift my discussion in a more textual direction, I propose to concentrate on three textual moments from the *Alien/s* films, and look more closely at the representations which are constructed. I intend to focus on three specifically and thematically connected scenes – one from each of the films. The scenes, for one reason or another, show Ripley in a state of undress. I have chosen to deal with the scenes chronologically, partly to affirm a sense of progression that must be acknowledged with respect to character and acting development, but mainly because the thirteen-year period in which the films were made corresponds to a period of changing theories of film spectatorship. As a device, it is also vital in that it allows us to view Ripley as she increasingly comes 'face to face', as it were, with herself.

It is important at this point to remember that Ripley, as played by Weaver, is probably the most constant factor in linking the three films together. When I examine a scene from each film, I am examining a scene directed by Ridley Scott, James Cameron and David Ficher respectively. Taubin claims that the trilogy comprises a slasher film, a war film and a film bordering on the avant-garde (Taubin 1992). So not only are their interests in creating spectacle different, but their distinctive directorial styles require them to employ quite different visual codes to do so. Because of the multitextual nature of film itself, factors of production, direction, authorship, acting and camerawork turn in on themselves and interplay with each other to form and inform the finished product. Despite differences in approach, each individual scene is a construct which has designs on our engagement, on our desire.

RIPLEY DISPLAYED

In *Alien*, the scene leading up to and including the final confrontation between Ripley and the alien is, perhaps, one of the most controversial in the film. It is the moment when O'Bannon's 'egalitarian' script (Penley 1989) would seem to be abandoned for the simple reason that it is difficult to imagine any of the male crew members being displayed in a similar fashion.

In general, Ripley is shot and lit from below, and for the most part it is a hand-held camera that is used to track her. She begins to undress mid-frame in a calm and relaxed manner. There is no tension in the scene at this point, and there is certainly no feeling that she is being watched. She does not look over her shoulder; she merely takes off her clothes layer by layer until she is in just a skimpy vest and an extremely undersized pair of knickers. While she is undressing she bends down to pull her trousers over her feet and the camera itself dips at the same time, indicating an audience or camera viewpoint. There are no shots which align the spectator with the monster (White 1991). Instead, Ripley is on display for the viewer/voyeur. She is calmly choreographed to provide a complete 360-degree pirouette as she struggles with her necklace and then sprawls over the instrument panel to check the controls with her rear view emphasized as sexually available. From the moment she touches the controls a flashing strobe light comes into play, erratic but slow enough to be reminiscent of a flashgun going off with Ripley in its sights. She is, in other words, like a pornographic model on display.

The mood of the scene proceeds to change when the xenomorph's hand then thrusts out from behind the instrument panel. The shock is made all the more effective and frightening by the fact that it was not signalled. From the moment the alien appears, the whole pace of the scene changes, menacing music begins and a process of fast intercut/multiple-camera action is used as Ripley runs and shuts herself in the closet. The acceler-ated pace established by the editing serves to generate both fear and tension.

At the point when the door closes behind Ripley, the pace once again slows and we are back to the hand-held camera as it pans Ripley's body. This technique accentuates the sense of claustrophobia and fear that is in turn further emphasized by the sound of her breathing. The lighting is again from below and Ripley is picked out in a golden light which caresses the contours of her flesh. A sequence of shots showing Ripley in the closet intercut with shots showing the darker area of the cabin are still not really point-of-view shots for either of the protagonists in this final conflict, but are more like point-of-view shots designed for the audience. Close-ups of Ripley's head register her expression and more particularly her eyes, which at this moment have become less fearful and more intent on finding a solution to her predicament. The close-ups on her head seem to serve the narrative by letting us know more about her character rather than making her head a fetish. It is other parts of her body that are fetishized. This is especially true of the moment when in preparation for squaring up to the xenomorph, she decides to cover her body with a spacesuit for protection. It is then the whole sequence of her dressing, as opposed to undressing, that becomes the centre of focus.

As she raises her leg to struggle into the spacesuit in the tight confines of the closet, the camera is held blatantly at crotch level, exposing the moulded triangle of material to our lingering gaze. When she has managed to step into the bottom half of the suit, the camera moves equally shamelessly to her breasts which are heaving both from exertion and fear.

Scott's direction of the filming until the end of this scene continues to control Ripley and invite voyeurism, but the way in which we are invited to look at Ripley does change. Once she is wearing the spacesuit, the scene begins another phase where, in terms of the narrative action, she confronts and defeats the alien. When she fits the helmet to the suit, her head is enclosed and Ripley's voice becomes a vocal track which is dissociated from her mouth movements. With the camera still filming her at an angle which is neutral to both of the combatants, it is what we hear that now becomes the most surprising feature of the scene. Ripley's mutterings and heavy breathing which, at the most dominant level express her terror, at much closer scrutiny sound like the soundtrack for a porno film. By breaking the link between what we hear and what we see, we are left with a soundtrack of a disembodied fucking scene complete with an intense climax which takes place both in terms of sound and narrative, when the huge phallic head of the alien rears up close to Ripley's head, and she pushes the release button for the pressurized door.

The interest of this scene for me is in how it is constructed for maximum voyeuristic effect. For a brief few minutes it sexualizes Ripley in a way that is not even hinted at in the rest of the film. The filming of her body emphasizes that she is female even if she is carrying out the function of the masculine role on the screen, and this is a vital ingredient in the textual equation between film and spectatorship. This scene, which is so blatantly voyeuristic, is an exceptional construct in this film. By design, however, it exploits our inherent drives to scopophilia and voyeurism, and this lure is, according to Metz, what makes film practices so successful. As he explains, the difference between cinema and other mediums, such as theatre, is that in cinema there is no direct interaction with the audience, and as a result the looks exchanged on the screen are recorded and therefore fixed. One of the most effective functions of film is that 'the actor should behave as though he is not being seen, and so cannot see him, the voyeur' (Metz, cited in Cook 1987, p. 247). Personally, when I examine my own drive to look, as a lesbian spectator, I find the construction of Ripley's vulnerability too overpowering to find much pleasure in her displayed body.

According to film theorists of the late 1970s such as Laura Mulvey, however, cinematic pleasure is strictly obtained through certain very specific ways of seeing and looking. They argue that how we see and look is governed by the binary constructs of masculinity and femininity in patriarchal society. According to Mulvey, 'mainstream film [has] coded the erotic into the language of the dominant patriarchal order' (Mulvey 1985, p. 206). The result, in Mulvey's view, is that women in film are placed in the subordinate position of object. In essence, therefore, women are in films to be seen/looked at, and men are there to act. Mulvey believed that an 'active/passive heterosexual division of labour has similarly controlled narrative structure', and that films are designed around the controlling role of the male which, in turn, creates a sense of identification between spectator and actor. The actor, therefore, is evolving into the spectator's screen surrogate (Mulvey 1985, p. 210), and does not allow for anything other than an active male gaze. Female activity is culturally denied once more.

It would seem that Ripley's role in *Alien*, and in particular within the scene that I have just analysed, corresponds to much of Mulvey's theory. The theory and the film both emerged in the late 1970s and it is possible that Scott would have been aware of it. One of the most obvious aspects in which it corresponds is in the way that Ripley is displayed in a directly sexualized manner, to provide what Mulvey calls 'moments of erotic contemplation' (ibid.). If, as Mulvey asserts, Hollywood film conceives of women as being the object of the controlling male gaze, then it would seem that Scott's conception of Ripley is tainted by this belief. Therefore, although he chose to make her the hero of the film, he also chose to inscribe her in such a way as to neutralize the significance of her threat in ascending into the male domain of movie hero. By rendering her available to male voyeurism, Scott's control of filming in the final scene ensures that in addition to the 'so-called' masculine traits of bravery, technical ability, and so on – all of which we have seen her demonstrate so well up to this point – she now signifies a wholly intelligible form of femininity.

This aspect of *Alien* surely indicates how and why Mulvey's theory was so influential in the late 1970s to early 1980s, given the impact and importance of radical feminism in both academic and cultural thought. As Lorraine Gamman and Margaret Marshment suggest, 'Mulvey's article paved the way for a great deal of interesting work on the representation of women' (Gamman and Marshment 1988, p. 5). The widespread acceptance of Mulvey's work has not, to say the least, been unproblematic. Although Gamman and Marshment acknowledge the pioneering importance of Mulvey's analysis, they also point to the fact that because the notion of a 'male gaze' came to be regarded almost as an orthodoxy in all mainstream genres, it created a situation where it became 'difficult, theoretically to move outside its parameters' (ibid., p. 5), especially for women as active spectators.

Since the radical feminist position privileges the universal oppression of all women above all other forms of oppression, it would be easy to view the scene that I have been discussing as epitomizing the force of patriarchal control over women. Yet this critical position surely has its shortcomings when we reflect on how until this moment Ripley has been represented as the autonomous protagonist and has only been displayed for the 'male gaze' in this one scene. But that is not to argue that *Alien* was made as part of some feminist project. Ripley emerged from the complex interplay of film genres as they have historically developed, and the film mediates current cultural concerns and specifically male anxieties about women's power and women's sexuality. It would seem that Ripley is not allowed to escape a token, if somewhat blatant, attempt to objectify her. Scott's construction of this moment of undressing provides what Clover calls a 'deflective convenience, for the male spectator (and film-maker)', by creating what she calls a 'female victim–hero' (Clover 1989, p. 120), a figure who is not yet a pure genre hero.

WHO'S SNOW WHITE?

The decision to make *Aliens* in the 1980s, and more specifically the decision to continue with Weaver in Ripley's role, was instrumental in changing some of the dynamics involved in her subsequent representations. *Alien* had established Ripley as both a star and a fledgeling hero, and the way in which her representation is designed for us is formed almost automatically by these factors. In addition, the idea that Ripley would be associated with an active role sets Weaver's performance in *Aliens* in immediate opposition to one of Mulvey's fundamental assumptions.

In her work, Mulvey seems to assume that, within patriarchy, the notions of femininity and masculinity are completely stable. Accordingly, it would seem that she makes no allowance for any negotiation as to how we may place ourselves in relation to these notions, in life or as spectators of film. Although the majority of mainstream Hollywood films probably do use women as a romantic disruption and object of the 'male gaze', it would be inadvisable to declare that no negotiation of masculinity and femininity takes place.

As Creed states, '*Aliens* is extremely self-conscious about its play with gender roles' (Creed 1987, p. 65), and the scene that I wish to discuss from the second film, although short, illustrates how *Aliens* problematizes sexual difference. The scene itself is of more narrative than visual importance, although it does create some striking images. Taking place early in the film, its purpose is both to introduce us to the troop of space marines, and to set into play ideas of sexual sameness and sexual difference. Because the marines are made up of men and women doing the same job, ideas about gender are liberated from the constructs created by a patriarchal division of labour. The effectiveness of the scene, therefore, depends on the use of other visual codes to indicate difference.

One of the areas of difference brought to our attention, here, is the difference between being a marine and being a civilian. Both visually and narratively this difference is established by the device of pairing Ripley and Vasquez. The pairing of these two characters also raises other questions about difference which point to the multiple possibilities of being a woman and being heroic. In addition, the comparison between the two female characters provides a space where a shallow exploration of lesbian representation is made possible.

The scene begins as the camera pans a row of sleep capsules. The lighting gradually becomes brighter to reveal a row of torsos. It would seem that the marines even sleep to attention, with one exception, which is Vasquez. We can only just make out that it is Vasquez, for she is barely in focus and appears more as a shadow, and in some ways she is paired as Ripley's shadow as the camera concentrates on Ripley's sleeping form. The camera is distanced to show Ripley asleep with her head on one side and looking relatively relaxed. As the capsules open, the marines stretch and cough as they come awake. Ripley, the outsider, is set up as such in camera shot. As the two male marines who have been asleep either side of Ripley wake up, they are seen to talk across her as if she was not there. As they all step from the capsules, Ripley's difference is noticeable in that she is the only one without very short hair and regulation army green, t-shirt style vest and shorts. Ripley's underclothes are grey, and she is once more in her feminine undersized knickers and vest. Unlike the first scene that I discussed, however, this time the camera does not linger on her body. Despite the short time that we are able to observe her, it is long enough to assess that her lack of muscle definition also sets her apart from the other marines.

There is no close-up work on Ripley here. In fact, Ripley is actually in motion for the most part, simply walking from the sleep capsule to the locker area. She is loose limbed as she walks into frame and is momentarily obscured by Vasquez, as Vasquez raises herself to do a pull-up on a bar suspended from the ceiling. A connection is again made between the two women as Ripley emerges from behind Vasquez's suspended body and the camera follows her as she walks over to the locker. At the locker she hesitates for a moment, and the tension created by the camera movement as it has followed her from the left of the frame suggests that Ripley has stopped because she is suddenly aware of Vasquez's gaze. The gaze is signalled but not seen. After Ripley's brief hesitation, the scene cuts to a full close-up of Vasquez. The focus is on Vasquez's head, shoulders and muscled upper arm as she exercises herself up and down on the bar. The focus is also on her dark Hispanic skin. These areas of Vasquez's body emphasize her physical contrast with Ripley. When Vasquez immediately asks another of the female troopers 'who's Snow White? ', the difference in skin colour as well as implied character is clearly reinforced. As Vasquez and her comrade's gaze travels over to where we know Ripley is standing, Vasquez's earlier unseen gaze is confirmed.

The following shot, where Vasquez once more returns to her pull-ups, this time in unison with a male trooper, not only reinforces that her muscles are so well-developed that she is as strong as many athletic men, but also further accentuates her prowess in an area which has been coded as a masculine activity. The self-conscious play with gender roles suggested by Creed is underlined by the exchange between the male trooper Hudson and Vasquez. He asks Vasquez if she has ever been mistaken for a man and her reply – 'No, have you? ' – is not only a smart deflationary comment but also foregrounds the overall narrative interest in sexual difference.[1]

One of the main concerns of this scene is to explore who is coded masculine and who is coded feminine in a setting which is, to all intents and purposes, androgynous in terms of division of labour and dress. Vasquez is not only coded as more masculine than Ripley but also as more masculine than most of the men. To the lesbian spectator she is represented by dress and disposition as both an exotic Amazon and a butch lesbian. In the last line of the scene, Vasquez exclaims 'Qué Bonita' with reference to Ripley, and the scene is edited so that the shot cuts immediately to the mess hall and to Ripley. Ripley is now fully dressed in a relatively unisex flight suit, and she is walking in the centre of the frame holding her tray. Behind her is Vasquez in full *Rambo* costume complete with a red bandana tied round her cropped hair and a cigarette in her mouth.

The edit to the mess hall serves to perform three functions. First, it once more reinforces the idea of pairing between Vasquez and Ripley. Second, it deflects Vasquez's declaration of admiration because emphasized lesbian desire would be too disruptive to the narrative. Finally, it succeeds in offering a surreptitious moment of lesbian desire for those who want to view it as such by providing what Annette Kuhn describes as a moment where contradictions emerge to allow an alternative reading (cited in Weiss 1992).

So far I have concentrated on the representation of Vasquez since the whole scene is constructed around her masculinized body. The design of the scene, however, tells a great deal (if indirectly) about how Ripley is represented. The introduction of Vasquez provides a device which allows an exploration of how powerful women can and might be represented. Vasquez's macho lesbian stereotype marks her as threatening to the identities of heterosexual men (Weiss 1992). Although I do not agree entirely with the critic who in a review of *Aliens* associated Ripley's image with that of Jean Arthur (*Monthly Film Bulletin* 1986), I would concur that Ripley is compared to Vasquez and found to be the 'acceptable' representation of a powerful woman in terms of Hollywood cinema and heterosexual spectatorship in the mid-1980s. The placing of Vasquez as a stereotype can also be seen, nonetheless, as a deflective device which is used to obscure the fact that it is Ripley who has all the power in the narrative, and that it is Ripley who is usurping the male role of hero in the film.

The examination of sexual difference and sameness in this scene creates several significant tensions. First, the comparison between Ripley and Vasquez shows that Ripley's role as hero is not simply one of reversal. As Marshment indicates, 'if a woman is represented as being "more like a man" – competent, intellectual, brave, strong, rich, powerful or whatever – this positive representation is one that holds up conventionally defined masculinity as a model of the *human*' (Marshment 1988, p. 29). Vasquez's coding as more masculine discloses that Ripley is allowed to be the hero but is also transgressively inscribed with feminine characteristics. If we adhere to the strict binaries of patriarchal gender codes, then the overall representation of Ripley in *Aliens* is that of the unthinkable – a strong woman *and* a woman hero.

PLAYING WITH A DIFFERENT SEX[2]

As the *Alien/s* trilogy moved into the 1990s with the release of *Alien 3*, the whole area of sexual difference continued to be problematized both culturally and politically. Mulvey's model of the controlling male gaze both within and outside the film began to be challenged. As Swanson (1986, p. 22) indicates, the whole theory was based on 'the preposterous equation of masculinity with activity', and it is impossible not to see the narratives of the first two *Alien/s* films as prime examples of female activity. Contesting the orthodoxy of the 'male' gaze created the possibility of new and stronger representations for women in film. In my third choice of scene, therefore, I hope to illustrate both a textual inscription of female activity and the possibility of a specifically female desire that is oppositional to patriarchal forces.

The scene that I wish to discuss from *Alien 3* is the encounter between Ripley and Clemons after they have just had off-screen sex. Surprisingly, considering the context, although Ripley is in a state of undress we are allowed to see less of her body than in the other two scenes I have discussed. The setting in which Ripley and Clemons wake up and exchange post-coital phrases before Clemons is called away to investigate a fatal 'accident' is dominated by shots of their heads and shoulders. In terms of narrative action the scene begins with a shot of Ripley's sleeping head, and as she wakes she turns over and her eyes linger on the tattooed barcode on the back of Clemons's head. The focus on the barcode both serves as a strategy of the narrative, adding an element of mystery to Clemons's character, and stages a moment of representational interest. The play with sexual difference and sameness is extended to the field of sexuality, and the iconography of two shaved heads on the pillow blurs the edges of sexual possibility. Conditioned by associated imagery of sexuality, at first glance it could be two gay men or two lesbians. It is, of course, a heterosexual couple, but a heterosexual couple where their representations are not governed by the binary division of masculine and feminine. The visual imagery created by using close-ups of their shoulders and heads emphasizes their sameness, especially as they both have shaved heads and are wearing the same style of khaki vest. In contrast, however, the use of dialogue expresses difference by way of reversing the recognized configurations of activity and passivity in the heterosexual encounter. Weaver's inclusion in the script of Ripley's initiative in the sexual encounter on screen (Pearce 1992) doubly reinforces the idea of an active female sexuality. This is further emphasized by Clemons when he thanks Ripley for her affections, for in the realms of male heterosexual culture, it is rare indeed for a man to acknowledge and express his need for affection as opposed to his sexual need for intercourse.

The combination of Weaver's influence as producer and Fincher's direction creates a particularly interesting constellation regarding Ripley's representation here. Fincher, who directed Madonna's video for the song *Vogue* (1990), obviously had some experience in experimenting with the visual codes of sexuality, and it was apparently his idea for Ripley to have her head shaved (Pearce 1992). By this action, he succeeded in adding a whole host of new associations and connotations to Ripley the female hero.

In both the history of film and also our cultural history, the shaving of women's heads signifies defeminization. Possibly the most famous image of a woman with a shaved head is that of Joan of Arc, and more specifically, Maria Falconetti's portrayal of her in the silent classic *La Passion de Jeanne d'Arc* (1928). The fact that Falconetti's film was silent further emphasizes aspects of voyeuristic and fetishistic interest in the representation of a woman with a shaved head. Although the Joan of Arc motif in *Alien 3* was picked up on by Kim Newman in his review of the film (Newman 1992), and although Taubin reflected upon the gay iconography of the male members of the cast having shaved heads (Taubin 1992), any reference to lesbian iconography, especially of the provocative kind expressed by the photographs of Della Grace, seems to have been over-looked. The result of the use of crossover iconography, however, creates a somewhat startling postmodern encounter, where Ripley is endowed with a lesbian aura and Clemons is visually coded as gay, and where they have sex while simultaneously reversing the norms of the heterosexual active and passive.

It would seem that both the look and the desire generated in this scene allow for a multiplicity of identifications from a multiplicity of positions *vis-à-vis* gender and sexuality, with the result that for a short while, at least, the dominance of the 'male' gaze is displaced. The participation of Weaver in both the production of the film and the screenplay, also negates the totalizing idea of the controlling male element in all Hollywood cinema. Because of her own financial input and the fact that it was impossible to imagine anyone other than Weaver playing the part of Ripley, Weaver was able to exert much more control over how her character was represented than is usually allowed. What is interesting, therefore, is how Ripley represents herself in this scene. As I have already mentioned, it was Weaver herself who demanded a love scene, and although it was off-screen, its particular design inscribed Ripley as being the subject of desire as opposed to existing completely as the object of desire. This decision is made all the more interesting by the fact that the use of close-ups, and specifically head-shots, to represent Ripley, also serves to create her as a fetish. In these shots she is calling on a whole history of a certain 'look' which has become encoded within Hollywood cinema. Ripley's 'look' is not only reminiscent of Falconetti's classic image as Joan of Arc, but also – given the beautiful way in which her close-ups are lit – they conjure up parallels with the likes of Garbo and Dietrich, who were two stars who specialized in the head-fetish shot. Because of Weaver's intimate involve-ment in the making of *Alien 3*, she is allowed to be the subject of desire even though the scene has been filmed in a style that is usually used to represent women as objects of desire.

The almost obsessive use of close-ups on Ripley's face provide also many instances of what Dyer refers to as 'the unmediated moment'. The function of these moments, according to Dyer, is to provide a 'transparent window to the soul' (Dyer 1987), whereby the intimacy created by being brought so near to the character, allows us the privilege of glimpsing the 'private self'. The scene would, therefore, seem to be designed in a way which brings us closer to Ripley and possibly also closer to Weaver herself.

CONCLUSION

Contextually, Ripley as a female action hero can be seen historically to be placed in extreme opposition to the exaggerated masculinity of her male counterparts such as Schwarzenegger. As Creed claims, masculinity in exaggeration stems from 'the failure of the paternal signifier and the current crisis in master narrative' (Creed 1987). Because film is such a male-dominated industry, the creation of Ripley might be interpreted as an attempt to come to terms with the rising power of feminism in the late 1970s, by presenting a strong woman character who was still ultimately under the control of a male director and a male-controlled industry. Although it is impossible to argue that Weaver's role was no longer under the influence of male control, I would say that in terms of both Ripley's development as a character, and the growth in Weaver's own ability to exert some degree of control over her own representation, it is, perhaps, possible to suggest that we might be able to detect some subtle shifts in power by the time that the films *Aliens* and *Alien 3* were made.

The changing representations of Ripley that take place in the three films have undoubtedly been informed by the cultural concerns of their time, otherwise the films would have proved unintelligible to the popular audience and would, consequently, have been unsuccessful. Because Ripley has developed into a figure of heroic transgression, she has become constructed in such a way as both to crossover, and yet include, many of the more positive gender characteristics that are currently associated with the two sexes. She provides a particularly interesting focus for debates of sexual difference in representation and sexual difference in spectatorship. By the second film, Ripley's role has moved far beyond anything that Mulvey would have thought possible – she is both active and heroic. Despite her active role she also continues to be objectified, although as I have indicated, in *Alien 3* it was Weaver herself who made many of the decisions about how this was to be done.

It is, perhaps, the interaction between being active, and yet simultaneously objectified, that places Ripley firmly within the debate on not only sexual difference but also sexual possibilities. The idea of one character encapsulating so many possibilities is one of the elements which draws me towards her as a character and elevates her in my affections. The complexity of her possibilities is also what leads me to believe that she is a valuable (if iconic) focus for the discussion of current lesbian perspectives on identity and spectatorship. The contradictory characteristics which are allowed to embody Ripley (and which most possibly embody us all), do not appear so contradictory when her success as a film character is taken into consideration. Creed (1987) associates Ripley with Propp's idea of a hybrid figure, but surely she is more an example of the ways in which a fluid identity can be constructed – one which is oblivious of gender prescriptions. Ripley allows for a position whereby a woman can be autonomous in desire and action without necessarily resorting to masculinization.

To the lesbian audience, the interplay between representation and gender characteristics is especially poignant because it has always informed both the representations of lesbians in film and the ways in which lesbians might represent themselves. Although I would not want to endorse the belief that there is any such phenomenon as a unitary lesbian category or position, I would like to suggest that the complexity of Ripley's representation might provide the focus for a range of possible lesbian affinities from a range of lesbian viewing positions.

Ripley's death at the end of *Alien 3* would seem to resign her to just a place in film history, but to many women spectators, and especially lesbian spectators, she has offered an occasion for an active and empowered gaze. As a fictive construction, Ripley has been a very personal and very specific representation of womanhood, one that has challenged the stereotypical role for women in films.

A publicity shot for *Alien 3*, which was printed in *Empire*,[3] shows Weaver in a crouched pose wearing a butch leather jacket and staring, with an unwavering gaze, straight at the camera and, therefore, also at the spectator. The light which frames her face highlights the redness of her lipstick and the slick texture of her cropped hair (which at this point in time had grown back to a length of two or three inches). The iconography employed in this marketing statement reflects the current matrix of concern in debates about lesbian representations and identities – wearing lipstick and a leather jacket can be as radical as either abandoning lipstick was for the early feminists or wearing a leather jacket has been for many lesbians.

When I left the cinema after seeing *Alien 3*, I experienced a feeling of sadness as I realized that the experiment in representation, which centred on Ripley, had come to an end. Not only that, but in our last encounter with Ripley she had declared her heterosexuality. On closer reflection, however, I am no longer disappointed. After all, in the mid-1990s we are as starved of positive lesbian representations on screen as we were in the late 1970s. Before she was killed off, Ripley, at least, managed to blur the categories of identity long enough to open a textual gap for lesbian affinities.

NOTES

1 I feel that it is important to point out director James Cameron's own personal interest in the representation of women who are highly muscled. Both the lingering camerawork on Vasquez and Cameron's influence as director in the physical reconstruction of Linda Hamilton in *Terminator II*, would seem to point to this. It is perhaps also significant that Hamilton is his partner and their interaction is not just professional.

2 *Playing with a Different Sex* was the title of an album recorded by the Au Pairs, Human Records, 1981.

3 Publicity still of Sigourney Weaver for *Alien 3* by Diego Uchital/Outline, *Empire*, September 1992, p. 61.

REFERENCES

Burroughs, W. (1983) *The Place of Dead Roads*, London: John Calder.

Clover, C. J. (1989) 'Her body himself: gender in the slasher film', in J. Donald (ed.), *Fantasy and the Cinema*, London: BFI Publishing.

Cook, P. (ed.) (1987) *The Cinema Book*, London: BFI Publishing.

Creed, B. (1987) 'From here to modernity: feminism and postmodernism', *Screen* 28, 2: 47–65.

Doane, M. A. (1982) 'Film and the masquerade: theorising the female spectator', *Screen* 23, 3/4: 74–87.

Dyer, R. (1987) *Heavenly Bodies: Film Stars and Society*, Basingstoke: BFI/Macmillan.

Gamman, L. and Marshment, M. (eds) (1988) *The Female Gaze: Women as Viewers of Popular Culture*, London: The Women's Press.

Marshment, M. (1988) 'Substantial women', in L. Gamman and M. Marshment (eds), *The Female Gaze: Women as Viewers of Popular Culture*, London: The Women's Press.

Monthly Film Bulletin (1986) 52, 632.

Mulvey, L. (1985) 'Visual pleasure and narrative cinema', in T. Bennett *et al.* (eds) *Popular Television and Film*, London: BFI/Open University.

Newman, K. (1992) 'Loving the alien', *Empire*, September 1992.

Pearce, G. (1992) 'Return to the forbidden planet', *Empire*, September 1992.

Penley, C. (1989) 'Time travel, primal scene and the critical dystopia', in J. Donald (ed.), *Fantasy and the Cinema*, London: BFI Publishing.

Sheldon, C. (1980) 'Lesbians and film: some thoughts', in R. Dyer (ed.), *Gays and Film*, London: BFI Publishing.

Swanson, G. (1986) 'Representation', *Screen* 27: 16–28.

Taubin, A. (1992) 'Invading bodies: *Alien 3* and the trilogy', *Sight & Sound* 2, 3: 8–10.

Weiss, A. (1992) *Vampires and Violets: Lesbians in the Cinema*, London: Jonathan Cape.

White, P. (1991) 'Female spectator, lesbian spector: *The Haunting*', in D. Fuss (ed.), *Inside/Out: Lesbians Theories, Gay Theories*, London: Routledge.

13

VISIBLE MORTALS

Andrea Weiss and Greta Schiller
interviewed by Nazreen Memon

INTRODUCTION

I originally went to interview Greta Schiller and Andrea Weiss at their London home in February 1993, just before the Berlin Film Festival. Andrea had contacted me following my interview with her about her newly published book, Vampires and Violets: Lesbians in the Cinema. *Her description of* Immortal, Invisible *was most tantalizing. It sounded like the kind of book I would want to rush out and buy.*

On the allotted evening of the interview, we started taping the questions and answers immediately after an early supper. The responses of these two film-makers were so gripping that I lost track of time and I missed the last bus home (although I was warmly invited to stay).

To cut a long story short, I found myself transcribing and editing those long conversations around the time of the Berlin Film Festival, one year later. This presented the chance for Andrea and Greta to update some of their responses. It was heartening to see how some of their film projects had finally secured funding or had been shot and completed. It was, however, very sad to have to update the mention of Andrea's collaborator on A Bit of Scarlet, *the British film-maker Stuart Marshall who died of an AIDS-related illness on 31 May 1993.*

INTERVIEW

NM: **In identifying the motives that drive you to make films, how large a part does the desire to expose lost or hidden lesbian histories play?**

AW: Different films have different motivations. With *Tiny and Ruby: Hell Divin' Women* it certainly was a big part.[1] There are so many lesbians with a significant place in American jazz history, but their sexuality is always ignored. For example, it's hardly ever acknowledged that Bessie Smith or Alberta Hunter were lesbians. Films are made about these people and it's missed out. *Tiny and Ruby* specifically grew out of *International Sweethearts of Rhythm* which, as an ensemble piece couldn't concentrate on any of the women's individual lives.[2] The fact that Tiny is a lesbian certainly had a lot to do with why we chose her to feature in a sequel.

GS: Yes, completely. Several of the Sweethearts had warned us about Tiny Davis, so we were really intrigued. They said we'd have to be really careful and edit out much of what she'd say. When I met her, I knew what they meant. She was going to talk about what really went on in that bus and who was sleeping with whom and stuff like that. Out of respect for the Sweethearts, we didn't include any of those direct references, but lesbian audiences get the innuendos. When I first went to visit Tiny, Ruby answered the door and said, 'why have they sent a white girl like you?', and I said 'well, I'm all they had'. Because obviously she didn't realize that Andrea and I were it, are it, there's no other 'they'.

Meeting them both was so exciting – it's not often you get to meet a lesbian couple who have been together for over forty years. We just had to go back and do a portrait of them as a couple, as a musical couple.

AW: So many aspects of them were fascinating. Originally, we had this particular image of Tiny. We knew she played the trumpet, we knew she was big and we knew she was a lesbian. When Greta first met her, she called me up and said, 'You're not going to believe this, but Tiny's a femme'. And it really challenged all of our assumptions about the visible person in the relationship being the butch and so on. Also, although it was a personal story about them, it gave us valuable insights into black lesbian lives that we had no idea about.

GS: As white film-makers documenting black women, the whole question of how much to 'expose' of their lives is really complex. So when the Sweethearts said things like, 'I don't want you to talk about certain things in the film because I now have grandchildren and am a member of the church blah, blah, blah', I have to respect that. I'm not interesting in outing people to uncover lesbian history. Women of our parents' generation often choose to discuss matters on a different level. If they want to be open and verbalize it, they have to be the ones to make that choice.

In *Before Stonewall: The Making of a Gay and Lesbian Community*, the idea of exposing hidden history was definitely the driving motivation of the film.[3] In some ways, making the film with two men was problematic. They knew how to pay lip service to equality but they didn't want to carry it through. When Andrea as research director said 'OK, I don't want to see any more men's photos or talk

Plate 20 Tiny from *Tiny and Ruby: Hell Divin' Women*. (Courtesy of the British Film Institute Stills Department.)

to any more men because we have limited resources and time', their response was, 'what if we miss that one great male picture?'. I had to say: 'So what?'

AW: There were other arguments. You asked the question about lesbian histories – plural. I think they had the idea of presenting one history, one kind of image. They didn't want to include a lesbian if she fell outside of it.

GS: For example, in *Before Stonewall*, Audré Lorde says that the white lesbian and gay culture of the 1950s was a reflection of the culture around it. There was a lot of racism amongst white lesbians. Now that's a pretty basic concept, but the others working on the film saw it as a sidetrack and were saying 'this film isn't about racism, it's about lesbian and gay history'.

In terms of current projects in development, some are lesbian and some are not. My last jazz film, *Maxine Sullivan: Love To Be In Love*, was a profile on someone who wasn't a lesbian.[4] She was a black woman whose life didn't fit in with the tragic story our culture loves to hear about blacks, and especially about black musicians. I had a terrible time getting any funding in the US for that film because her inspirational story wasn't considered dramatic enough, that is, tragic enough. Documentaries are often dependent on funding from television and it is very rare for television to fund gay or black subjects. The Channel Four *Out* series is unique in the world,[5] but as a magazine show, most of my film projects are too big for them. Television is the dominant media culture and there's not a lot of room for diversity. It's hard because it's expensive to make films and by not funding certain projects, it's their main way of maintaining dominance.

NM: **Do you ever feel daunted by the fact that most television documentaries are transmitted once and never shown again?**

AW: Actually, it is incredible to see how long a life these films are having. *International Sweethearts of Rhythm* and *Tiny and Ruby* have shown on television stations all across Europe and America.

GS: Yes, and that's a really good feeling. They're really what we call 'evergreens', which means they're always of interest. They don't get outdated.

NM: **So, creating an 'evergreen' durability is an important intention behind the documentaries you make.**

AW: Yes, and I would like to see documentaries restored to their original status in two ways. First, to more of an auteur kind of film-making

Plate 21 Maxine Sullivan: Love To Be In Love, directed by Greta Schiller.
(Courtesy of Jezebel Productions.)

mode instead of television's current tendency to opt for a journal-
istic or magazine style. Because if a documentary is author-led or
presented by somebody offering his (usually it's 'his' rather than
'her'') perspective, then where is the point of view of the film-
maker? Second, I'd like to see more documentaries shown in movie
theatres. The documentary has a long tradition as a cinematic form.

211

GS: A lot of documentaries are really entertaining. Certainly the films we've made are. And they should be seen on the big screen, not just on television. But, you know, I'm not God, and I don't control the world. Unfortunately cinemas very rarely show documentaries and many documentary film-makers don't actually work in celluloid anymore. It's so expensive, relatively slow and cumbersome, and as documentaries aren't shown much on the big screen anyway they work in video. I think the fact that we've always made our films on film gives them a resilience, more of a permanency.

NM: **Can you talk about the techniques and forms you have utilized to challenge mainstream offerings and represent lesbians in different ways?**

GS: In my most recent film, a fiction called *Woman of the Wolf*, I was deliberately subverting the style of the mainstream costume drama and especially how women are portrayed in it.[6]

In *Tiny and Ruby* we made use of a combination of techniques. A sort of home-movie style created a sense of intimacy, as if you were at home with them. We intercut those scenes with animation sequences which were narrated by using poetry written by a contemporary black lesbian, Cheryl Clarke, as a way of bridging the gap between generations.

AW: In terms of challenging the mainstream, there aren't that many mainstream offerings of black lesbians to challenge. With *Tiny and Ruby* we were at a disadvantage in that we were filling in an absolute void in terms of visual representations. *Before Stonewall* was a more conscious effort to look at mainstream images of homosexuality through the years. We tried to show two parallel histories. The history of the dominant representation and the history of the subculture of people's actual lives. In many cases that history contradicted the mainstream images, and that was the tension we tried to create in the film.

NM: **How does your approach change from documentary to feature? Do you tightly structure each film project in advance with strict storyboards or use filming as part of the research process, then construct the film in the edit suite? Is there ever a great disparity between your initial vision of a film and the final outcome?**

GS: I freely adapted the script for *Woman of the Wolf* from a story written by Renee Vivien in 1904, and I worked with Andrea and the director of photography to design the shots which were then storyboarded. The production designer, cinematographer, costume

Plate 22 Woman of the Wolf, directed by Greta Schiller. (Courtesy of Jezebel
Productions)

designer and editor were all crucial in visualizing my script. And I think the final film is very close to the original script and storyboad.

This is so different to how we've worked in the past, especially with *Tiny and Ruby* and *Sweethearts*. Those were films which, in very large measure, got made in the editing room. Partly because of the way we worked, and partly because of the American independent way of not receiving the funding all at one time. If someone had given us $50,000 and said 'go and do this film', it would have been completely different. We wouldn't have had all the stops and starts and maybe I wouldn't have spent all those weeks alone in the editing room trying to sort out a structure.

There was a huge disparity between the earlier version and what came out in the end with *Tiny and Ruby*. The original idea had been to make a cinema verité film. But the thing is, they're show people. Tiny would say things like, 'Oh, she's just making a movie, so act real nice now'. She was almost like a codirector. Equally unexpected was how the first shoot turned out. It was Tiny's birthday party, and I really wanted to capture it for the film. But the cameraman I'd brought out with me to Chicago got totally stoned (the birthday party was quite a wild event), and so much of the footage was out of focus or badly shot. By the time we raised the money to go back, we realized the whole cinema verité style just wasn't right. The second time around we structured it very carefully – it wasn't verité but more like a 'closely observed' style. By then Tiny and Ruby were more comfortable with me, and I just hung out and shot it myself. I was able to get things like Ruby cooking and yelling at me for leaving my dish in the sink.

When we started to edit the material, we realized it just wasn't coming together. We felt it needed a narrator but didn't want the tone of a detached official one. That's when we came up with the idea of using Cheryl Clarke's poetry to create a sense of their lives. At the end, we brought in a coeditor, Peter Friedman (assistant editor on *Before Stonewall* whose most recent film is *Silverlake Life*), who understood our aesthetic.[7] As a middle-class, gay, white man working in the industry, he also brought a certain eye and sensibility which, through arguments, forced me to defend my thinking. For example, earlier when we were working on *Before Stonewall*, there was a part where a woman talks about passing and explains that it was a really serious thing in working-class areas of Chicago. If you wanted to take your girl out to dinner, you would really have to pass as a man when you were driving the car, because otherwise, you could get the shit kicked out of you. Trying to pass convincingly was deadly serious – it wasn't like the butch/femme playing around of today, and he just refused to believe that. The thing is, as the director, I would have had the last word, but it really helped to sharpen that scene because I was forced to think it through carefully and structure it so her words seemed plausible to people today.

NM: **Do you generally identify and target audiences for each film? How much does an awareness of their eventual viewing influence the film you are creating?**

AW: I don't really think about the audience, but if I did I'd want to attract people who are more interested in cinema than in television; who actively engage in cinema instead of being just passive viewers. Indirectly, my latest film is about the history of the cinema and will have many recognizable references to other films.

GS: I know a lesbian or gay audience are going to pick up different nuances and laugh in different places than straight people. Lesbians could easily see the lead character in *Woman of the Wolf* as a lesbian, although straight women can also identify with her refusal to accept the male character's world. But I don't target the films with only lesbians in mind. I think more about having integrity to the film itself. If it's a documentary, I feel particularly responsible to the people it is about.

AW: Neither of us have ever felt that we only want lesbians to see our work. I'm thrilled when people like our films, whoever they are. If it reaches them on some level, then it's really important to me.

GS: Yes, once at the Berlin Film Festival an older, white, German woman came up to me and said: 'I really like your *Tiny and Ruby*. I identified so much with them.' And I thought: 'What is she talking about? Is it the same movie?', and then I realized she really had found something that spoke to her as an older, creative, working woman.

GS: I remember when Peter Adair, who made *Word Is Out* and a number of gay documentaries, said at a conference 'I really loved how you brought out the lesbianism of some of the women in *Sweethearts*'.[8] The whole audience of around fifty people then broke up into this big debate, because half the people, or maybe three-quarters, didn't have any idea of what he was talking about. They didn't hear any references in the film to lesbianism or sexuality, while the others were so happy to pick up those references.

AW: Similarly, when we show *Sweethearts* or *Tiny and Ruby* to all black audiences, especially older black audiences who remember them from the 1940s, it's amazing how the things they pick up are completely different to what a white, gay audience would. That's why I love attending screenings of our work. It's always really interesting to hear different audience responses. And to wonder who these people are and why they're responding in this particular way.

GS: And what about the reaction of that sound-mixer on *Tiny and Ruby*!

AW: Yes, he was incredible. Right at the very end of the sound mix, he asked 'are those ladies gay?'. He'd been listening to the cracks and pops and different sound problems for hours and hours, but never really to what was being said, and I just thought that was startling.

GS: And then he tried to convince Andrea she was really talented and cute and blah, blah, blah. That she should go into making films on other subjects and that it would be better for her career, or whatever. It was really offensive.

NM: **You were talking earlier about how some of the people involved in making *Before Stonewall* were very reluctant to expose some of the racism that existed in the lesbian and gay communities. What is your stance on the positive images debate? Do you ever actively avoid lesbian representations which may be attacked as negative portrayals?**

GS: My position on the positive-images debate is that it is totally subjective and personal because positive imagery is individual. Some people might think that *Tiny and Ruby* is not a positive image of black lesbians. I mean what's positive and what's negative? As a film-maker, I resent anyone telling me what I should or shouldn't make. It's boring and really annoying. On the other hand, as a movie-goer, I want to have a say in what is made. In the case of *Basic Instinct*, I get terribly depressed, because Hollywood can make that movie but never one with a so-called 'positive image'.[9] They can't even make one in which a lesbian remains a lesbian.

AW: Yes, but it's naive to think you can stamp and kick your feet and then Daddy's going to make a nice movie for you. I mean, Hollywood is Hollywood. In a way, I get more annoyed by independent film-makers, perhaps because I expect so much more. Especially by some younger film-makers who trash the generation that came before them. Although, I guess every generation does that. It's part of a backlash within the lesbian and gay community that takes for granted some of the hard-won gains of the last two decades. These young film-makers look back at the so-called positive images of the 1970s and 1980s, to the work of other lesbian and gay film-makers, and make fun of it because it's now dated and not in vogue anymore.

I don't think they understand how those films, in many ways, their films possible.

GS: Completely. I mean, if Peter Adair hadn't made *Word Is Out* we wouldn't have been able to make *Before Stonewall*. If we hadn't made *Before Stonewall*, then Gregg Araki and those adolescent boys would have not been able to make their movies. I developed my formative views at a time when we believed that we could change the world. We believed that humanity was basically good and that as human beings we could take control of our lives and planet and turn things around. Along with most people under thirty, these film-makers have a belief system that the world is awful, that there's no hope for change and that people are powerless.

We grew up in a time of sexual freedom and sexual experimenta-tion. But today it's so different. AIDS has made them very angry, because they can't have the same kind of freedom. And I can understand that anger because 90 per cent of the whole group of people I came of age with as a gay person, who were my first gay friends, are dead. But that anger is no excuse for ignorance about history.

NM: **How do you feel about representations of explicit lesbian sex on the screen? That extraordinary scene at the Lesbian Summer School (when the tape of *She Must Be Seeing Things* was seized by women who hadn't even seen it) seemed to split lesbians into two fiercely opposing camps.[10]**

GS: And that's such an innocuous film. Where is the S/M in that? People always refer to it, but I've never been able to see any!

My position on sex in movies is that the more sex the better. Monica Treut was attacked for her first film and repeatedly asked 'what do you feel about men coming to your films and maybe getting turned on?', and she would say 'I don't care who gets turned on by my films', and I feel the same way. I mean I don't really care. What annoys me is the notion of censorship and the idea that the audience dictates what the film-maker does.

I once made an erotic lesbian video tape. It was called *Waking Up* and was a lot of fun to make.[11] My main problem was that the producer was trying to draw a line between erotica and pornography. I said, 'listen, why do you think people want to watch sex movies in the privacy of their own homes?'. For me, the more raunchy the sex the better. The more pornographic the better. I wanted more butch/femme and interracial sex in it, but the producer didn't. But that's OK – it was her film.

One of my current projects is an interracial lesbian romantic

d there will be sex in it and I know that one of the
vill sell to a straight audience is because it will feature
l lesbian sex. And I don't care. I really don't care. I mean
ire going to enjoy it a lot more than anyone else. Most
ers are hard-pushed to name more than two lesbian sex
⌐ in the history of mainstream cinema.

Susie Bright does an incredible, rich and diverse presentation on the history of lesbian erotica in film, but of course there's a distinct absence of mainstream clips.

GS: I've never seen her public presentation, but I've stayed at her home and experienced one of her private shows. She gets it all cued up then just leaves the house and you get to have your own fun. A real joy!

AW: I feel just the opposite. I'm certainly not against putting sex in films, but so often explicit sex is used out of lack of imagination. I think that there are a lot of films that are very erotic without being explicit. And in a way maybe more erotic, for being less explicit.

GS: You mean, for example, Marlene Dietrich's movies which, I agree, are certainly some of the sexiest movies ever made and there's never any actual fucking in them. But we're in a different era now.

NM: Do you have any taboos, or boundaries you would be reluctant to cross?

AW: My next film takes place in a lesbian nightclub during the Nazi period. Although the Weimar period in Germany and its lesbian bar lifestyle has a kind of magic for me, I deliberately situated it after that in the early Nazi period and felt a huge responsibility to set the context really well. I had to come up with formal ways of showing that this actually wasn't a wonderful nostalgic period. It wasn't even diametrically opposed to what was going on around it and, in fact, there was an integral kind of relationship to it. It's not a taboo or boundary, but a responsibility I take seriously as a film-maker. If you deal with that kind of heavy subject matter, it's important not to romanticize it or be flippant or nostalgic about it, so that people don't end up with a totally misconstrued idea of history.

As a viewer, I've always felt very uncomfortable with a certain kind of documentary. There are lots of them in America, where for example, the film-makers would go to Nashville and make fun of all the people who visit Elvis's grave, or something like that. I don't mean all the films which look at the mainstream culture as somehow peculiar and worthy of an 'ethnographic study' are necessarily making fun of their subjects. Louis Malle went into a Christian, middle-America town and made *God's Country*, and it was one of the most sensitive and illuminating documentaries I've seen.[12] I'm talking about the ones in which the whole point is to ridicule people and show how silly they are, so everyone can have a good laugh at their expense. Those are the kind of films I never want to make. Being a film-maker is such hard work – why would you want to make a film that you didn't care deeply about?

GS: Yes, I would say that if there was any taboo for me it would be to lose integrity to the subject matter, whether it's a documentary or fiction. For me, it's really important to try not to be exploitative.

NM: **What are the problems and benefits of being out lesbian film-makers?**

GS: Gay people have more media images now than ever before and there are many gay people in independent cinema, so it's a relief not to get as many 'oh, you're not representing me' responses. And there's nothing that's so exhilarating as an appreciative audience, especially an all lesbian and gay audience, because those are the people who are going to be the most critical.

However, being out absolutely adversely affects funding. Every lesbian film-maker that I know who works in the mainstream removes the word lesbian from their resumé. Even films made for *Out* will describe it as a 'magazine series for Channel 4'. Fortunately, I've been lucky enough to make films that are good enough to continue to be sold and screened outside of just the lesbian and gay ghetto. But I'm sure that because I am a lesbian it's harder to get funding. Absolutely. But actually, it's hard to get funding as an independent film-maker at all.

AW: Yes, the funding is such a hurdle. Greta and I are in really different positions, because she is very focussed on the technical side of cinema. If she can't make lesbian films then she'll do other films, because her goal is to work in film production exclusively. I don't think I would ever work as a director for hire. This has lead me to explore writing and some theatre projects in between film projects.

NM: **What do you feel about the relationship between lesbian identity and the tradition of using more marginalized forms of cinema? How easy or important is it to make your work accessible without compromising experimentation with conventional cinematic forms?**

AW: My next film, the one I mentioned earlier that is set in Nazi Germany, is an experimental narrative which mixes fiction, documentary and archival footage with nightclub scenes which are like a musical. But I think it is accessible. I hope it will have a very appealing style where diverse forms all work together. Traditional elements like the structure, character and plot will remain important.

GS: I'm really interested in people who work in experimental forms and textures. I've always been a fan of Su Friedrich's work for example. She works in a more experimental form and so she's even more marginalized than we are. It's just once in a blue moon that her films will get picked up by television, whereas for us television provides a fairly regular source of funding. We want to nurture diversity in the broad spectrum of lesbian cinema. This is why we formed Jezebel Productions, a non-profit-making production company in New York with Su, so that resources could be shared between the three of us.

I'm not really sure what accessible means – it depends what you bring to it. I find Su's films to be incredibly accessible – maybe not in a traditional storytelling way – but even *Sink or Swim* is very methodically structured and tells a series of stories.[13] Unfortunately, the difference is that if you work in an experimental form and it's a form people aren't used to seeing on television, there's only going to be a small percentage of people who are interested enough in being challenged by it.

It's not necessarily true that lesbians are more interested in marginalized film styles. Lesbians are challenged in nearly every aspect of life: who you want to be out to; how you dress; what work you choose; how to relate to your family. So I can understand why lesbians don't want to go to the cinema and continue to be challenged. I can really understand where that would come from. Just like anybody else, lesbians get home videos and watch television and that's where they get their cultural references. Most lesbians don't want to watch all this 'weird' stuff.

NM: **Have you rejected the notion of New Queer Cinema as a redundant marketing ploy useful only to promote work by white gay men, or do you feel there are potential benefits some lesbian film-makers can gain by using the label?**

GS: The article by B. Ruby Rich that gave birth to the label was only about the boys.[14] I don't think Ruby intended to invent it as a marketing ploy, but I think it's been picked up and used that way. When she was on the New York State Council for the Arts, she was a very important person in terms of helping to fund independent cinema. This included lesbian and gay cinema, and she was also instrumental in launching lesbian and gay festivals. But I still think I disagreed with almost everything she said in that article. While I greatly admire the work of Todd Haynes, I'm not a fan of Tom Kalin's *Swoon* or anything by Gregg Araki.[15]

I think Ruby did a big disservice to lesbian film-makers by writing that article and not mentioning the lesbian film-makers that do exist or why lesbian features seldom get made. It isn't just because lesbians don't want to make features, it's because lesbians are women and gay men are men. That's essentially it. It's really simple. It boils down to gender. And money and power. It's 1994 and only one woman director has ever been nominated for an Academy Award.

AW: My problem with the term queer is that it tends to gloss over the really deep divide between men and women. Which in large measure is a financial one, among other things. Queer makes it seem like we're all in the same boat when, in fact, the situation is horrifically different.

NM: **Do you feel your work is in danger of being ghettoized into a restricted circuit of lesbian and gay film festivals? How can this be counteracted?**

GS: On the one hand, the gay film festival circuit was integral to launching my career in terms of building an audience and a word-of-mouth demand for the films. And events like the Jewish Film Festival, the Lesbian and Gay Film Festival or black film festivals are really important in terms of a community and an audience. But I don't understand the policy of festivals like the Lesbian and Gay Film Festival in London insisting on premieres.

AW: It's a Catch 22. The premiere rule means that you can't show your film anywhere else. I would like all my films to be in gay and lesbian film festivals, but only after they've been in other festivals where buyers and distributors can see them. As a film-maker, you need that to survive. And also, we need lesbian and gay films in mainstream festivals. If lesbian and gay festivals insist on premieres, then those other festivals are going to be let off the hook. If lesbian and gay films are not available for them to premiere, then they don't have to show them. Then we will only have succeeded in marginalizing ourselves even further.

NM: **What are the inspirations behind your current projects? How radically do they differ from previous films? Has the funding been difficult to secure?**

GS: One of my features in development is an uncompromising lesbian love story set in New York and London. The other project in production, *Paris Was A Woman*, is a documentary on one of the most famous lesbian communities in the history of the world – a community of women that lived between the First and Second

221

World Wars.[6] It is a major project in the same way as *Before Stonewall* was, involving primary research and complex historical and literary ideas. Every woman I describe the project to in television thinks it's wonderful. They have heard about these women, read some of the novels or maybe some of the biographies and are totally inspired. And men almost always ask, 'well who are the leaders?'. Some say that Paris in this period has already been covered many times – we've already done Picasso, James Joyce or Hemingway. They don't get it – that what they're saying just proves the point. Others want it to be a biography of just one of the women or ask what it's about. I tell them it is about creating community space.

AW: The film I'm most involved with right now is *Ticket To Anywhere*, a feature which is really different to my other work, although there are connections.[17] Like *Sweethearts*, it is about a multicultural group of women, is set in the past, uses archival footage and relies heavily on music. It also deals with how women's personal lives are affected or influenced by larger historical forces outside of themselves. In contrast, it is explicitly lesbian, will be shot in black and white and make use of experimental forms.

Plate 23 Greta Schiller (left) and Andrea Weiss shooting studies in the Berlin Olympic Stadium for *Ticket to Anywhere*. (Courtesy of Andrea Weiss.)

I have a really deep interest in the early Nazi period in Berlin. I want to look at why Jews did or didn't leave. Why other people did or didn't leave and what their lives were like. It's a very intimate story in that it's not directly about the 'big themes' like the rise of Nazism and how it was possible. Instead, it's about people's personal life choices and their daily decisions.

I also have a feature documentary called *A Bit of Scarlet* which I started with Stuart Marshall.[18] It looks at the history of gay and lesbian representation in British cinema and relies heavily on archive films. Stuart and I decided to collaborate when I was still living in New York. He would write something and then fax it to me, and then I would inch it a little further and fax it back to him until I came to London. Then we spent a lot of time together in the archives, which sometimes felt like looking for a needle in a haystack. It's been a long time waiting for the funding, but now it's finally going ahead, unfortunately without Stuart who died last year with an AIDS-related illness. It will have a limited theatrical release and then be transmitted on Channel 4 television.

NM: If you were offered unlimited funding with no strings attached, what kind of a film would you make?

Plate 24 Greta and Andrea at work on *Ticket to Anywhere*. (Courtesy of Andrea Weiss.)

GS: I have so many films I would make if I had unlimited funding – I'd make a film every year. I'd keep making documentaries. I'd love to do a series on the environment, on the Great Lakes of the American mid-West where I come from. I would also make historical epics and dramas. There are so many novels I would like to adapt and they would require a lot of money. I'd want much, much bigger budgets.

AW: I would make exactly the film I'm making now. It doesn't need very much money at all, but if I had more money I would just make it look more sumptuous. It is exactly the film I want to be making.

GS: I know. Isn't it nice to be content . . .

NOTES

1 *Tiny and Ruby: Hell Divin' Women,* directed by Greta Schiller and Andrea Weiss, USA 1988.
2 *International Sweethearts of Rhythm*, directed by Greta Schiller and Andrea Weiss, USA 1986.
3 *Before Stonewall*: *The Making Of A Gay And Lesbian Community*, directed by Greta Schiller, USA 1984.
4 *Maxine Sullivan: Love To Be In Love*, directed by Greta Schiller, USA/UK/France 1991.
5 *Out* (originally *Out On Tuesday*), commissioning editor Caroline Spry, UK. Annual Channel Four series transmitted since 1989 (apart from 1993).
6 *Woman Of The Wolf*, directed by Greta Schiller, USA/UK 1994.
7 *Silverlake Life: A View From Here*, directed by Tom Joslin and Peter Friedman, USA 1993.
8 *Word Is Out*, directed by Peter Adair, USA 1977.
9 *Basic Instinct*, directed by Paul Verheven, USA 1992.
10 *She Must Be Seeing Things*, directed by Sheila McLaughlin, USA 1989.
11 *Waking Up*, directed by Greta Schiller, USA 1989.
12 *God's Country*, directed by Louis Malle, USA 1985.
13 *Sink or Swim*, directed by Su Friedrich, USA 1990.
14 B. Ruby Rich, 'A queer sensation', *The Village Voice*, 24 March 1992.
15 *Swoon*, directed by Tom Kalin, USA 1992.
16 *Paris Was A Woman*, to be directed by Greta Schiller. In development.
17 *Ticket To Anywhere* to be directed by Andrea Weiss. In development.
18 *A Bit of Scarlet*, directed by Andrea Weiss. In production.

FILMOGRAPHY

Alien, US (1979) dir.: Ridley Scott
Aliens, US (1986) dir.: James Cameron
Alien 3, US (1992) dir.: David Giler
Anne of the Indies, US (1951) dir.: Jacques Tourneur
Anne Trister, Canada (1986) dir.: Lea Pool
Another Way, Hungary (1982) dir.: Karoly Makk
At Land (1944) dir.: Maya Deren
Bagdad Cafe, West Germany (1988) dir.: Percy Adlon
Basic Instinct, US (1991) dir.: Paul Verhoeven
Before Stonewall: The Making of a Gay and Lesbian Community, US (1984) dir.:
  Greta Schiller
Blue Velvet, US (1986) dir.: David Lynch
Bondage, West Germany (1983) dir.: Monika Treut
Brief Encounter, GB (1945) dir.: David Lean
The Brood, US (1979) dir.: Carol Spier
Camille, US (1937) dir.: George Cukor
Cat People, US (1942) dir.: Jacques Tourneur
The Children's Hour, US (1961) dir.: William Wyler
Claire of the Moon, US (1992) dir.: Nicole Conn
The Color Purple, US (1985) dir.: Stephen Spielberg
The Cotton Club, US (1984) dir.: Francis Coppola
Coup de Foudre, France (aka at First Sight/Entre Nous) (1983) dir.: Diane Kurys
The Crying Game, GB (1992) dir.: Neil Jordan
Daughters of Darkness, Belgium (1970) dir.: Harry Kumel
Desert Hearts, US (1985) dir.: Donna Deitch
Desperate Remedies, Aus. (1993) dir.: Stewart Main and Peter Wells
Doctor Paglia, Germany (1992) dir.: Monika Treut
Drugstore Cowboy, US (1989) dir.: Gus van Sant
Falling in Love, US (1984) dir.: Ulu Grosbard
Female Misbehaviour, Germany (1992) dir.: Monika Treut
Frankie and Johnnie, US (1991) dir.: Frederick de Cordova
Fried Green Tomatoes at the Whistle Stop Cafe, US (1991) dir.: Jon Avnet
Gaslight, GB (1940) dir.: Thorold Dickinson
God's Country, US (1985) dir.: Louis Malle
Hairspray, US (1988) dir.: John Waters
I've Heard the Mermaids Singing, Canada (1987) dir.: Patricia Rozema
Internal Affairs, US (1990) dir.: Mike Figgis

International Sweethearts of Rhythm, US (1986) dir.: Greta Schiller and Andrea Weiss

Johnny Guitar, US (1953) dir.: Nicholas Ray

The Killing of Sister George, US (1969) dir.: Robert Aldrich

Lianna, US (1983) dir.: John Sayles

Madame X: An Absolute Ruler (*Madame X: Eine Absolute Herrscherin*), West Germany (1977) dir.: Ulrike Ottinger

Making Love, US (1982) dir.: Arthur Hiller

Max, Germany (1992) dir.: Monika Treut

Maxine Sullivan: Love to Be in Love, USA/GB/France (1991) dir.: Greta Schiller

Morocco, US (1930) dir.: Josef von Sternberg

Mildred Pierce, US (1945) dir.: Michael Curtiz

Mississippi Masala, US (1991) dir.: Mira Nair

Much Ado About Nothing, GB (1993) dir.: Kenneth Branagh

My Beautiful Laundrette, GB (1985) dir.: Stephen Frears

My Father is Coming, Germany, (1991) dir.: Monika Treut

My Own Private Idaho, US (1991) dir.: Gus van Sant

November Moon (*Novembermond*), Germany (1984) dir.: Alexandra von Grote

Oranges are Not the Only Fruit GB (1990) dir.: Beeban Kidron (TV serialization)

Orlando, GB (1992) dir.: Sally Potter

Out of Africa, US/GB (1985) dir.: Sydney Pollack

Parting Glances, US (1985) dir.: Bill Sherwood

Partners, US (1982) dir.: James Burrows

Peeping Tom, US (1959) dir.: Michael Powell

Personal Best, (1982) dir.: Robert Towne

Portrait of a Marriage, GB (1990) dir.: Stephen Whittaker (serialized for TV)

Pretty Woman, US (1990) dir.: Guy Green

Pumping Iron II: The Women, US (1984) dir.: George Butler

Queen Christina, US (1933) dir.: Rouben Mamoulian

Rachel, Rachel, US (1968) dir.: Paul Newman

Rebecca, US (1940) dir.: Alfred Hitchcock

Rebel without a Cause, US (1955) dir.: Nicholas Ray

Red Sonja, US (1985) dir.: Richard Fleischer

Rispondetemi, Canada (1992) dir.: Lea Pool

Rope, US (1948) dir.: Alfred Hitchcock

Rosemary's Baby, US (1968) dir.: Roman Polanski

Salmonberries, Germany (1991) dir.: Percy Adlon

Salome, GB (1987) dir.: Ken Russell

Seduction: The Cruel Woman, West Germany (1985) dir.: Monika Treut and Elfi Mikesch

Seven Women, US (1966) dir.: John Ford

She Must Be Seeing Things, US (1987) Sheila McLaughlin

Silence of the Lambs, US (1990) dir.: Jonathan Demme

Silkwood US (1983) dir.: Mike Nichols

Silverlake Life: The View from Here, US (1993) dir.: Tom Joslin and Peter Friedman

Sink or Swim, US (1990) dir.: Sue Friedrich

Star Wars, (1977) dir.: George Lucas

Strictly Ballroom, Aus. (1992) dir.: Baz Luhrmann

Sunday, Bloody Sunday, GB (1971) dir.: John Schlesinger

Switching Tracks, GB (1993) dir.: Alison King (video)

Swoon, US (1992) dir.: Tom Kalin

Tea and Sympathy, US (1956) dir.: Vincente Minnelli

Terminator 2: Judgement Day, US (1991) dir.: James Cameron

Thelma and Louise, US (1991) dir.: Ridley Scott

Tiny and Ruby, Hell Divin' Women, US (1988) dir.: Greta Schiller and Andrea Weiss

Tongues Untied, US (1989) dir.: Marlon Riggs

Torch Song Trilogy, US (1988) dir.: Paul Bogart

Touristinnen, Germany (1986) dir.: Ulrike Zimmerman

Track 29, GB (1988) dir.: Nicolas Roeg

Truly, Madly, Deeply, GB (1990) dir.: Anthony Minghella

2001: A Space Odyssey, GB (1968) dir.: Stanley Kubrick

Victim, GB (1961) dir.: Basil Dearden

Virgin Machine, West Germany (1988) Monika Treut

Woman of the Wolf, US/GB (1994) dir.: Greta Schiller

Word is Out, US (1977) dir.: Peter Adair

INDEX

Note: Numbers in *italics* refer to pages with illustrations. Numbers in **bold** refer to main references.

Adair, Peter 215, 217
Adam, Parveen 127
Adlon, Percy 73
AIDS *see* HIV/AIDS
Akers, Andre **99**
Alien/s trilogy (1979, 1986, 1992) 17, 179, 187, **193–205**
Allen, Louise 113
Amazon *see* boy/girl/Amazon
androcentrism 7
androphobia 31
Anita: Dances of Vice (1987) 50
Anne of the Indies (1951) 16, *169*, 178
Anne Trister (1986) 15, **131–41**, *134*, *135*, *138*
Annie (1989) 40
Another Way (1982) 97, 98, 131
Araki, Gregg 147, 217, 220
Archivi Lesbici Italiani 13
Ardill, S., and O'Sullivan, S. 184
Armatrading, Joan 79
art 14, 57, 58–9
'art cinema' 59, 60
'art television' 59
Arthur, Jean 201
Arzner, Dorothy 13
At Land (1944) 141
audience/s 4, 148; analysis of 75; creating/targeting 46–8, 215–16; interaction 146; as judge 187–9; queer 147
auto-ethnography 147, 160
Axton, E. 163

Babuscio, Jack 165

Bagdad Café (1987) 73
Bancroft, Anne 169, *176*
Barker, Liz 54
Barthes, Roland 165
Basic Instinct (1992) 27, 31, 46, 93, 164, 179, 216
Baudrillard, Jean 184
BBFC *see* British Board of Film Censors
Beauty and the Beast (1992) 74–5, 76
BECTU *see* Broadcasting Entertainment Cinematograph and Theatre Union
Before Stonewall: The Making of a Gay and Lesbian Community (1984) 208, 210, 212, 214, 217, 222
Bildungsroman 55
binarism 202
Birmingham Post 60
bisexual 21, 193
A Bit of Scarlet (*in production*) 207, 223
'black' 83
Blackeyes (1989) 59–60
Blue Velvet (1987) 21, 28
Blum, Ina 48, *49*
the body 184–6; in crisis 189–91; gendered 74; images of 187–9
Bogarde, Dirk 10
Bondage (1983) 34, 40
Bourdieu, Pierre 73, 83
Bowie, Malcolm 128
boy/girl/Amazon 168–73, *174*, *175*, *177*, 200
Brideshead Revisited (Waugh) 58

228

Brief Encounter (1945) 97
Bright, Susie 40, 218
British Board of Film Censors (BBFC) 10–11
Broadcasting Entertainment Cinematograph and Theatre Union (BECTU) 121
The Brood (1979) 187
Brookside 93
Brown, Rita Mae 53
buddy tropes 31–2
Burroughs, W. 193
Burton, Peter 152
Bussman, Tony 58
butch/femme 14, 70, 72–83, 86, 91, 104–5, 107, 113, 200, 214, 217; black/white 82–3; eroticization of 77, 80
Butler, Alison 9
Butler, Dean 98
Butler, Judith 3, 74, 77, 125, 165, 183, 185

Calamity Jane (1953) 97
Cameron, James 194, 205
Camille (1936) 97
camp 106, 144–5, 163–4, 182; academic 164–7; feminist 173–7; gay male 81, 165, 168, 178; lesbian 15, 16, 177–80; popular 170–3; subcultural 167–70; subversive 183
'camp trace' 152
'Capra-porn' 40
Carr, C. 36, 42
Case, Sue Ellen 74, 75
Cat People (1982) 187
C.B. 36, 43
The Celluloid Closet (1981) 26
censorship 13–14, 25, 89, 91
Chapman, Tracey 79
Charbonneau, Patricia 95, 104
Cher 27
The Children's Hour (1961) 97, 98, 111
Chunn, Louise 58
cinema *see* films
cinematic contract 1, 16, 151–2
Claire of the Moon (1992) 93
Clarke, Cheryl 212, 214
Clary, Julian 161
Cline, Patsy 81
Clinton, Bill 28
Clips 37

Clover, C.J. 198
Clute, John 53
Cohen, S., and Taylor, L. 156, 157
Collis, R. 157
The Color Purple (1985) 93
Conan cycle (1982–4) 171, 178
confidentiality 127
Cook, P. 197
costume drama 118–19
The Cotton Club (1984) 27
country and western 72, 81, 96
Coup de Foudre/At First Sight (*Entre Nous*, US) (1983) 97, 98
Crawford, Joan 169, 175
Creed, B. 187, 191, 198, 203–4
cross-dressing 27, 127, 168–70, 175, 177, 185
The Crying Game (1992) 27
cultural capital 73
culture 77

Dallas 81
darkness *see* whiteness/darkness
Daughters of Darkness (1971) 174, 179
de Lauretis, Teresa 95, 157
de Sade, Marquis 42
Dean, James 81, 83
Dearden, Basil 10
Deitch, Donna 4, 15, 94, 96, 103
Demme, Jonathan 46
Deren, Maya 141
Desert of the Heart (Rule) 94
Desert Hearts (1985) 4, 15, 23, 26, 73, 81, **92–112**, 94–6, 99, 101, 104, 110, 131; external characteristics 98–102; happy ending 110–12, 113; internal characteristics 102–10; sex scene 107–8; shower scene 106
Desperate Remedies (1993) 146, 157, 161
deviant female 182
Dietrich, Marlene 2, 169, 174, 203, 218
Divine 16, 183, 189, 191
Doane, Mary Ann 153, 155, 158, 194
documentaries 210–12, 221
dominance 82, 83, 168
domination–submission 42
Dr Paglia (1992) 35, 45
drag 16
Drewal, Margaret Thompson 152
Drugstore Cowboy (1989) 28
Dunye, Cheryl 4

Dyer, Richard 9, 13, 77, 92, 144, 151, 156, 157, 203

Edel, Alfred 37
Edwards, T. 151
Emmerdale Farm 93
Empire magazine 205
the erotic 7, 8
essentialism 18
ethnicity 14
Evening Standard 55

Fairbairns, Zoe 53, 54
Falconetti, Maria 202, 203
Falling In Love (1984) 97
Fatal Attraction (1987) 20
Fatale Videos 37
Female Trouble (1978) 183, 191
female victim/hero 198
the feminine 16, 168, 176–7, 178
feminism 9–10, 87, 148, 164–5, 182–4
femme *see* butch/femme
Ficher, David 194
film festivals 93, 221; Berlin (1985) 41; Berlin (1993) 207, 215; London (1988) 36; London (1994) 11; San Francisco (1986) 35, 50; Toronto (1986) 41; Toronto (1988) 45
film genres 25–8; and gender 30–1
film theory, and identification 145–7; psychoanalytic framework 143–5, 156–7, 165
films, aqueous images 139, 141–2; black film-making 166; as controversial 40–3; fantasy 159; happy endings in 111, 113; importance of, as physical environment 160; lesbian disaster movies 97–8; as lesbian-negative 179; 'malestream' 120; 'primitive' narration in 119, 120; romance in *see* romance; as unclassifiable 39–40; voiceovers 120
Finch, M. 94, 107, 170
Fincher, David 202
Firstein, Harvey 24
Florence, Penny 92, 95, 144, 146
The Forsyte Saga (1967) 116
'fort-da' 136–7
Foto Fantasy Guys 155
Foucault, Michel 167, 192
frame-within-a-frame 109

Frameline Film Festival (1991) 36
Frankie and Johnny (1991) 97
Freud, Sigmund 15–16, 25, 132, 140, 143, 153, 156, 157
Fried Green Tomatoes at the Whistle Stop Café (1991) 93
Friedman, Peter 214
Friedrich, Sue 220
From Wimps to Warriors (1991) 192
Fuss, D. 125, 182

Gamman, Lorraine 197–8
Garber, M. 127
Garbo, Greta 1, 2, 203
Garcia, Andy 28–32
Gaslight (1939/43) 25
gay 16, 21, 22, 94, 123, 129, 145, 152, 180, 182, 191; and maleness 8
Gay Times 34, 36, 147, 152, 155
gaze 155; ownership of 143
gender 3, 16, 74–7, 159, 204; conformity 27; confusion 71; positive/negative 165; representation 191; roles 198, 200; theory 182–3; trespass 185, 189
gender–power relations 167, 182
Gere, Richard 28–32
Gever, Martha 11
Gilman, Sander 158
God's Country (1985) 218–19
Golding, Sue 83
Grace, Della 127, 129, 203
Graham, P. 182
Grahn, Judy 75
Graulau, Mary Lou 46
Great Dyke Rewrite 7
Greyson, John 11
Guardian 56, 58
Guthmann, E. 37, 46

Hairspray (1988) 152
Halperin, D.M. 8
Hamilton, Linda 179, 205
Hammer, Barbara 4, 10
Hanson, Ellis 6
Harris, D. 37
Harvey, D. 42, 46, 47
Haynes, Todd 220
Hays Code (1930) 11, 22, 25–6
heterobinarism 9–10
heteromasculinity 28, 29, 30–1
heteropatriarchy 184

heterosexual 122, 125, 153
HIV/AIDS 11–12, 20–1, 22–3, 147–50, 160, 217, 223
homoerotic 31, 32
homophobia 3, 31, 33, 102, 107, 109, 152, 159, 164
homosexual 8–9, 11, 22, 26, 122–3, 125, 128, 153, 180; as secret trope 31
hooks, bell 74, 76
Hudson, Rock 21
Hungry Heart 37
Hunter, Alberta 207
hybrid figure 204

identity 5, 111, 124, 182, 191, 219–20; escaping from 156; lesbian 70–2, 74, 125–7, 158; loss of 137; masculine 177–8; and money 125; performative 73–7, 82–3, 159, 163, 165; racial 70–2, 82–3; search for 70–83; sex/gender 148; and social control 119; and use of signs and symbols 23–4, 72, 74, 79, 104, 202–3
image/music dialogue 96, 103, 106, 109, 110, 190, 192, 195
immortality 1
incest 136, 141
Internal Affairs (1988) 12–13, 20–2, 27–32
International Sweethearts of Rhythm (1986) 208, 210, 214, 215, 222
invisibility *see* visibility
Irigaray, Luce 15, 31, 121, 131–3, 136–8, 141
I've Heard the Mermaids Singing (1987) 93

Jack Babuscio Award 34, 38, 48
Jacobus, M. *et al.* 185
James, Clive 52
Jarman, Derek 6
Jewel in the Crown (1984) 58
Jewish Film Festival 221
Jezebel Productions 220
Johnny Guitar (1953) 169, 175, 177

Kalin, Tom 220
Kaplan, E. Ann 141
Kidron, Beeban 13
The Killing of Sister George (1968) 23, 26
King, Alison 11

Kleinhans, Chuck 145, 152
Knight, Julia 5, 46
Koenig Quart 95
Kotz, Liz 9
Kristeva, Julia 157, 158
Krutnik, Frank 132
Kubrick, Stanley 6
Kuhn, Annette 124, 200

La Passion de Jeanne d'Arc (1928) 202
Labourdette, Kati 100
Lacan, Jacques 16, 132, 141, 156, 157
Lancashire Evening Telegraph 56, 60
lang, kd 14, **70–83**, *80*, 139; consumption of 73, 80–1; her identity 79; as lesbian idol 70, 73, 82
Lauretis, Teresa de 23
Lebow, Alisa 4–5, 7
Lesbian Herstory Archive 88
Lesbian Summer School (1988) 86–91
lesbians of colour 2
lesbians/lesbianism 22–4, 94, 123, 148; cinematically marginalized/repressed 131; 'community' 14; definitions of 3–6, 111; and femaleness 8; ignored 124; as 'other' 14, 117; positive image 216–17; statistically significant number 160; as suspended 2–3
Lewis, R. 156
Lianna (1982) 4, 26, 98, 131
Liberator 54
Lindley, Audrey 95
Linton, James 151
Lipman, A. 103
The Living End (1992) 15, **147–52**, 155, 159
Local Government Act, Section 28 (1988) 57, 85, 88, 93, 112, 129
Lodge, David 58, 59–60
The Lone Ranger 81
Longfellow, B. 14
Lorde, Audré 210
Love Story (1970) 97
Lowry, L.S. 53

McArthur, Alex 99
Mackenzie, S. 94
McLaughlin, Sheila 14, 86, 93
Madame X – An Absolute Ruler (1977) 35–6
Made in America (1993) 97

Madonna 152, 184, 202
Main, Stewart 161
Making Love (1982) 23–4, 26
male gaze 191–2, 197–8, 201–3
male psychosis 29
Malle, Louis 218
marriage 122, 129
Mars, Shelley 48, *49*
Marshall, Stuart 207, 223
Marshment, Margaret 197, 201
masquerade 73, 75
master/slave 166
Max (1992) 40, 45
Maxine Sullivan: Love To Be In Love
  (1991) 210, *211*
Mayne, Judith 119
Medhurst, A. 170, 191
Mercer, K. 166
Merck, Mandy 95, 103, 104, 124
Mercurio, Paul 155
Merle, Robert 38
Metz 196–7
Meyer, M. 144
Mikesch, Elfi 35, 41, 50
Mildred Pierce (1945) 23, 25
mind/body dualism 103–4, 107, 185
miscegenation 25
Mississippi Masala (1991) 97
Modleski, Tania 174
money-power 118, 119, 128, 221
Monroe, Marilyn 77
monstrous feminine 183, 191
Monthly Film Bulletin 201
Morice, Tara 155, 161
Morrill, Cynthia 144–5
Mortimer, Penelope 129
mother–daughter relationship 100–1,
  131–3, 135–7, 139–41
Ms magazine 53, 55
Much Ado About Nothing (1993) 97
Mulvey, Laura 144, 156, 174, 197–8,
  201
music *see* image/music dialogue
mutual gaze 139, 141
My Beautiful Laundrette (1985) 111
My Father Is Coming (1991) 36, 37,
  38–9, 40, 44, 45–8
My Own Private Idaho (1991) 81

narcissism 134
narrative, closure 176–7; desire and

tension 97, 113; disturbance 120;
  girl-meets-girl 93
Nazimova 23
Neale, S. 178
Nestle, Joan 14–15, 88, 91, 107
New American Gothic 28
New Left 164
'new man' 91
New Queer Cinema 6, 38, 40, 147, 163,
  220–1
New Queer Wave 7
New Right 93
New Statesman and Society 53, 65
Newman, Kim 202
Nice Work (Lodge) 58, 59
Nielson, Birgitta 173, *179*
Nietzsche, Friedrich 192
November Moon (1984) 111

Observer 55, 60
O'Connor, Flannery 53
Oedipus complex 132
Olivieri, G. 4
On Our Backs 35
Oranges Are Not the Only Fruit
  (Winterson) 5, 13, **52–68**, 93;
  ambiguous cultural status of 52–3; as
  successful 52; televized adaptation
  56–66; universal appeal of 66–8
orientalism 173, 175
Orlando (1992) 119–20
Ottinger, Ulrike 35
Out 93, 94, 179, 210, 219
Out of Africa (1985) 97
Out On A Limb 36
Out on Tuesday 93

Paglia, Camille 35, 47–8, 50
Paris Was A Woman (*in development*)
  221–2
Parmar, Pratibha 11
Partington, Angela 72–3, 75
Partners 26
The Passion (Winterson) 52
Patton, Cindy 9, 17, 143
Pearce, G. 202
Pearce, Lynne 111, 113
Peeping Tom (1959) 128
performance 74–77
Personal Best (1982) 4, 26, 97, 98, 131,
  134
perversion 25

Perversions: Deviant Readings (Merck) 95
Peter, Jean 169
phallic-feminine images 173–7
phallocentrism 7, 15, 148, 168, 175, 178, 180, 191
phallomorphism 132, 141
Phoenix, River 1, 81
Playing with a Different Sex (Au Pairs, 1981) 201, 205
Plummer, Ken 2
Poitier, Sydney 24
Pool, Lea 131, 133, 134, 139–40
pornography 37, 86, 89, 91, 163, 195
Portrait of a Marriage (1990) 15, 93, *115*, **115–27**, *126*
post-queer 13, 38
postmodernism 7, 184–5
poststructural 164
Potter, Denis 58, 59–60, 67
Potter, Sally 119–20, 128
Powell, Michael 128
The Powerhaus club 81
pre-Oedipal 134–5, 174
Pressburger, Emeric 128
Pretty Woman (1990) 97
production processes, and TV culture 116–27
psychoanalysis 9, 15, 16, 117, 119, 120, 122, 128, 145, 146, 182
public/private 97, 107, 109, 111
Publisher's Weekly 55
Pumping Iron II: The Women (1984) 16, **182–92**

queer 6–9, 10, 24, 94, 123, 148, 152, 163–4, 180, 221; cinema 93, 112; politics 183

Rachel, Rachel (1968) 26
racial difference 14, 24, 71–83, 104–5
racism 210, 216–17
Radio Times 129
The Rainbow (Lawrence) 63, 69
Rainer, Yvonne 5
realism 166–7
Rebecca (1940) 97
Rebel Without a Cause (1955) 81
Red Sonja (1985) 16, 170–3, 174–7, *179*
religion, 'unsafe sects' 61–2
Relph, Michael 10

representation 89, 117, 203–5; cinematic 12–15, 32–3; strategies 123–5; of women 197–8
A Restricted Country (Nestle) 15, 88
Rich, B. Ruby 6–7, 38, 94, 96, 104, 220–1
Richardson, Colin 40
Ripploh, F. 41, 43
risk 20–2, 93, 163–4
Rispondetemi (1991) 133, 140
Robertson, J.C. 11
Rocky III 94
Rodgerson, Gillian 41
romance 15, 218; conventional 73, 96–8, 106, 109, 111, 113; lesbian **92–112**, 131; popular 92
Roof, J. 104, 106, 116
Root, J. 94
Rope (1948) 25
Rose, Jacqueline 120, 128
Rosemary's Baby (1968) 187
Rosen, S. 37, 47
Rowe, Martha 53
Rule, Jane 94

S/M practices 37, 42, 43–4, 127, 129, 152, 217; debate on 86, 88, 90–1 *see* sadomasochism
Saalfield, C. 41, 42
Sacher-Masoch, Leopold von 42
Sackville-West, Vita 15, 115
sadomasochism 40, 42–3
Salmonberries (1991) 14, **70–83**, *78*, *80*, *139*; productive readings of 72–4; race, gender and performance in 74–7, 82–3; whiteness and lesbian identity in 77–81
Salome (1975) 23
The Satanic Verses (Rushdie) 57
Schiller, Greta 4, 17, *222*, *223*; interview **207–24**
Schlüpmann, Heidi 156
Schroeter, Werner 35
Schwartzberg, S. 37, 38, 47–8
Schwarzenegger, Arnold 16, 203
Scott, Ridley 194, 196
Section 28 (of Local Government Act 1988) *see* Local Government Act
Sedgwick, Eve 30
Seduction: The Cruel Woman (1985) 35, 36, 40–3, 44

See Red Women's Poster Workshop 192

Seven Women (1966) 175, *176*

sex 159, 217–18; scenes 62–5; toys 42, 45

sexual, choice 43–4; desire 7; difference 17, 71, 121, 158, 199–201, 202, 204; politics 8, 85, 89

sexuality 3, 16, 77; ignorance and silence 157–8; lesbian 133–7; multi-faceted and mutable character of 4–5; use of metaphors 139, 141

Shaver, Helen 95

She Must Be Seeing Things (1988) 14, 18, 86, 87, 88, 91, 93, 217

Sheldon, Caroline 194

Sight & Sound 38

The Silence of the Lambs (1990) 46

Silkwood (1984) 27

Silverlake Life: A View From Here (1993) 214

Simpson, Mark 147–8

The Singing Detective (Potter) 58

Single White Female (1992) 93, 135

Sink or Swim (1990) 220

Sleepless in Seattle (1993) 97

Smith, Bessie 207

Smyth, Cherry 7, 64, 65

social reality 75

sociology of escapism 156–7

Sontag, Susan 144, 167, 170

2001: A Space Odyssey 6, 190

Spare Rib 53, 58, 64–5

Spark, Muriel 52

spectatorship 5, 16, 116, 143–5, 144–5, 156, 194, 195; as active process 160; and engagement strategies 151, 160; gay male 173–5; as hard work 157–9; heterosexual 201; and sensuous/social experience 146–7; social/political location 147–51

Spiro, Ellen 4

Split Britches 74

Sprinkle, Annie 37, 39, 45, 47

Square Peg (1988) 37

Stacey, Jackie 73, 97, 116, 145, 146, 157, 158, 160

Stage, Screen and Radio 121

Stein, Gertrude 67

stereotypes 20–1, 22–4, 103, 105, 113, 148, 168, 175, 201

Steyn, Mark 63

Stone, Sharon 179

Strauss, Richard 192

Strictly Ballroom (1992) 97, 147, **152–5**, *154*, 156–7, 161

Stryker, Jeff 155

Studlar, G. 173

subject 125

subjectivity 132–3, 166–7

subordination 83

Sullivan, Maxine *211*

Summer's Out 93

Swanson, G. 201

Switching Tracks (1993) 11–12

Swoon (1992) 93, 220

symbolization 133–7

tart-with-a-heart 168–70, 176, 177

Taubin, Amy 7, 194, 202

Tea and Sympathy (1956) 26

television, and deregulation 117–18, 121; economic dimension 123–5; and genre 118–20; producer choice 117, 128; production (of) values 120–1; and production processes 116–17

Television Today 58

Terminator II: Judgement Day (1991) 179, 205

text determinism 147

textual jouissance 165

Thelma and Louise (1991) 139

Ticket To Anywhere (*in development*) 222

Time Out 53, 54

Tiny and Ruby: Hell Divin' Women (1988) 207–8, *209*, 212, 214, 215–16

Today 56, 60

Torch Song Trilogy 24

Touristinnen (1986) 141

Track 29 28

transformation 103, 107–8

transgression 7, 40, 112, 128, 167

transsexuality, female-to-male 37, 39, 40

transsexuals 45, 47

Traub, V. 6, 144

Trefusis, Violet 15, 115

Treut, Monika 5, 13, 47, 146, 217; as controversial 40–3; asks for tolerance 45–6; as lesbian film-maker 34–8, 48–9; and promotion of sexual choice 43–4; relative neglect 50

Truly, Madly, Deeply (1991) 97

Tucker, Colin 129
Tuskegee 150, 160–1
Twin Peaks 81

Vampires and Violets: Lesbians in the Cinema (Weiss) 95, 207
Vanity Fair 82
Venus Rising club 81
The Village Voice 147
Virgin Machine (1988) 34–5, 36, 37, 40, 43–4, 45, 48, *49*, 146
The Virility Factor (Merle) 38
visibility/invisibility 1–2, 23–4, 71, 76–7, 145
Vivien, Renee 212
Vogue (1990) 202
von Praunheim, Rosa 35, 50
voyeurism 195, 196–7

Waking Up (1989) 217
Walker, Lisa M. 74, 75, 76–7
Walsh, Andrea 24
Warren, S. 37
Weaver, Sigourney 17, 179, **193–205**
Weiss, Andrea 4, 17, 36, 50, 93, 95, 116, 200–1, *222, 223*; interview **207–24**
Wells, Peter 157, 161

We've Been Framed (1992) 94
Whitbread Prize 52, 53–4, 58
'White Goddess' 77
White, P. 195
whiteness/darkness 72, 104–5, 113; and lesbian identity 77–81
Whitford, Margaret 141
Williams, Linda 134
Wilson, Elizabeth 128
Wilton, Tamsin 9, 141
Winterson, Jeanette 5, 52
Wolfenden Report 11
Woman of the Wolf (1994) 212, *213*, 215
women, as economically dependent 122, 129; in exile from language 140; images of 163–4; representation of 197–8
Wood, R. 183
Woolf, Virginia 118
Word Is Out (1977) 215, 217

Zech, Rosel 70
Zeig, S. 37–8, 46, 47
Zerstreuung 156
Zimmermann, Ulrike 141
Zorro 81